War at Every Door

CIVIL WAR AMERICA *Gary W. Gallagher, editor*

War at Every Door

Partisan Politics
and Guerrilla Violence
in East Tennessee,
1860–1869

NOEL C. FISHER

The University of North Carolina Press

Chapel Hill and London

© 1997
The University of North Carolina Press
All rights reserved
Set in Janson
by G&S Typesetters
Manufactured in the United States of America
Library of Congress Cataloging-in-Publication Data
Fisher, Noel C.
War at every door : partisan politics and guerrilla violence
in East Tennessee, 1860–1869 / by Noel C. Fisher.
p. cm. — (Civil War America)
Includes bibliographical references and index.
ISBN 0-8078-2367-8 (alk. paper)
1. Tennessee, East—History—Civil War, 1861–1865.
2. Guerrillas—Tennessee, East—History—19th century.
3. United States—History—Civil War, 1861–1865—
Underground movements. 4. Reconstruction—Tennessee,
East. I. Title. II. Series.
E531.F57   1997
976.8′04—dc21   97-9886
                    CIP
Portions of this work appeared earlier, in somewhat
different form, in "'The Leniency Shown Them Has Been
Unavailing': The Confederate Occupation of East Tennessee,"
Civil War History 40 (1994): 275–91, and are reprinted here
with permission of the Kent State University Press.
01 00 99 98 97   5 4 3 2 1

CONTENTS

TABLES, MAPS, AND ILLUSTRATIONS

ACKNOWLEDGMENTS

A great many people contributed to this work in some way, and I am grateful and humbled to remember them. Professor Allan Millett first pointed me to this project, directed it through a dissertation, and made numerous suggestions that greatly increased my understanding of the partisan war. Professor Joan Cashin shared with me her considerable knowledge of Southern history, critiqued my writing style, and provided valuable advice on a great many things. Professor Stephen V. Ash, Dr. B. Franklin Cooling, Professor Peter Maslowski, and the two readers at the University of North Carolina Press all reviewed this manuscript with great care, provided countless useful suggestions, and helped transform a dissertation into a book.

Many people made the research for this project both fruitful and enjoyable. The staffs of the Tennessee State Library and Archives, the University of Tennessee Library Special Collections, the McClung Collection, the Southern Historical Collection, the Manuscript Division of the William R. Perkins Library at Duke University, the National Archives, the Manuscript Division of the Library of Congress, the North Carolina State Archives, and the Federal Records Center in Atlanta were all knowledgeable, friendly, and efficient. Ms. Ruth Sloan of the Grandview Heights Public Library went beyond the call of duty in locating a number of sources for me, and the Alumni Research Fund of the Graduate School at the Ohio State University provided funding for much of the research. Dr. Carl Beamer made his extensive Civil War library available to me. And Barb and Jerry Ryan made my stay in Durham, North Carolina, unforgettably pleasant.

My deepest thanks are reserved for my wife, Angela, who traveled with me, participated in the research, supported my work, and lived with this project for many years. Her patience and long suffering are remarkable.

War at Every Door

November 5, 1861. Crab Orchard, Kentucky. Despite a lack of men, a shortage of supplies and transport, and an incessant rain that has turned roads into muddy streams, Brigadier General George H. Thomas continues preparations for a movement into East Tennessee. He is now only forty miles from his destination, and his scouts have probed almost to the border. But Brigadier General William T. Sherman, commander of the Department of the Cumberland, does not share Thomas's resolve. Doubtful that his troops can take and hold East Tennessee, overcome by fears for the security of his position in Kentucky, and on the verge of nervous collapse, Sherman calls off the invasion. Thomas protests but complies, and his forces remain at Crab Orchard, unable to intervene in the events that will soon transpire.

November 8, 1861. Jacksborough, East Tennessee. Brigadier General Felix K. Zollicoffer, commander of the Confederate Department of East Tennessee, watches apprehensively for the large Union force reported just across the border in Kentucky. For the past weeks he has been increasingly burdened by the conflicting demands of this inhospitable region, attempting with his inadequate force both to defend his department and pacify a hostile population. In the last few days he has marched constantly from one point to another, chasing vague reports of massing Federal troops, and the strain is evident in his recent dispatches. The threat in his front will soon dissolve into phantoms, but even now the enemy in his rear is poised for action. In a few hours the population that he hoped had become reconciled to Southern rule will rise up and attempt to break free from the hated Confederate grasp.

November 8, 1861. Knoxville, Tennessee. Colonel William B. Wood, post commander at Knoxville, also waits, not for an invasion but for the rebellion he senses is imminent. Unlike Zollicoffer, Wood has no illusions concerning the loyalties of this people. He knows that Unionist partisans outnumber Confederate forces, and he has detected an increasing restlessness among the loyalist population in the past few weeks. He is certain that in some fashion, and soon, disaffection will boil over into rebellion. Wood can only hope that the reinforcements for which he has pleaded will arrive first.

November 8, 1861. Hamilton County, Tennessee. Convinced that Federal troops will soon enter East Tennessee, three men cautiously make their way through the trees toward the wooden bridge that carries the East Tennessee and Georgia Railroad across Chickamauga Creek. Nervously alert for Confederate guards, they quickly douse the span with turpentine and apply their matches. The dry wood quickly ignites, and within moments timbers are crashing into the stream below. The war for East Tennessee has begun.

The American Civil War had many faces. The first and most familiar was the conventional struggle between the Confederate and
Union armies, a conflict that was fought under the authority of national governments, conducted by commissioned officers and organized forces, and, in theory at least, waged according to a recognized
code of conduct. This dimension of the war has been treated in hundreds of accounts of campaigns, battles, mobilization, army organization, command, strategy, politics, and diplomacy.

A second face of the war was the unorganized conflict between
Unionist and secessionist partisans. This struggle pitted region
against region, community against community, and members of the
same community against each other. It was decentralized, local, and
often surprisingly detached from the conventional war, and its character varied from place to place. In Middle Tennessee secessionists
formed partisan bands to deter the Unionist minority from chal-
lenging Confederate rule and fought an increasingly effective war of
sabotage and ambush against Federal forces. In many parts of North
Carolina loyalists encouraged desertion, harbored draft evaders, harassed Confederate authorities, resisted conscription, and fought
against the state militia and Confederate troops. In Missouri Confederate guerrillas fought a savage war against Unionist partisans
and Federal troops. And in parts of Alabama, Florida, Kentucky,
Louisiana, Mississippi, Texas, and Virginia loyalist and secessionist
partisans harassed enemy troops, spread dissent, and battled each
other for political control. This second dimension of the Civil War
was seemingly less honorable and more brutal than the conventional
war. Yet it was equally important in determining the loyalties of
thousands of communities, the fate of the Union, and the shape of
postwar Southern politics and society.[1]

The relationship between the conventional war and the partisan
conflict was complex. Both Confederate and Union officers condemned guerrilla violence as criminal and dishonorable, and they
were frequently appalled at the viciousness and recklessness of
their partisan allies. Yet both sides also tolerated the operations of
friendly guerrillas and employed partisan bands when it suited their

purposes. Further, both dimensions of the Civil War were remarkably savage. Unionist and secessionist partisans shot, hanged, beat, and whipped their civilian and military enemies, plundered and burned homes, executed prisoners, and on occasion raped women and assaulted children. The partisan conflict allowed the worst human impulses to flourish, and guerrillas used the war to justify the harshest measures. Yet, as recent studies of Civil War combat have made increasingly clear, the fighting on the battlefield was also vicious and often marred by atrocities.[2]

East Tennessee was the site of particularly intense fighting between Unionist and secessionist partisans. In June 1861 East Tennesseans rejected secession by a margin of more than two to one. Though the rest of the state overwhelmingly supported separation, loyalists refused to accept Confederate rule. They defied Confederate officials, assaulted Southern troops, evaded conscription and war taxes, and intimidated and drove out secessionists. The Confederate government responded with increasing repression, and local secessionists fought back against Unionist violence. This conflict quickly spread to every county in East Tennessee as well as neighboring regions in Georgia, North Carolina, and Kentucky.

The division between East Tennessee Unionists and the Confederacy proved unbridgeable. Despite evidence to the contrary, loyalists were convinced, as were President Abraham Lincoln and many other Republicans, that the majority of Southerners actually opposed separation from the Union. In their view secession was a conspiracy, developed in the 1850s by Southern radicals and imposed on the Southern states through fraud, manipulation, and intimidation. Unionists therefore concluded that Tennessee's act of secession was invalid and argued that their resistance to the Confederate government was justified. Confederates, in turn, were baffled by Unionists' obstinate refusal to join their war in defense of Southern rights. They concluded that Unionism originated in the lies and manipulations of loyalist leaders, who turned the region's population against the Confederate government to preserve their own power. Southern officials viewed East Tennessee Unionists as ignorant and deluded and were unable to see that their loyalties were deep and enduring. Thus, Confederates never understood Unionist fears of Southern rule, while East Tennessee loyalists had little sympathy for Southern grievances. The result was a tragic conflict that could be resolved only by force.

This is a study of the political and military conflict for control of East Tennessee. It begins with the division of the East Tennessee population into Unionist and secessionist factions in 1860, and it ends with the resolution of their conflict during Reconstruction. The first chapters examine the bases of Unionism in East Tennessee, the roots of the Unionist-secessionist conflict, the nature of the struggle between Unionist and secessionist partisans, the relationship between the war in East Tennessee and similar conflicts in Middle Tennessee and western North Carolina, and the use by both sides of intimidation, violence, legal harassment, economic deprivation, and propaganda. The work then traces the attempts by the Confederate and Union governments to occupy and control this region, the development of policies to suppress guerrilla violence and other forms of dissent, the struggle between partisans and regular troops, and the intersection of the East Tennessee conflict with the conventional war. Finally, it considers the political and military significance of the guerrilla conflict and the link between the struggle in East Tennessee and the policies of Tennessee's Reconstruction government. Readers should be warned that this work does not pretend to offer a comprehensive account of the Civil War and Reconstruction period in East Tennessee and that it notes only briefly such topics as the social and economic impact of the war on this region, the demise of slavery, changes in racial relations, and the attempts to alter Tennessee's social and economic structure during Reconstruction. This work focuses on the massive political violence that convulsed East Tennessee in the Civil War period, the way in which that violence helped determine the fate of this region, and its significance to the history of the Civil War, the South, and nineteenth-century American politics.[3]

1 The Switzerland of America

East Tennessee's position in the antebellum South was ambivalent. The mountain ranges that enclose this area on all sides cut East Tennessee off from ready communication with other regions, created a sense of isolation, and produced a set of distinct economic and cultural characteristics. East Tennessee was relatively poor in comparison with other parts of the Confederacy, and staple crop agriculture was largely absent. It relied little on slavery, and there are indications that by 1860 a free labor ideology had begun to take hold. At the same time, East Tennessee's rural structure was similar to that of other regions of the state, its manufacturing sector was still small, and its transportation systems provided links not with the North but rather with its Southern neighbors. Further, East Tennessee's political leaders, both Whig and Democrat, proudly identified themselves as Southerners, defended the institution of slavery, and supported Southern interests in Congress. East Tennessee's location in the Appalachians did not in itself separate it from the rest of the South. As John S. Inscoe and Kenneth Noe amply demonstrated, western North Carolina and southwest Virginia, Appalachian regions with economic structures similar to East Tennessee's, fully supported secession and supplied thousands of recruits to the Confederate army.[1]

The territory that became known as East Tennessee was not penetrated by Europeans until the late colonial period. Many of these early settlers came west from Virginia and North Carolina, while others drifted down the valleys from Pennsylvania. They gathered in four settlements on the Watauga, Nolichucky, and Holston Rivers and engaged in hunting, farming, trade with Native Americans, and land speculation. Their first years were chaotic and their future uncertain, for this land belonged to the Cherokee and by

British regulations was closed to settlement. The white communities evaded British orders to withdraw behind the dividing line established by the Proclamation of 1763; they then attempted first to lease this area and then to purchase it outright. Many Cherokee resented the trespassers, however, and in 1776 tensions between the two groups erupted into war. The white settlers suffered considerable losses, but in 1777, aided by troops from North Carolina, they defeated the Cherokee and forced them to cede thousands of acres.[2]

The early settlements were also threatened by political disorder. Because surveys lagged behind settlement, it was unclear whether this territory belonged to Virginia or North Carolina. As a consequence, East Tennesseans lacked both legal and political institutions. To fill this political vacuum, in 1772 delegates established a new government, the Watauga Association, which consisted of a court of five members with both legislative and executive powers, a clerk, and a sheriff. It governed the settlements until 1776, when North Carolina formally annexed this region. The Watauga Association had many flaws, but it provided a measure of law and order, and East Tennessee's early historians proudly pointed to it as the first written constitution west of the Appalachian Mountains.[3]

The East Tennessee settlements were largely untouched by the first years of the Revolutionary War. But in 1780, after British forces had occupied much of North Carolina, the loyalist commander Major Patrick Ferguson demanded that the settlers on the frontier acknowledge British authority and threatened to raze their homes if they refused. In response, about one thousand volunteers from East Tennessee, North Carolina, and western Virginia marched across the mountains, overtook a loyalist force at King's Mountain, and nearly annihilated it. This victory, in conjunction with numerous American triumphs in the South in 1780 and 1781, ended the British threat. King's Mountain also established a powerful tradition of patriotism and national loyalty in East Tennessee.[4]

The conclusion of the Revolutionary War did not bring stability to East Tennessee. Despite its annexation of this region, North Carolina had been slow to incorporate the new settlements. The North Carolina legislature had established three counties, Washington, Greene, and Sullivan, with rudimentary governments, but the settlers still lacked effective representation in the state legislature, legal institutions, and security from Native American raids. This situation worsened in early 1784, when North Carolina ceded its western lands to the Confederation government, leaving the frontier settle-

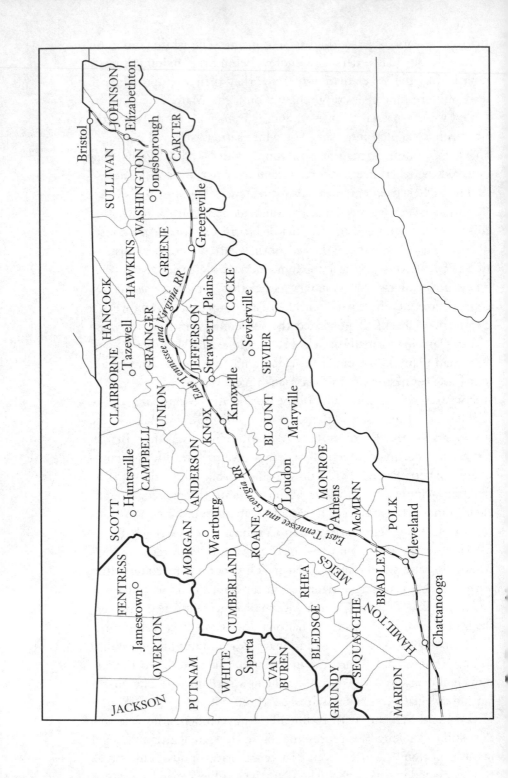

ments in a political limbo and depriving East Tennessee of government. Angry at their position, in late 1784 East Tennessee delegates again met in a convention, proclaimed their region the state of Franklin, organized a government, and applied to Congress for admission.

The premature bid for statehood proved disastrous. In response to North Carolina's opposition, Congress rejected petitions from Franklin for admission in both 1785 and 1786. North Carolina's governor then threatened to arrest the leaders of the Franklin movement and try them for treason. East Tennessee settlers split into pro- and anti-Franklin factions, the former headed by John Sevier and the latter by John Tipton, both wealthy land speculators and ambitious politicians. The two groups formed armed bands and struggled for control of political and judicial offices. The crisis peaked in 1788, when Tipton and his supporters arrested Sevier and took him to North Carolina for trial. The position of the Franklin government was further damaged by renewed war with the Cherokee in 1786–88. At the same time, the statehood movement spurred North Carolina to remedy its neglect of the frontier. In late 1784 North Carolina repealed the cession of its frontier lands, appointed a superior court judge and an Indian commissioner for the region, and established a militia. It also dropped its charges against Sevier and allowed him to return to East Tennessee. This combination of threats and improved government proved effective, and in 1789 the Franklin government collapsed. Nevertheless, the experience of Franklin and the desire for a separate East Tennessee state were not forgotten.[5]

From this point on, the fortunes of the East Tennessee settlers improved dramatically. In 1789 North Carolina again ceded its public lands to the new Federal government, opening huge tracts for sale and reviving hopes of self-government. In 1790 Congress organized East Tennessee and other frontier areas into the Southwest Territory, and President George Washington appointed William Blount, a wealthy land speculator and an early settler in East Tennessee, as governor. By 1795 the settlements in what would become East and Middle Tennessee had reached a sufficient population to apply for statehood, and in 1796 Congress, over Federalist objections, admitted the state of Tennessee. Rapid expansion followed political stability, and throughout the 1790s and early 1800s the Cherokee were repeatedly forced to cede land and move south to accommodate the region's rapidly growing white population. In 1817 and 1819 most Cherokee signed treaties giving up their remaining land in East Tennessee in exchange for territory across the Mississippi River, and in 1835 the few remaining families in the southeastern corner of East Tennessee were forcibly removed.[6]

In its early years Tennessee was a Republican state, for most inhabitants despised the Federalist Party for its perceived advocacy of Eastern interests at the expense of the frontier. Politics were based on faction rather than party, and for three decades two Republican contingents competed with each other for office. The first, based in Middle Tennessee, was led by William Blount, the former governor of the Southwest Territory and the state's first senator. The second faction was headed by John Sevier, a land speculator who rose to prominence as a militia leader in the wars against the Cherokee. This group found most of its support in East Tennessee, and initially it dominated state politics. Sevier skillfully parlayed military fame into votes, and he served as governor from 1795 through 1801 and 1805 through 1809. But Middle Tennessee's population rapidly overtook East Tennessee's, and by 1815 the Blount faction had ousted Sevier. Blount was aided not only by demographics but also by superior talent, particularly Willie Blount, Felix Grundy, Sam Houston, and most importantly Andrew Jackson. By contrast, Sevier was followed by less prominent and less politically shrewd figures such as William Carroll and John Williams.[7]

In the 1830s party replaced faction, however. Influenced by Andrew Jackson's great popularity and his advocacy of Western interests, large numbers of Tennessee voters initially embraced the new Democratic Party that formed around him. But Jackson's assertion of broad presidential powers, his opposition to Federal aid for transportation improvements, and his political appointments angered many voters, even in Tennessee. An opposition movement coalesced around John Bell of Nashville and Judge Hugh Lawson White of Knoxville and took shape as the Whig Party of Tennessee. By 1836 both Whigs and Democrats were fully organized, and for the next decade and a half the two parties fiercely competed for national, state, and local offices. Until 1852 Whigs won the majority of national and state elections, but the two parties were remarkably well matched. The breakup of the national Whig Party in the early 1850s shifted the advantage to the Democrats, but throughout the rest of the decade Whigs, sometimes under the guise of other parties such as the Know-Nothings, continued to compete effectively for office.[8]

Political loyalties in antebellum Tennessee were tenacious, and between 1836 and 1852 the vote of most counties could be predicted with great accuracy. But the reasons for party preference are less clear. The most thorough studies of voter behavior in antebellum Tennessee have found no correlation between party affiliation and either slaveholding or wealth. Rather, they have concluded that the most significant factors influencing voting were residence and occupation. Town-based groups, such as merchants and lawyers, and residents of more economically developed rural areas tended to support the Whig Party. Democrats, conversely, controlled rural areas not experiencing significant economic change. This pattern changed somewhat in the late antebellum period. After 1854 merchants, lawyers, and other urban professionals tended to drift out of Whig ranks in West Tennessee, while making up an increasingly large percentage of the Whig Party in East Tennessee. During this same period new voters in West Tennessee tended to join the Democratic Party, but in East Tennessee favored the Whigs. These trends reflected the increasing influence of the sectional crisis on voting in Tennessee. All these connections were tenuous, however, and local factors may have been more influential.[9]

Both the Whig and Democratic Parties were well represented in East Tennessee. Until the early 1850s twelve counties tended to vote for Whig candidates, eleven typically favored the Democracy, and six were unpredictable. Central East Tennessee had a particularly strong Whig following, while the northeastern counties were the home of Andrew Johnson and the Democrats. The dissolution of the national Whig Party did not alter this pattern substantially. The majority of East Tennessee Whigs moved into the American, the Opposition, and the Constitutional Union Parties and continued to win many elections.[10]

Politics in East Tennessee were intensely personalized and frequently marred by violence. Party institutions were not sufficiently developed to transform political contests into objective, impersonal contests, and elections were characterized by slander and abuse. Further, the leadership circle in East Tennessee was small, and grievances and feuds were perpetuated in election after election. Political contests, thus, tended to generate considerable personal hostilities and resentments.

At the center of many of these conflicts was William G. Brownlow, an editor of legendary ferocity who would become the chief spokesman of the East Tennessee Unionists. Brownlow was born to a poor family in Virginia and was apprenticed to a carpenter at age fourteen. After his conversion at a Methodist camp meeting, however, Brownlow became a minister and spent several years riding circuits in Tennessee, Virginia, and North Carolina. Brownlow apparently carried out his duties faithfully, but his true calling was politics, as he demonstrated in battles with his Presbyterian and Baptist rivals and in debates over slavery. Brownlow did not simply argue with his opponents; he sought to intimidate and humiliate them so severely that they would never cross him again. He possessed a vicious wit, and he employed insults, caricatures, insinuations, half-truths, and lies to devastating effect.[11]

In 1839 Brownlow resigned his pastorship, moved to Elizabethton, Tennessee, and founded the *Elizabethton Whig*. There he made his first prominent enemy, Landon Carter Haynes, the son of wealthy parents in northeastern East Tennessee and a future Confederate senator. Brownlow and Haynes first encountered one another when they supported opposing candidates for the First District U.S. House seat, a nasty campaign that left many wounds. The following year Brownlow moved his sheet to Jonesborough, while Haynes became editor of the rival Democratic paper, the *Jonesborough Sentinel*. Brownlow immediately declared war. He portrayed Haynes as an untalented hack who had stolen other students' speeches at Washington College and passed them off as his own and taunted Haynes for living off his family's wealth. Haynes in turn charged that Brownlow was illegitimate. After several exchanges of slander the conflict took a new turn. On the evening of March 2 an assailant fired at Brownlow while he was seated in his house. Brownlow rushed out and fired back, and the next week he publicly accused Haynes of attempting to kill him. Two months later Brownlow accosted Haynes on the streets of Jonesborough and began beating him with his cane. Haynes in turn pulled out his pistol and shot Brownlow in the leg. Shortly thereafter Haynes, unwilling or unable to sustain the conflict, gave up his editorship.[12]

In 1849 Brownlow moved his paper to Knoxville and acquired several new enemies. Brownlow had announced in advance his intention to supplant Knoxville's two existing papers, the Whig *Register* and the Democratic *Sentinel*. His reputation for combativeness preceded him, and both papers made plans to destroy the new enterprise. The *Register*'s funders, who included John Crozier, William G. Swan, William H. Sneed, and Thomas W. Humes, pooled $6,000 to fight off Brownlow's challenge. Their first opportunity to damage the *Whig* came soon. Brownlow, apparently unaware of Crozier's enmity, shipped his press in Crozier's care. The press was purposely left on the docks, and, though one of Brownlow's friends discovered and rescued the shipment, this incident alerted Brownlow to his danger. In one of his first editions Brownlow accused the *Register*'s supporters of secretly planning to burn his office, and he and a number of friends stood guard for several nights. It is not clear whether the accusations were based on real evidence or were simply a publicity stunt, but they further heightened the conflict. Tensions soon became so high that Knoxville's leaders called a town meeting to plead for an end to the feuding.[13]

Brownlow eventually triumphed in Knoxville. In 1851 the *Sentinel* folded, and soon thereafter the *Register* converted to a Democratic press. Not content with his victory, Brownlow continued to ridicule the *Register*'s editor, James Sperry, as "a man of bad morals, bad associations, and the tool of the worst class of men in Knoxville" and to dismiss his paper as a sheet with "but a limited circulation, and no character for anything but lying." A final challenge came in the early 1850s, when William G. Swan attempted to establish a second Democratic sheet in Knoxville, the *Southern Citizen*. After some written sparring Brownlow came to Swan's house one night, brandished a pistol, and challenged him to a duel. Swan declined, and Brownlow publicly accused his rival of cowardice. In 1856 Swan's enterprise collapsed. By the late 1850s Brownlow's *Whig* had become the most influential paper in East Tennessee and one of the largest in the South. Brownlow's victory resulted partly from his combativeness, but partly also from his shrewd political instincts and his keen understanding of the East Tennessee population.[14]

Brownlow's enemies were not confined to journalistic rivals. In 1856, in response to worsening economic conditions, the Knoxville branch of the Bank of Tennessee suspended specie payments. Two Democratic businessmen, J. G. M. Ramsey and Major Thomas C. Lyon, were appointed to examine the bank's accounts and repay depositors. The examiners moved slowly, and Brownlow, along with Whig businessman George W. Ross, filed suit in Knox County Chancery Court against the bank's former president, William W. Churchwell, to recover depositors' funds. Churchwell hired John Crozier to defend him. Brownlow and Ross won their suit, and the state supreme court upheld that ruling, though the onset of secession prevented Brownlow and Ross from collecting any of the judgment. Brownlow also used the *Whig* to accuse the examiners of incompetence, favoritism in making repayments, and fraud. Thus, by 1860 Brownlow had acquired the enmity of the future secessionist leaders Ramsey, Lyon, Crozier, and Churchwell as well as Sneed, Swan, and Haynes.[15]

Brownlow's most enduring and formidable enemy was Andrew Johnson, the leader of the East Tennessee Democrats. Brownlow and Johnson shared many characteristics. Both had risen from obscurity, both resented the influence of large slaveholders over Southern politics, and both were passionately devoted to the interests of East Tennessee. But where Brownlow saw East Tennessee's salvation in the developmental policies of the Whig Party, Johnson favored limited government, the restriction of business privileges, and the protection of the common people from economic exploitation. Johnson attacked bank and railroad charters, introduced a homestead bill that would open land to poorer white families, and advocated the determination of representation on the basis of white population alone.

Brownlow encountered Johnson directly in politics only once, when both were candidates for the First District congressional seat. Brownlow lost that contest decisively, and he developed a certain respect for Johnson's political skills. But Brownlow never gave up attempts to damage the Democratic leader. He not only attacked Johnson's political views but also portrayed him as morally unfit to hold office. Brownlow accused Johnson of being an atheist, an infidel, and a Catholic. He further claimed that Johnson beat his wife, regularly visited prostitutes, and drank heavily. Finally, in a favorite charge, Brownlow exploited Johnson's obscure past and accused him of being illegitimate. Johnson in turn depicted Brownlow as a tool of the East Tennessee elite, accused him of favoring government interference in private morality, and condemned him for promoting hatred and intolerance. The two men despised one another, but they remained impervious to each other's assaults. Brownlow proved unable to block Johnson's political ascension, but he retained his considerable influence over Whig voters.[16]

Party loyalties were not the only dividing factor in antebellum Tennessee. The separation of Tennessee into three regions, West, Middle, and East, is central to the state's history. East and Middle Tennessee had originated as separate enterprises and had functioned independently for two decades. West Tennessee was not settled until the 1820s, and its frontier heritage was still evident in 1860. Following geography and history, the constitution of 1834 established three "grand divisions" for purposes of taxation, appropriations, and some political appointments. Many religious denominations organized three separate conferences in Tennessee, one for each division. Even the state's railroad lines did not link its divisions together, but instead tied each section to markets and transportation centers in neighboring states.[17]

Tennessee's three sections competed with each other for political dominance, revenues, and funding for internal improvements. From the state's founding to the first decade of the nineteenth century East Tennessee supplied most of the state's governors, controlled the state legislature, and monopolized at least one Senate seat. But in 1812 rapid population growth and congressional redistricting threw the advantage to Middle Tennessee. The subsequent political decline of East Tennessee, symbolized by the removal of the state capital from Knoxville to Nashville, was deep and painful. Between 1819 and 1860 only a single candidate from the eastern counties, Andrew Johnson, reached the governor's chair, and after 1840 East Tennessee lost its claim to one Senate seat. Three defeats late in the antebellum period particularly embittered East Tennessee Whig leaders. In both 1851 and 1853 T. A. R. Nelson, one of East Tennessee's most respected Whig leaders, was a candidate for a U.S. Senate seat, but both times the state legislature instead selected a Middle Tennessee candidate. Then, in 1857, John Netherland lost badly to Isham G. Harris in the governor's race, a defeat that further emphasized East Tennessee's political weakness. Whigs in East and West Tennessee frequently allied against Democratic Middle Tennessee, but representatives from the middle counties nonetheless tended to dominate the state legislature.[18]

Occasionally sectional disputes threatened to split the state. In the late 1830s Middle Tennessee legislators blocked several bills funding railroad and road projects in the other two sections. In turn, representatives from East and West Tennessee accused Middle Tennessee of monopolizing state funds to build its own road network. Their dispute became so divisive that in 1841 East Tennessee congressmen introduced bills in the Tennessee House and Senate authorizing the eastern counties to form a new state. These bills received the support of both Whigs and Democrats, including William G. Brownlow and Andrew Johnson. The Senate actually approved the statehood measure in 1842, but the House added an amendment requiring a referendum on the issue of separation. The

Senate refused to accept this amendment, and the measure died. East Tennessee legislators introduced a similar statehood bill in 1843, but it again failed. Nevertheless, the desire for an East Tennessee state, a desire fueled partly by history and partly by resentment of Middle Tennessee, remained.[19]

The antislavery movement came to East Tennessee in the early nineteenth century, and in some locations lingered until the Civil War. Several manumission societies were founded in the 1810s and 1820s, and three antislavery papers, the *Manumission Intelligencer*, the *Emancipator*, and the *Genius of Universal Emancipation*, were published briefly in Jonesborough and Greeneville during this period. The movement flagged in the late 1820s, and all three papers moved north. But the issue of slavery emerged again in the early 1830s when Tennessee delegates debating proposed revisions of the Tennessee constitution also considered a measure for the gradual abolition of slavery. Thirteen of twenty delegates who supported this move represented East Tennessee, and East Tennessee voters sent the majority of petitions in favor of this measure. East Tennessee thus gained a reputation as a haven for antislavery sentiment, and in locations such as Maryville antislavery views may have continued to circulate and shape political leanings. But on the whole the antislavery movement was neither influential nor enduring. Early manumission societies in East Tennessee were small and attracted few major figures, and the antislavery publications had only limited circulation. While many East Tennesseans despised large slaveholders and resented their political influence, they firmly believed in black inferiority and had little interest in the fate of slaves.[20]

East Tennessee comprises three distinct geographical sections and exhibits great variations in terrain, climate, and soil quality, not only from section to section but also within each geographic division. The counties bordering North Carolina lie within the Unaka Mountain Range and are characterized by high, steep slopes and a rugged, heavily wooded terrain. In most of this area the soil is poor and agricultural potential limited, but the resources of timber and ores are rich. The western counties, which are situated on the edge of the Cumberland Plateau, are also mountainous, though slightly less rugged. While parts of this region are level and productive, much of the land is cut with ridges that limit agricultural production. In this section were found some of the most isolated and undeveloped counties in antebellum East Tennessee, particularly Scott, Morgan, and Cumberland. The final section, the Greater Valley of

East Tennessee, separates the two mountain sections and comprises about half the territory of the region. Here level fields alternate with rolling hills, and this region contains extensive areas of good soil that allows a variety of agricultural pursuits. This mixed terrain of slopes, pastures, and cultivated fields gave East Tennessee its nineteenth-century designation as "the Switzerland of America." Thus, while antebellum East Tennessee lacked the rich soil and agricultural productivity of other areas of the South, it did not fit the simple nineteenth- and twentieth-century stereotype of a Southern "mountain" region.[21]

Agriculture in East Tennessee was highly diversified. East Tennessee farmers raised considerable quantities of wheat, corn, oats, hay, and fruit, grazed large herds of cattle and hogs, and kept honeybees and silkworms. Farms ranged in size from small subsistence plots to large market enterprises, and agricultural practices varied widely. Holdings in the river valleys were intensively cultivated, and some farmers employed advanced agricultural methods and bred high-quality livestock. Conversely, most of the land in the mountain counties remained in pasture and timber, and unfenced grazing was common. In 1860 57 percent of East Tennessee families owned land, and the majority of farms were in the range of fifty to two hundred acres.[22]

The manufacturing sector in East Tennessee grew rapidly in the late antebellum period and was just beginning to transform the region's economy. Most production was limited to basic processing of the region's resources, and grain mills, iron and copper works, lumber mills, and alcohol distilleries were common. But in towns such as Knoxville, Chattanooga, Greeneville, and Jonesborough a number of more specialized establishments also existed, including foundries, wagon and carriage shops, and boot and shoe manufacturers. East Tennessee's per capita investment in manufacturing and production exceeded that of Middle and West Tennessee, and by 1860 the region's resources in coal, ores, and timber made the potential for rapid industrialization clear. Even so, East Tennessee's urban population was small. Knoxville, East Tennessee's political and economic center, had about 3,000 inhabitants in 1860, while Chattanooga had only 1,500. Other important towns, such as Athens, Cleveland, Greeneville, and Kingston, had fewer than 1,000 residents. These villages served largely as commercial and government centers for the surrounding rural areas.[23]

The economy of East Tennessee was hampered by the poor soil

in many regions and by a climate that precluded the production of valuable staple crops, particularly cotton. But the greatest barrier to economic development was the lack of transportation. The Tennessee, French Broad, Holston, and Watauga Rivers provided local movement of goods, but numerous obstructions on the Tennessee River impeded extensive shipping and blocked access to the South's major river systems and ports. Further, unlike Middle Tennessee, the eastern counties lacked the private capital to construct a network of hard-surface roads. Until the 1850s goods moved into East Tennessee from Baltimore, Philadelphia, Richmond, and Nashville on large wagon trains, and East Tennesseans drove herds of cattle and hogs to market in neighboring states.[24]

The potential of the railroad for overcoming these transportation barriers was quickly recognized. In the 1830s a group of East Tennessee businessmen led by Dr. J. G. M. Ramsey organized the Hiwassee Railroad, which was projected to run from Knoxville to the Georgia border and to link up with the proposed Louisville, Cincinnati and Charleston Railroad. This project, unfortunately, soon collapsed for lack of funds. The railroad movement revived in the late 1840s, however, when the Western and Atlantic was completed from Atlanta to Chattanooga. Taking advantage of extensive state aid, East Tennessee companies had completed by 1855 two lines, the East Tennessee and Georgia and the East Tennessee and Virginia Railroads. Running from Bristol to Chattanooga, these lines provided service to the entire East Tennessee Valley and linked the region with the Atlantic seaboard and the Gulf coast. The railroads left many counties without service, and in the mountain areas transportation remained a serious problem. But they also spurred increased trade, manufacturing, and tourism, allowed farmers to market more grain, and accounted for a boom in wheat production in the 1850s.[25]

By greatly increasing contacts between East Tennessee and the rest of the South, the railroads had unexpected effects on the region's economic and political development. Wheat merchants established business contacts and friendships with Southern merchants in Georgia and other states. Increasing numbers of Southern travelers visited East Tennessee's mountain resorts, and East Tennesseans made more frequent visits to friends and relatives in Southern states. The result, at least among certain groups in East Tennessee, was an increasing identification with the South. Merchants and lawyers involved in Southern trade linked their own prosperity with the

TABLE 1. *Sectional Comparisons, Tennessee, 1860*

	East	Middle	West	State
Land Values ($ per acre)	8.51	14.54	12.16	11.82
Farm Value ($ per farm)	2,772	3,261	3,433	3,117
Improved Acreage (percent)	28.27	33.55	31.41	31.14
Farms of 500 Acres or More (percent)	1.00	1.01	2.24	1.27
Capital Invested in Manufacturing ($ per capita)	21.50	16.33	8.66	16.61

South's, while increased personal contacts led to a greater awareness of, and sympathy with, Southern grievances against the North.[26]

By many measures the economic structure of rural East Tennessee differed little from that of the rest of the state. The percentage of East Tennessee families who owned land was only slightly smaller than in Middle and West Tennessee, and farm sizes were similar. Land values in East Tennessee were somewhat lower, farms tended to be less intensively cultivated, and East Tennessee had fewer large enterprises. But the differences between the eastern counties and the rest of the state were only moderate. For example, the average percent of improved acres on East Tennessee farms was 28.3 percent, only slightly behind Middle Tennessee's 33.6 percent. Similarly, in both East and Middle Tennessee only 1 percent of farms exceeded 500 acres, while in West Tennessee the figure was 2 percent. Equally important, in all three regions land values, land holdings, and agricultural development varied widely. For example, land prices in East Tennessee ranged from less than $2 per acre in the mountain counties of Cumberland, Morgan, and Scott to more than $13 per acre in the valley. In Middle Tennessee land values varied from $5 to $33 per acre, and in West Tennessee they ranged from $4 to $19.[27]

Nonetheless, in four areas—staple crop production, levels of wealth, and percentages of slaveholding families and of slaves in the population—East Tennessee sharply diverged from other regions of Tennessee and the South. Seventeen of East Tennessee's thirty-one counties grew no cotton at all in 1860, and only one, Monroe, exceeded the state's production mean. By contrast, only three counties in the rest of the state planted no cotton. Production of tobacco was

TABLE 2. *Sectional Distinctions, Tennessee, 1860*

	East	Middle	West	State
Cotton (bales per farm)	0.25	3.45	9.93	3.66
Tobacco (pounds per farm)	27	525	1,052	454
Wheat (bushels per farm)	97	51	46	66
Slaveholders (percent)	10.26	25.85	32.24	21.50
Planters (percent)	0.33	1.89	3.57	1.68
Aggregate Wealth ($ per capita)	454	934	1,243	823

only moderately higher. Every county in East Tennessee planted at least a small amount of this crop, but on average East Tennessee farms produced only one-twentieth as much as Middle Tennessee and one-fortieth as much as West Tennessee. Many East Tennessee farmers turned to wheat as a substitute market crop, but that commodity could not compete with cotton or tobacco as a moneymaker.[28]

The lack of a high-value money crop in East Tennessee not only kept wealth and income levels relatively low, it also took away much of the incentive and ability to acquire slaves. In only three East Tennessee counties did slaveholding families make up 15 percent or more of the population, and in none did they constitute more than 20 percent. By contrast, twenty of thirty-five counties in Middle Tennessee and fourteen of eighteen in West Tennessee had slaveholder populations above 20 percent, while four counties in each section exceeded 40 percent. Overall, in East Tennessee slaveholders made up only one-tenth of the population, compared with about a quarter in Middle Tennessee and one-third in West Tennessee. The percentages of planters and slaves in the population followed a similar pattern. Most slaves in East Tennessee were found on the commercial farms along the Holston and French Broad River valleys and in the larger towns.[29]

Finally, East Tennessee lagged significantly behind the rest of the state in wealth. In 1860 the aggregate wealth (real plus personal property) per capita was only $454. By contrast, the per capita aggregate wealth in Middle and West Tennessee was $934 and $1,243, respectively. The highest per capita wealth in East Tennessee was $730, in Jefferson County, while the top figures for Middle and West Tennessee were $2,600 and $3,300.[30]

These figures must be used with caution. Land values, for example, reflected a wide range of factors, including agricultural potential, demand, capital availability, population density, transportation facilities, and the market for commodities produced. Likewise, levels of wealth in the antebellum South were closely linked to both slaveholding and land values, and they may reveal very little about actual income levels or standard of living. Nonetheless, these figures suggest sharp economic and social differences between East Tennessee and the rest of the state.

Antebellum East Tennessee was a region for which the economic and political future was uncertain. Many East Tennesseans craved development that would improve the region's economic position, but while some promoted industrial expansion and exploitation of the region's resources, others feared the effects of manufacturing on the region's social and racial structure and favored continued reliance on agriculture and trade. The promise of favorable industrial and trade policies drew Whigs to the national government, as did their memories of King's Mountain and their reverence for the American Union. But other East Tennesseans identified strongly with the South and shared Southern fears of the North. Most East Tennesseans participated only peripherally in economic institutions fundamental to other parts of the South, yet the fortunes of a minority were increasingly dependent on slavery and Southern trade. Antislavery agitation in the North continued to repel almost all East Tennesseans, but at the same time many also resented the influence of large slaveholders over political affairs. Sadly, East Tennessee fit comfortably with neither the North nor the South, and whether it could find a home anywhere was a question with no easy answer.[31]

2 Hewers of Wood and Drawers of Water

East Tennessee gave few indications in the antebellum period that it would divide so completely from the rest of the South. East Tennessee leaders had not differed noticeably from the rest of the state on sectional issues, and Knoxville had hosted the 1857 Southern Convention. Both Whigs and Democrats had defended the institution of slavery, attacked Northern abolitionists, and promoted Southern expansion and economic development. Nonetheless, when war came the majority of East Tennesseans refused to leave the Union, and neither appeals nor threats would move them from this position.

In the antebellum period most Tennessee leaders had adopted a moderate position on sectional issues. Democrats tended to be more outspoken than Whigs in defense of Southern rights, but both parties had rejected radical measures. In 1847 the Tennessee Senate declared its opposition to the Wilmot Proviso, but voted down proposals to nullify any Federal statutes barring slavery in the territories. The majority of Tennesseans apparently supported the Compromise of 1850, and few Tennessee delegates attended a Southern convention held in Nashville in 1851 to discuss Southern grievances. Senator John Bell opposed both the Kansas-Nebraska Act and the LeCompton Constitution. And after John Brown's raid on Harpers Ferry, Representative T. A. R. Nelson condemned agitation of the slavery issue by both Southerners and Northerners.[1]

Moderation likewise prevailed in the presidential election of 1860. Tennessee played a leading role in the organization of the Constitutional Union Party, provided the new party with its presidential candidate, John Bell, and gave Bell twelve of his thirty-nine electoral votes. Tennessee's voting in this election followed established political patterns, and Democrats and Whigs each carried their usual counties. But Democrats split their votes between Stephen Douglas and John C. Breckinridge, allowing Bell to win a plurality. Most voters apparently did not view the election as a referendum on the sectional crisis, and even Andrew Johnson, destined to become the staunchest of Southern Unionists, reluctantly supported Breckinridge.[2]

Most Tennesseans reacted to Abraham Lincoln's election with caution. Moderates and conservatives alike were distressed at the triumph of a "Black Republican," but they also rejected immediate secession and favored waiting to see what course the new president would take. South Carolina's departure in December aroused little sympathy, and many Tennesseans angrily condemned that state's independent action. William G. McAdoo, a Knoxville Democrat who later became a staunch Confederate supporter, reacted to South Carolina's secession with contempt: "God speed her. I am willing to go with spade and pickaxe and work a month to ditch around her and float her out into the Atlantic a thousand miles."[3]

East Tennessee did not differ markedly from the rest of the state in its voting in 1860. Sixteen counties supported Bell and twelve Breckinridge, a division that closely matched the voting tendencies of these counties in the antebellum period. But the specter of secession was not entirely absent. William G. Brownlow repeatedly accused Breckinridge and his supporters of plotting to break up the Union and proclaimed his determination to defend the Federal government. The Reverend Nathaniel G. Taylor, state representative from Carter County, asserted that the consequence of Breckinridge's election would be civil war and insisted that East Tennessee would fight against the Deep South. Lincoln's election also aroused some concerns. A public meeting in Greeneville, home of Senator Andrew Johnson and Representative T. A. R. Nelson, issued resolutions asserting the right of Southerners to take slaves into all the territories, criticizing antislavery agitation, and deploring the election of a sectional president. Johnson's proposed resolution declaring secession illegal was voted down, and Andrew Jackson Fletcher, a Greeneville Whig who would become Tennessee's secretary of state in the Reconstruction period, concluded that the Union was effectively dissolved. But the excitement soon passed, and the pleas of Whig leaders for caution prevailed. Brownlow, Nelson, Oliver P. Temple, and others insisted that Lincoln's election was legitimate and asserted that the new president was simply an old-line Whig of the Henry Clay school who harbored no evil intentions toward the South.[4]

But moderates did not monopolize the political scene in Tennessee. On January 7, 1861, Governor Isham G. Harris, an outspoken secessionist, called the legislature into special session to discuss the current crisis. In his opening address Harris proposed submitting a compromise plan to the other Southern states. The basis of this plan was five constitutional amendments that would increase protection of slavery: extension of the Missouri Compromise line to the Pacific; a stronger fugitive slave law that would include compensation for unrecoverable slaves; protection of the rights of slaveholders temporarily residing in Northern states; the preservation of slavery in Washington, D.C.; and a requirement that any future amendments concerning slavery gain the consent of all slaveholding states. After presenting this plan, though, Harris admitted that he had little faith in the possibility of compromise and asserted that the only true question before the legislature was whether Tennessee would stand with the North or the South. The governor therefore pressed for prompt passage of an ordinance of secession. Most legislators were cautious, however, and refused to follow his lead. They authorized a referendum on secession for February 9, but allowed Tennessee voters not only to elect delegates to a state convention but also to determine whether or not they wished such a convention to be held at all.[5]

The results of the February referendum reflected Tennessee's political moderation. The proposal to hold a convention failed 68,282 to 59,449, while antisecession delegates outpolled secessionists 88,803 to 24,749. West Tennessee gave a decisive majority for the convention, but Middle and East Tennessee both voted the proposal down. Only three counties in East Tennessee recorded votes favorable to a convention, and none elected secessionist delegates.[6]

At the beginning of the secession crisis it was not obvious that East Tennessee would become a Unionist stronghold. Several prominent men, including future Confederate district attorney John Crozier Ramsey, Knoxville postmaster C. W. Charleton, lawyer and former congressman William H. Sneed, attorney John H. Crozier, physician and historian Dr. J. G. M. Ramsey, and railroad president W. W. Wallace actively supported secession, while many others expressed uncertainty about what course to take. But Whig leaders in Knoxville, supported by a majority of the population, outflanked

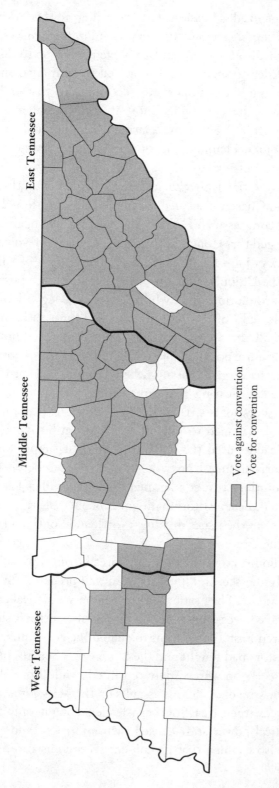

East Tennessee

Middle Tennessee

West Tennessee

■ Vote against convention

☐ Vote for convention

MAP 2. *Results of Special Election, February 9, 1861*

and outorganized secessionists. According to his own account, Oliver P. Temple, a successful lawyer and influential Whig spokesman, returned to Knoxville in late November 1860 to discover that local Confederate supporters had seized the initiative and were attempting to mobilize support for secession. To that end, they had scheduled a public meeting in Knoxville for November 25 to discuss the current crisis. The news alarmed Temple, and he met with Brownlow, John Fleming, and other Whigs to devise a strategy to counter the secessionists.

Speakers at the Knoxville meeting divided into three groups. Crozier and Charleton argued for immediate secession. Temple and Tennessee congressman Horace Maynard warned against hasty action and urged that Congress be given a chance to resolve the crisis. And attorneys John Baxter and W. B. Reece, both of whom would later take the Unionist side, proposed a compromise position. They introduced resolutions that, while denying the legality of secession, asserted the right of revolution and called for a gathering of delegates from all the Southern states to agree on a common course. This compromise position apparently reflected the majority opinion and was on the verge of passing when Temple, Maynard, and Fleming intervened. Fearing that any such convention would be controlled by secessionists, they raised a cloud of parliamentary objections and managed to put off the vote until a second meeting. Unionist leaders used the delay to rally their supporters from the districts surrounding Knoxville, and on December 8 they easily passed resolutions that condemned secession as illegal and unnecessary, asserted the constitutionality of Lincoln's election, and urged a compromise of the issues dividing North and South and the preservation of the Union.[7]

The Unionist movement quickly spread from Knoxville throughout East Tennessee, and loyalists were well prepared for the February referendum. They saturated the region with speakers and leaflets, portrayed secession as a conspiracy of Southern slaveholders, and implored East Tennesseans to defend the government for which their ancestors had fought and died. Johnson's Senate speeches condemning secession were widely reprinted, while Brownlow spewed out a steady stream of vicious assaults on the secessionist movement. Brownlow charged that Southern leaders sought only to preserve their political power and accused them of gross fraud and corruption. He also claimed that prominent secessionists in South Caro-

lina all had Tory ancestors and offered this prayer for preservation
of the country:

> Almighty God, our heavenly Father, in whose hands are the
> hearts of men, and the issues of events, not mixed up with Loco-
> focoism, nor rendered offensive in thy sight by being identified
> with men of corrupt minds, evil designs, and damnable purposes,
> such as are seeking to upturn the best form of government on
> earth, Thou hast graciously promised to hear the prayers of those
> in a humble spirit, and with true faith—such as no Secessionist
> can bring into exercise—call upon Thee. Be pleased, we beseech
> Thee, favorably to look upon and bless the Union men of this
> Commonwealth . . . Possess their minds with the spirit of true pa-
> triotism, enlightened wisdom, and of persevering hostility toward
> those traitors, political gamblers, and selfish demagogues who are
> seeking to build up a miserable Southern Confederacy, and under
> it to inaugurate a new reading of the Ten Commandments, so as
> to teach that the *chief end of man is Nigger!* [8]

The magnitude of the February victory, though gratifying to
moderate leaders, obscured both the fragility of Tennessee Unionism and the potential split between the eastern counties and the rest
of the state. Contrary to the belief of loyalist leaders in East Tennessee and Northern observers, Tennessee's vote did not constitute
an absolute rejection of secession. The continued loyalty of many
who had voted for Unionist delegates depended on two unlikely oc-
currences: Congress devising an effective, lasting settlement of sectional conflicts; and the Lincoln administration avoiding an armed
clash with Southern forces. Further, leading secessionists, including
Governor Harris, did not accept the February vote as final, but continued to labor for separation. Finally, the coalition that had defeated secession was itself fragile. A conglomeration of Democrats
and Whigs, conservatives and moderates, slaveholders and yeoman
farmers, it was held together only by the common threat of secession. This diversity of interests made it difficult to agree on a general platform beyond the immediate preservation of the Union. [9]

The Unionist coalition in Tennessee began to unravel almost as
soon as the campaign was over. A few weeks of cooperation could
not erase years of bitter party competition, and in early March old
enemies began to squabble over the distribution of Federal patronage in the state. Whig office-seekers, who made up a majority of the

coalition, expected favorable treatment from the Lincoln administration. But Lincoln assumed that he could rely on the loyalty of southern Whigs and concluded that it would be more profitable to reward Unionist Democrats. He therefore granted control of the patronage to Senator Andrew Johnson and Representative Emerson Etheridge. Johnson, concerned with his own political future, used his power to strengthen his personal following and retain some ties to the Democratic Party. Johnson's partisanship angered and embittered Tennessee Whigs, divided the coalition on old party lines, and demoralized Whig voters. His choice of the known secessionist John L. Hopkins as district attorney for East Tennessee particularly angered Unionists there, and several correspondents warned Johnson that suspicions and recriminations were corrupting the coalition and undermining Unionist unity.[10]

At the same time that the Unionist coalition was splitting internally, the foundations upon which conditional Unionism rested were crumbling. Efforts to resolve the sectional crisis and devise a compromise satisfactory to both sides floundered, and the two sides edged closer to an armed clash over the continued Federal occupation of Fort Sumter in South Carolina and Fort Pickens in Florida. Upper South Unionists, including Johnson and Nelson, offered a number of proposals in Congress, but, given their position as moderates in a time of extremism, they exercised little influence. Unionists failed to sway either Republicans or Southern partisans, and the defeat of the Crittenden Compromise and the failure of the Washington Peace Conference dashed their hopes for a satisfactory settlement.

The Confederate attack on Fort Sumter and Lincoln's subsequent call for troops gave the final blow to the precarious middle ground that conditional Unionists had occupied. Although a few proposed the formation of a border state confederacy and the maintenance of neutrality, most Upper South moderates concluded that the only choice left was on which side they would fight. In Middle and West Tennessee the Unionist coalition dissolved, and leaders who wished to retain power had little choice but to ride the secessionist tide. On April 18 eleven influential Whigs led by John Bell published a circular that condemned Lincoln's attempt to coerce the South and declared the Union effectively dissolved. Other former Unionist leaders soon followed. A few prominent men, including former Governor William B. Campbell and Representatives Emerson Etheridge and William B. Stokes, refused to bend, but they were a minority. Most attempts to speak against secession were feeble and quickly suppressed.[11]

Secessionist leaders moved quickly to exploit this shift in public opinion. Eleven days after Fort Sumter's surrender the Tennessee legislature again met in special session and with little debate took their state out of the Union. Basing their actions not on the doctrine of secession but rather on the right of revolution, the legislators passed a Declaration of Independence from the United States and a measure authorizing representation in the Confederate States government. Both measures were submitted to a referendum scheduled for June 8. But the legislature refused to wait for formal public sanction of its actions and immediately began placing Tennessee on a war footing. Harris authorized Southern forces to erect batteries on the Tennessee portion of the Mississippi River and sent W. C. Whitthorn, speaker of the Tennessee House of Representatives, to coordinate military preparations with the Confederate War Department. On May 7 the legislature ratified a Military League with the Confederate States and granted the governor authority to issue war bonds, raise and equip a state army, and commission officers.[12]

The specter of civil war dismayed and confused even Unionists in East Tennessee, and a minority, unable to fight against their Southern brothers, embraced secession. But the majority held firm and, while deploring the prospect of internecine conflict, announced their refusal to join an unjust war against the Federal government. East Tennessee loyalists were in fact confident of a second victory at the polls, and they quickly mobilized for the June referendum. Their confidence reflected a dangerous ignorance of political affairs in the rest of the state. Loyalist leaders had convinced themselves that secession in the rest of the South had been imposed on an unwilling people by scheming, unprincipled leaders. They claimed that the majority of Tennesseans opposed secession and, if allowed to vote freely, would defeat the measure on June 8. Their misperception of the political environment created a dangerous situation.[13]

Reinforced by the return from Washington of Johnson, Nelson, and Maynard, Unionist leaders launched a determined campaign. Johnson and Nelson undertook a strenuous joint canvass of the entire region, while local leaders mobilized their respective districts. Unionist rallies were held in almost every county of East Tennessee and were attended by hundreds, sometimes thousands, of supporters. Waving U.S. flags and sometimes carrying guns, loyalist voters cheered while speakers extolled the government of their forefathers and blasted the attempts of secessionists to destroy the nation. The stakes in this election were higher than they had ever been, and Unionist orators employed harsh and sometimes violent rhetoric.[14]

The speeches and writings of East Tennessee Unionists during this campaign reveal that they genuinely felt threatened by Confederate rule and alienated from the rest of the South. Loyalists repeatedly argued that the Confederate government endangered their status as free white men and invoked the image of slavery to depict their future status in the Confederacy. In his speeches to the Senate in the winter of 1860–61 Johnson portrayed the national crisis as a contest between democracy and aristocracy. He referred to Confederate president Jefferson Davis as a tyrant, and he warned that "the people of Tennessee are to be handed over to the Confederacy like sheep to the shearers." But Johnson also fiercely asserted that "whatever they may do . . . they never can, while God reigns, make East Tennessee a land of slaves." Likewise, Brownlow charged that the impending war would be fought by "the honest yeomanry of these border states, whose families live by their hard licks, four-fifths of whom own no negroes and never expect to own any," while "the purse-proud aristocrats of the Cotton States" remained at home. He concluded, therefore, that East Tennesseans "can never live in a Southern Confederacy and be made the hewers of wood and drawers of water for a set of aristocrats and overbearing tyrants." Brownlow also accused South Carolina's leaders of aristocratic leanings and concluded that "these are not the people to head a Confederacy for Tennesseans to fall into. . . . Let Tennessee once go into this *Empire of Cotton States*, and all poor men will at once become the *free negroes of the Empire*."[15]

Other leaders voiced similar fears. Horace Maynard condemned secession as "the uprising of the few against the many; the assertion of the rights of property in disregard of personal rights." Oliver P. Temple described the Confederacy as "a splendid aristocracy of slaveholders" and argued that such a government would inevitably threaten the status of the common people, for "large slaveholding communities were always inimical to non-slaveholding men." And William Randolph Carter, who fought with the First Tennessee Cavalry (Union) and later wrote the history of that regiment, blasted Governor Harris for attempting to "sell" Tennessee to the Confederacy and asserted, "The loyal people of East Tennessee . . . determined never to submit to this attempt to take away their liberty, destroy the government, and foster the yoke of slavery upon them. . . . [I]n the language of Patrick Henry, it was 'Give me liberty or give me death.'" [16]

Less prominent Unionists shared these sentiments. In June fourteen loyalists from Clinton reported to former governor William B. Campbell that "while King Harris is drilling his men for the purpose of awing, intimidating, and finally coercing us into subjection to him and his associated tyrants, we as Free men, are rubbing up our Riffles . . . and drilling for the purpose of defending ourselves, and protecting our liberties, and dying if need be." Another Unionist urged Nelson's son, David, to "go among the hills and the valleys of Carter and Johnson and rouse the people to stand firm for their rights. . . . Surely it is impossible that the mountaineers of East Tennessee will *ever* succumb to the So. Ca. traitors—to the minions of King Cotton." And the secessionist David Key complained that Nelson and Johnson had convinced "our backwoods yeomanry" that if secession passed the Confederacy would "elect a King to rule over them and grind them into powder." [17]

These fears of Confederate oppression derived from at least three sources. First, many East Tennesseans despised the large slaveholders who, they believed, controlled not only their state but also most of the South, and they did not wish to live in a nation dominated by this group. Though sometimes expressed by men of wealth, these sentiments reflected deep class resentments. Johnson's hatred of the so-called Southern aristocracy was particularly well known. He ridiculed the Tennessee elite as "an upstart, gulled headed, iron heeled, bobtailed aristocracy, who infest all our little towns and villages," and he condemned Southern rights leaders as "an illegitimate, swaggering, bastard, scrub aristocracy." Brownlow dismissed Southern planters as "descendants in direct line from some old foreigners who had been sold out upon shares to pay their passage to this country . . . who had taken their start in life by peddling upon pins and needles, by spading up gardens for other people, or by entering other people's lands, and, by hook or crook, securing their titles." Less prominent loyalists voiced similar antagonisms. In June 1861 one man from Harrison expressed his apprehensions concerning "the oppressions and degrading exactions that will no doubt be attempted to be imposed by the Rebel leaders in Tenn," while another Unionist looked forward to the time when East Tennessee would be "unpolluted by the tread of those who wear the chains of King Cotton, or cling to a supercilious and would be aristocracy." East Tennessee Unionists despised abolitionists as much as advocates of secession and argued that secession itself, which led inevitably to civil war, posed the greatest threat to that institution. But many Unionists also greatly resented the perceived privileges and domination of large slaveholders.[18]

Second, the manner in which secession was accomplished in Tennessee seemed to confirm Unionist suspicions of tyranny and triggered their republican fears. Unionists saw secession as a conspiracy developed in the 1850s by Southern Democrats. Foreseeing their loss of political dominance, Southern leaders deliberately split the Democratic Party and ensured Lincoln's election. They then took their states out of the Union through fraud, intimidation, and force. Unionists charged that the same tactics were used in Tennessee. They believed that Governor Harris had attempted to undermine the results of the February vote against separation, and they characterized his use of the legislature to pass the ordinance of secession, rather than calling a state convention to decide the issue, as unconstitutional. Finally, loyalists pointed out that the legislature had established the Military League with the Confederacy and raised troops almost a month before Tennessee voters had actually approved secession. In the eyes of East Tennessee Unionists, all these irregularities were simply manifestations of the tyranny and corruption against which they must fight.[19]

Finally, East Tennessee did not share the economic structure of the Deep South, and many Unionists feared that the Confederate government would create a political economy detrimental to their interests. Brownlow asserted that "we have no interest in common with the Cotton States. We are a grain growing and stock raising people, and we can conduct a cheap government, inhabiting the Switzerland of America." Nelson pointed out that the Confederate Constitution prohibited both a protective tariff and national aid for internal improvements, measures seen as important to East Tennessee's economic development. Even A. W. Howe, a Greeneville Democrat hostile to the Unionist movement, worried that "the Hemp, Rice, Sugar, and cotton planters of the extreme South, will want free ports, and will want revenue raised by taxation," thereby destroying the interests of the manufacturing sector. Loyalists were also convinced that, once secession passed, the political structure of South Carolina would be imposed on the whole Confederacy. Nonslaveholders would thereby lose the right to vote and hold office and would become second-class citizens at the mercy of the large slaveholders.[20]

The June campaign occurred in the midst of mobilization for war, and it is no surprise that it was characterized by fraud, intimidation, and violence on both sides. In Carter, Johnson, Knox, and many other counties Unionists threatened violence against anyone voting for secession, while in Polk County Confederate recruits intimidated the Unionist minority. A citizens' committee at Blountville requested that Johnson and Nelson cancel their appointment to speak there for fear of violence, and angry secessionists at Kingsport, Jonesborough, and Cleveland attempted to silence Johnson and Nelson when they appeared to speak. The scene at Jonesborough was particularly frightening: "He [Johnson] rose to speak. The crowd at once commenced *booing booing* until it fairly deafened you. . . . They cursed him for a *God Damned Traitor*—told him that he was hired by Lincoln to make speeches. . . . When he went to start out to Nelson's they raised the shout—groaned and *booed* him out of Town. . . . [Y]ou never seen such a time men on horses whipping up and down the street screaming upon the tops of their voices *you damned Traitor you damned Traitor*." Tensions were also reported to be very high in Madisonville, Jasper, and other communities.[21]

The presence of large numbers of Confederate troops in East Tennessee added to these tensions. Their de facto occupation of the region well before the June referendum inflamed Unionist tempers, while Confederate soldiers viewed the Unionists as traitors to the South. At Rogersville a Confederate company strode into a Unionist meeting and ordered Johnson to stop speaking. Johnson immediately took the initiative and asked whether anyone in the audience wanted him to cease. When no one responded he went right on, while the Confederates stalked out. At least two Confederate officers proposed using their troops to break up Unionist rallies and arrest the speakers, but they were restrained by authorities in Richmond. In Knoxville two Confederate companies and a military band deliberately marched past a street corner where Johnson was speaking. The noise of the band forced Johnson to halt, and as the procession neared angry Unionists reached for their weapons. A violent clash appeared certain, but bloodshed was averted when a prominent Confederate supporter, Colonel David Cummings, silenced the band and directed the procession down another street. But not all encounters were resolved peacefully. In early May 1861 Charles Douglass, a Knoxville Unionist, got into a heated debate with Major Wright Morgan over secession. Morgan pulled his pistol and attempted to fire, but Douglass fled to safety. Cummings prevented

Confederate soldiers from marching into Knoxville to punish Douglass, but a few days later an unknown sniper shot the Unionist dead in his home.[22]

The most serious clash between Confederate troops and East Tennessee loyalists occurred on May 5 at Strawberry Plains, where several hundred Unionists had gathered for a rally. The farm at which they were meeting was situated close to the tracks of the East Tennessee and Virginia Railroad, which was packed with cars carrying troops to Virginia. Just after the Unionists had gathered, a train of Alabama recruits pulled out of the Strawberry Plains depot. As it slowly passed, one soldier threw a stone at the speaker, then other soldiers seated on top of the cars began firing at the crowd. Armed Unionists fired back, and when the train had passed they rushed the tracks and attempted to tear them up. No one in the crowd was hurt, and Oliver P. Temple, who was present, concluded that the soldiers, meaning only to intimidate the Unionists, had deliberately fired over their heads. Nonetheless the incident frightened loyalists and further increased their resentment.[23]

The secessionist position achieved only a limited hearing in the June campaign. Local secessionists were reinforced by speakers from other parts of the Confederacy, including former Tennessee governor Gustavus A. Henry, former Mississippi governor Henry S. Foote, and Senators William Lowndes Yancey and John Bell, but they could not compete with the influence of Johnson, Nelson, and Maynard. Secessionist leaders found significant support in southern East Tennessee and in several towns along the line of the East Tennessee and Virginia and East Tennessee and Georgia Railroads, but in many other areas Unionist sentiment was so fierce that Confederate supporters could hardly campaign at all. Thus some secessionists resorted to more devious methods. C. W. Charleton used his position as Knoxville postmaster to hamper delivery of Brownlow's *Whig* and other Unionist literature, and he monitored the activities of the Unionists by reading their mail. Charleton and other secessionists also attempted to embarrass Johnson by forging a correspondence between the senator and Boston abolitionist Amos Lawrence and publishing it in the *Knoxville Register*.[24]

The network of loyalist leaders that directed the February and June campaigns assumed a more formal status at the Knoxville Convention of May 30–31, a gathering of 469 Unionists representing twenty-seven East Tennessee and two Middle Tennessee counties. Many of these delegates had been elected at county rallies, while others were self-selected. With the vote on secession yet one week away, the convention had no real agenda, and its immediate purpose was to solidify the Unionist front and create a formal organization for future contingencies. The resolutions that were adopted simply repeated the established Unionist platform: that secession was illegal and unconstitutional; that its passage would force Tennessee into a calamitous civil war; that in the existing Confederate states secession had been achieved not by democratic processes but by conspiracy and usurpation; and that the recent acts of the Tennessee legislature authorizing the June referendum and establishing a military alliance with the Confederacy were unconstitutional and therefore nonbinding. The resolutions also praised Kentucky for its neutrality and urged Tennessee to adopt the same policy.[25]

In spite of the tensions and irregularities that characterized the campaign, the actual voting went off quietly, with none of the violence that many had feared. The results stunned loyalists. The Unionist vote in East Tennessee declined from about 80 percent to 69 percent, but even so their second victory was decisive. The proposed measures for independence and Confederate representation went down by a margin of more than two to one, and only six of twenty-nine counties gave majorities for separation. But in Middle and West Tennessee secession triumphed by majorities of 50,000 and 23,000, respectively. The West Tennessee vote was no great surprise, but the support for secession in Middle Tennessee greatly distressed Unionist leaders. It also aroused their suspicions. That almost twenty thousand Middle Tennesseans could have reversed their position in only four months seemed impossible, as did the extremely lopsided results in many counties. Three Middle Tennessee counties recorded not a single vote against secession, while in twenty-two others secessionists won 80 percent or more of the total. Reports of illegal voting by Confederate soldiers, intimidation of loyalist voters, and suppression of Unionist speakers in Middle and West Tennessee quickly reached loyalist leaders, and an examination of the published returns confirmed their belief that the election had been fraudulent.[26]

The June campaign took place in an atmosphere that precluded normal voting, and there is no doubt that the results were distorted. Effectively the government of Tennessee and two-thirds of the state had already separated from the Union before the referendum votes were cast, and the election itself was a mere formality. Even more distorting was the fact that the campaign took place in a state that

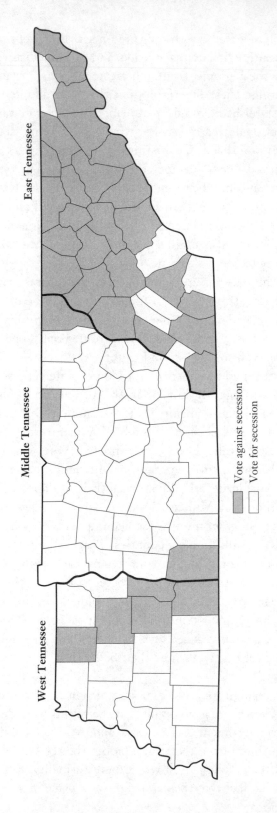

East Tennessee

Middle Tennessee

West Tennessee

Vote against secession

Vote for secession

MAP 3. *Results of Special Election, June 8, 1861*

was already at war. Thousands of men were drilling in camps, the railroads were flooded with military transport, and the government was erecting fortifications, issuing war bonds, and purchasing military supplies. Even friendly observers termed Knoxville a "military camp," with troops stationed just outside town at the fairgrounds, Home Guards drilling in the streets, and troop trains passing "day and night." A special act of the state legislature authorized Tennessee troops to vote in the district in which they were stationed, and in Knoxville soldiers marched to the polls, company by company, to cast their votes for secession. In other places soldiers remained at the polls all day to observe the voting and to hiss anyone with a Unionist ticket. But secessionists also complained of loyalist intimidation, while both Unionists and secessionists reported that at some locations ballots were marked and lists kept of voters who opposed the majority position.[27]

The accusation of fraud is more difficult to evaluate. The editors of the Johnson Papers concluded that circumstantial evidence does point to irregularities, particularly the fact that not only the official state returns but also the official totals of several counties simply disappeared. A marked difference between the margin of victory in East Tennessee and the rest of the state also raises questions. Only six counties in East Tennessee recorded majorities of 80 percent or more, while the average margin of victory was 49 percent. Conversely, twenty-four of thirty-four counties in Middle Tennessee, and seven of eighteen in the West, approved secession by a margin of 80 percent or more, while the average margin of victory was 78 percent and 66 percent, respectively. (See Appendix C.) It is likely, then, that the charges of fraud and manipulation possessed some validity. But while a fair election might have increased the Unionist vote, it would not have altered the final results, for the onset of war eliminated the hopes for compromise and threw conditional Unionists into the Confederate camp. Virginia, North Carolina, and Tennessee all exhibited similar pre-Sumter alignments, and the beginning of hostilities produced similar results in all three states.[28]

Nine days after the June vote 292 Unionist delegates assembled a second time, this time at Greeneville, in a world that had totally changed. The outcome of the June 8 election presented the East Tennessee Unionists with a situation for which they were sadly unprepared. Some delegates had been profoundly ignorant of the political situation in the rest of the state and had been stunned by the results of the referendum. Others had been better informed but had been reluctant to consider what they might do if secession passed. But now these leaders were called to face the crisis to which events, and their own actions, had brought them. Up to this point most of the actions of the Unionists had fallen within the safe, familiar realm of constitutional processes, of speeches, campaigns, and elections. The men meeting at Greeneville, however, now confronted a situation that would not be resolved through normal political means. The convention itself was considered an illegal gathering, and they risked arrest by meeting. These facts considerably influenced the attitudes of the men present, particularly the more conservative delegates.

Unlike the Knoxville gathering, the Greeneville Convention was marred by disharmony. The first day's proceedings split the delegates into two groups: the radicals, headed by Nelson, Brownlow, and local leaders such as Thomas D. Arnold, Andrew Jackson Fletcher, and William Clift; and the conservatives, led by Temple and Baxter. Nelson set forth the radical position in two documents, a Declaration of Grievances and a set of resolutions. Nelson's papers constituted a thinly veiled proclamation of rebellion. They declared that the Tennessee Declaration of Independence and the other acts of the Tennessee government relating to separation were unconstitutional and void, and they asserted that East Tennessee and the Unionist counties of Middle Tennessee would continue to constitute the true state of Tennessee. Nelson inserted a note of conciliation by promising that, if left alone, East Tennessee would remain neutral in the conflict. But he also asserted that if the Confederacy moved against East Tennessee, Unionists would defend themselves, call on the Federal government for protection, and if necessary retaliate against Confederate forces and the secessionist population. Nelson recommended that in preparation for this contingency every loyal county promptly raise and equip self-defense companies. Other radical delegates went even further and proposed that the convention itself raise an army of at least ten thousand men.

The Business Committee initially approved Nelson's documents with little debate, and the majority of delegates appeared ready to follow. But the fiery resolutions raised a storm among conservative leaders, who believed that such open defiance would invite Confederate repression. Their protests launched two days of intense, often recriminatory debate between the two groups, with the conservatives warning against the recklessness of the radical course and Nelson's supporters accusing the conservatives of cowardice. In the end, caution and moderation triumphed. The Business Committee completely rewrote Nelson's resolutions, and the convention delegates limited direct action to three cautious steps. First, they appointed a committee of three men to present a memorial to the Tennessee legislature requesting that East Tennessee and the Unionist counties of Middle Tennessee be allowed to form a separate state. Second, they authorized elections for delegates to a third Unionist convention to be held in Kingston in August, presumably for the purpose of organizing the new state. Finally, the convention established an executive committee of five men—Temple, Fleming, John Williams, Connelly F. Trigg, and Abner G. Jackson—to direct Unionist affairs until the Kingston Convention met. In a show of formal harmony, all but two delegates approved the final platform. But a number of radicals did not in fact accede to the conservative course, and after adjournment several met in secret and pledged to raise forces to resist Confederate rule.[29]

The Greeneville Convention revealed the essential conservatism of the senior Unionist leadership. Unionist spokesmen had stepped to the brink of revolution, then recoiled. Whigs, lawyers, and politicians, men who had thrived in and were devoted to the established political system, they could not bring themselves to abandon that system and plunge into the dark unknown of revolution and civil war. Thus they rejected the radical course and took refuge in the few constitutional options left to them. Their course was not unwise. It is likely that if Nelson's resolutions had passed Confederate authorities would have resorted to immediate, harsh repression, for no government, particularly one struggling for its life, could tolerate such disloyalty. Thus the armed struggle for East Tennessee would have begun in June rather than November. The hope that Unionist East Tennessee could exist uneasily within the Confederacy until rescued by Federal troops was also somewhat realistic. The conservative course held out the chance of escaping the horrors of repression and civil war, and this fact, as well as constitutional restraints, influenced the Greeneville delegates.[30]

But the possible wisdom of their course does not relieve the Greeneville delegates from all blame. The failure of Baxter, Temple, and other moderates was not their decision to take a cautious stance, but rather their having inflamed the East Tennessee population to the point of rebellion and then, at the point of crisis, attempting to reverse course. In the campaigns of February and June Unionist speakers, staking everything on a victory at the polls, had employed a rhetoric that was dangerously harsh and inflammatory even by the standards of the antebellum South. They had equated Confederate rule with slavery, portrayed secession as a plot to destroy the rights and liberties of common free men, and called on the Unionist masses to fight and die rather than submit to such bondage. This rhetoric of slavery and freedom, tyranny and liberty, was a common feature of antebellum politics and was not always dangerous. But Unionists in 1861 had taken it literally, and Temple admitted that more than once Unionist leaders had to dissuade their followers from violence: "[Their] zeal and indignation outran that of the speakers, and they became ready to take up arms. This feeling never abated." In these circumstances the conservative resolutions of the Greeneville Convention were absurd. After being convinced that Confederate rule was tantamount to slavery, how could Unionists now acquiesce in it? It is no surprise that conservative attempts to prevent violence failed. For there were other men in East Tennessee who did not shy away from the prospect of bloodshed, and after the Greeneville Convention control of the resistance would shift increasingly from prominent lawyers and politicians into the hands of farmers, merchants, county officials, and other local leaders.[31]

3 A State of Rebellion

The Unionist attempt to form a separate state of East Tennessee was a forlorn hope. The Tennessee legislature politely referred the loyalist memorial to a committee, which voiced doubts that the petition expressed the will of most East Tennesseans and concluded that the present legislature should take no action on the matter. Moderate Unionists were disappointed, but they counseled their followers to be patient and avoid a confrontation with Confederate authorities. Many loyalists, however, refused to accept that counsel, and despite Confederate efforts at conciliation they remained intransigent.[1]

After June 8 the Unionist campaign to throw off Confederate rule became increasingly violent. Loyalists organized and drilled military companies, seized political control of many counties, attempted to acquire weapons and ammunition, and initiated contacts with the Union army in Kentucky and with the Lincoln administration. In response, Federal forces developed plans to aid the Unionists and invade East Tennessee. Thousands of loyalists escaped to Kentucky to join the Federal army, while others remained in East Tennessee to harass Confederate troops and assault Southern supporters. Open Unionist resistance eventually culminated in mass uprising against the occupying forces.

The same conditions that allowed the Union and Confederate governments rapidly to recruit thousands of men were equally favorable to the formation of irregular forces. Given the state's militia structure, the presence of a few trained officers, and ready availability of firearms, rough forces could be quickly organized. The mobilization of partisan forces was primarily a decentralized process, but some prominent Unionists coordinated efforts in several counties. William G. McAdoo noted in August that the Sevier County Home

Guard was organized a few days after John Fleming had visited the county, though McAdoo also believed that Willie Homer, a brick-mason, was the principal leader. And after the Greeneville Convention at least eight delegates met to concert their efforts to raise troops.[2]

The Unionist mobilization was rapid and widespread, and within a few weeks loyalists were prepared to challenge Confederate rule. On July 6 reports spread that a Confederate force had entered Bradley County, and within a few hours seven hundred Unionists, most carrying some type of weapon, had assembled to meet them. On August 15 Confederate troops were rushed from Knoxville to Kingston in response to reports that three hundred armed Unionists had gathered there. In Hancock County rival Unionist and secessionist Home Guard units, each numbering two hundred or more, gathered in nearby camps and created a dangerous standoff that Confederate officers defused only with great difficulty. In Hamilton County perhaps five hundred Unionists assembled at the farm of William Clift, a wealthy merchant and farmer. They had originally congregated there in preparation for an escape to Kentucky, but soon so many had arrived that Clift established an armed camp, complete with fortifications and wooden cannon. R. A. Crawford reported to Nelson that 1,800 Unionists were drilling in Greene County and that most already had guns and ammunition. They had sent a trunk of sulfur and saltpeter to Knoxville in exchange for gunpowder, but Confederate authorities had intercepted the shipment. Samuel Bush informed Johnson that the Unionists of Fentress County were also eager to fight. They were short of arms, but they were seeking one thousand rifles or muskets from the Federal government. Admittedly, these Unionist companies lacked proper training, leadership, and equipment, and they could not stand up against regular troops. Nonetheless they represented a significant threat to Confederate control.[3]

Violence flared throughout East Tennessee in the summer and fall of 1861. In August Unionists in Carter and Johnson Counties killed at least two secessionists, wounded several others, persuaded the Confederate clerk of the court in Johnson County to resign, and reportedly forced numerous other Confederate supporters to flee to Virginia or North Carolina for safety. In Greene County Confederate troops feared being overrun and had to be reinforced. In Fentress County Unionist partisans ambushed a small group of Confederate troops and left one man for dead, while in Scott County three

Unionists surprised a dispatch rider and almost killed him. And when Confederate troops at Huntsville attempted to arrest a loyalist suspected of carrying communications to Kentucky, they were ambushed by Unionist bushwhackers, and Confederate officers had to send a second company to support the first.[4]

Unionists suffered from Confederate violence in turn. In July four Southern soldiers in Fentress County assaulted an outspoken Unionist. When a Knoxville Unionist got drunk and publicly gave three cheers for Lincoln, several Mississippi soldiers chased him down and beat him up. Other Mississippi troops attempted to hang a Unionist guilty of a similar indiscretion but were stopped by an officer. In October drunken soldiers clashed with police and citizens in Knoxville, and post commander Colonel William B. Wood, who believed that loyalists had deliberately provoked the confrontation, brought two companies into Knoxville to apprehend the aggressors. Wood threatened to burn down any building in which the Unionists were found, but fortunately for Knoxville the men had already fled.[5]

Confederate troops also targeted Unionist leaders. One night in August 1861 eight Confederate soldiers broke into the home of Andrew Jackson Fletcher, a prominent Greeneville loyalist and a delegate to the Knoxville and Greeneville Conventions, and attempted to kill him. Fletcher fought back and escaped, but the incident terrified him so much that he fled East Tennessee and spent the war in the safety of Indiana. As late as 1864 Fletcher still seemed shaken, writing that "here I fear no more the advance and retreat—the brutal soldiery or the assassin. Walk the streets all hours without arms and lie down at night and sleep serenely." Fletcher claimed, probably correctly, that secessionists in Greeneville had sent the soldiers to his house. Confederate soldiers also targeted John Baxter. After the Greeneville Convention Baxter had publicly recognized the Confederate government and announced his candidacy for a seat in the Confederate House of Representatives. Baxter still rejected the constitutionality of secession, but he believed that the Union was permanently severed, and he argued that the best course for Unionists was to occupy Confederate offices and thereby moderate Southern policies. Secessionists were suspicious of Baxter's intentions, and on August 15 several Confederate soldiers threatened to kill him in his hotel room in Tazewell. Baxter barricaded the door, held the soldiers off with a pistol, and made his campaign speech as planned. Unlike Fletcher, he also remained in East Tennessee.[6]

These encounters led to increasing tensions between Unionists and Confederate troops. When a troop train crashed on August 19 and killed five Mississippi soldiers, many Confederates blamed Major S. Temple, brother of Oliver P. Temple and superintendent of the railroad. That same month wild rumors spread among Confederate troops stationed outside Knoxville that Unionists had poisoned their food supply and that twenty men had already died. And H. C. Watterson, a Hawkins County secessionist, feared that his son's regiment would be trapped by Unionists in Knoxville "somewhat like a Missouri regt. near St. Louis was not long since."[7]

Confederate officials recognized the threat posed by East Tennessee loyalists. But they continued to hope that Unionists might still be won over to the Southern cause. Tennessee governor Isham G. Harris had received numerous reports that the resistance in East Tennessee was due primarily to the malignant influence of a few demagogic leaders and to the misapprehensions that they had created. To demonstrate Confederate goodwill, Harris urged President Jefferson Davis to station as few forces in East Tennessee as possible, employ only Tennessee regiments, and appoint a moderate and prudent man as commander. Harris also drew Davis's attention to the fact that the first three Tennesseans appointed generals were all Middle Tennessee Democrats and requested that the next commissions go to former Whigs from the other two sections.[8]

Except for his place of residence, the first commander of the Department of East Tennessee, Brigadier General Felix K. Zollicoffer, perfectly fit these criteria. Zollicoffer had begun his political career as a journalist and, after working on smaller papers in Columbia and Knoxville, had reached the position of assistant editor of the influential *Nashville Republican Banner*. By the early 1840s he had achieved a reputation, somewhat exaggerated, as a kingmaker in the Tennessee Whig Party. In 1849 Zollicoffer won a seat in the Tennessee Senate; then from 1853 through 1859 he represented Tennessee's important Eighth (Nashville) District in the U.S. House. When the secession crisis emerged in 1860 Zollicoffer exerted all his influence for compromise. He helped organize the Constitutional Union Party, stumped his district for John Bell, represented Tennessee in the Washington Peace Conference, and campaigned against secession in the February referendum. Like many other Southern Unionists, Zollicoffer clung to the Union until the fighting had actually begun: "I would have given all I had to preserve the Union, and the rights and honor of the South. But our reasonable demands were refused — equality and security of rights denied us." Elsewhere he asserted that "we must not, cannot, stand neutral and see our Southern brothers butchered." Nonetheless Zollicoffer remained sensitive to the fears of Southern Unionists.[9]

Zollicoffer arrived in Knoxville in late July. His initial orders from Secretary of War Judah P. Benjamin stated that his primary responsibility was to secure the rail lines in his department and block Northern attempts to smuggle arms into the region. His second was to break up the Unionist political and military organizations and if necessary aid civilian authorities in suppressing treason. At the same time, Benjamin instructed Zollicoffer to make every attempt to win over the rebellious population to the Confederate cause. How the new commander was to implement these conflicting responsibilities the secretary of war did not specify.[10]

Zollicoffer's first major act upon taking command was to issue a general proclamation to the loyalist population. The new commander first made clear that he would tolerate no resistance to Confederate rule. He stated unequivocally that the Confederate government considered the June referendum to be final and binding and warned that he would immediately suppress any rebellious activities. But Zollicoffer then attempted to calm Unionist fears concerning Confederate rule. He promised that if Unionists refrained from giving aid to the North they would be allowed to carry on normal activities: "No man's rights, property, or privileges shall be disturbed. All who desire peace can have peace, by quietly and harmlessly pursuing their lawful avocation." Essentially the new commander offered Unionists the refuge of neutrality. Zollicoffer was willing to tolerate Unionist sentiments as long as they did not lead to rebellious actions, and he demanded no token of loyalty or service to the Confederacy. But in his conclusion Zollicoffer warned that the price of continued resistance would be civil war within East Tennessee.[11]

Zollicoffer's attempts to conciliate Unionists were sincere and deliberately obvious. He enforced strict discipline among his troops, ordered his men to treat the population with respect, and attempted to minimize contact between Confederate troops and civilians by confining soldiers to their camps. Zollicoffer also maintained friendly relations with many Knoxville Unionists. According to one account, he refused to arrest loyalists whose letters to Northerners had been intercepted by postal authorities, and he welcomed old Whig acquaintances who came to see him. And in spite of mounting criticism by local secessionists, Zollicoffer allowed Brownlow to continue publication of the *Whig*, even when the publisher defiantly turned out editorials ridiculing Southern pretensions to greatness, accusing the Confederate War Department of corruption, and questioning the courage of local secessionists who declined to enlist.[12]

Confederate officers also protected citizens as much as possible from the burden of supporting Southern forces. Brigadier General William Caswell, who organized the initial Confederate mobilization in East Tennessee, issued very strict orders against taking any supplies from citizens and required officers to turn over soldiers who disobeyed to the civilian authorities for punishment. Caswell feared that depredations would damage the war effort, and he warned that lawless behavior would undermine Confederate policy by "falsify[ing] the assurances given by the military authorities" concerning the protection of private property. Zollicoffer altered these orders slightly, but his policies on foraging remained conservative. Zollicoffer recognized that Confederate troops might be forced to secure some subsistence from the population, but he specified that supplies not be taken from citizens unless absolutely essential for the welfare of the troops, and he limited foraging to quartermasters, commissaries, or specially appointed officers.[13]

Other Confederate authorities also attempted to woo the East Tennessee Unionists. In late July Major General Leonidas Polk persuaded four Tennessee moderates, Colonel Robertson Topp, Judge R. Caruthers, Dr. Jeptha Fowlkes, and D. M. Leatherman, to undertake a peace mission to East Tennessee to convince Unionists that Confederate rule posed no threat to their interests and that Southern troops were stationed in East Tennessee only to prevent a Northern invasion. At the same time President Davis appointed A. M. Lea, Zollicoffer's brigade commissary, an "emissary" to East Tennessee and instructed him to work out a reconciliation with loyalist leaders. These men, Topp in particular, traveled throughout East Tennessee, met with Unionist leaders, and discussed loyalist grievances. Topp also sent reports to Richmond and apparently met with President Davis in person concerning his findings. Lea also talked with a number of Unionist leaders, and he claimed to have published a handbill containing Zollicoffer's proclamation, a letter of submission from T. A. R. Nelson, and endorsements from other loyalist leaders. But neither Topp nor Lea altered the Unionist determination to resist Confederate rule. Several loyalists, in fact, claimed that Lea came to Knoxville not to make peace but to offer an ultimatum to Unionist leaders to submit or suffer imprisonment.[14]

The first test of Confederate policy came almost immediately after Zollicoffer's appointment. On August 1 Tennessee was scheduled to hold its first state elections under Confederate rule, but
many Confederates believed that conditions in East Tennessee were
too unsettled to risk another political campaign. Confederate senator Landon Carter Haynes urged Harris to suspend the elections in
the eastern counties, arguing that a campaign at this time would
simply encourage further resistance and suggesting that the governor appoint provisional representatives instead. Haynes and J. G. M.
Ramsey both reported that Unionists were organizing into military
companies and talked openly of revolt and the coming of the Union
army. Other secessionists warned of threats to the East Tennessee
railroads, claimed that the Lincoln administration had shipped ten
thousand muskets to Cincinnati with the intention of smuggling
them into East Tennessee, and pointed out that loyalists had not
abandoned plans to hold a third convention in August. But Harris
and Zollicoffer believed that the risk of opening the polls was justified. Free elections might demonstrate that Confederate rule posed
no threat to the rights of East Tennesseans and counter the asser-
tions of Unionist leaders.[15]

Secessionist fears proved fully justified, for Unionists still harbored hopes of recapturing control of the state government in the
August elections and reversing Tennessee's secession. Attempting to
appeal to a broad segment of moderate and conservative sentiment,
they rejected William G. Brownlow's bid for the governorship and
instead nominated William B. Campbell, a former popular governor who had spoken out against secession in Middle Tennessee. But
Campbell recognized that the cause was hopeless and withdrew,
leaving William H. Polk to take his place. Polk ran a feeble campaign, and the gubernatorial election repeated the results of the
June referendum. Polk easily won East Tennessee but lost disas-
trously in the rest of the state. East Tennessee Unionists enjoyed
greater success in the congressional elections, however. In each of
the region's three districts a Unionist candidate running avowedly
for the U.S. Congress opposed the Confederate candidate. In the
First and Second Districts the loyalist candidates, Nelson and Maynard, won decisively. In the Third District both candidates claimed
victory, but it is likely that the Unionist George Bridges received
the majority of votes. Loyalists also dominated most county and
municipal elections.[16]

Harris and Zollicoffer refrained from interfering in the campaign, even when Unionist candidates repeatedly condemned the Confederacy. But both men were embarrassed and angered at the

results of the August elections, and both displayed a marked change in attitude. On August 3 Harris stated, "I fear we will have to adopt a decided and energetic policy with the people of that section," and on August 16 he requested that the War Department station twelve to fourteen thousand troops in the region to "crush out rebellion there without firing a gun." On August 6 Zollicoffer concluded that "there are very many Lincoln men here who will be restrained from cooperating [with a Union invasion] only by consideration of policy or apprehension of the circumstances," and one recruit claimed to have heard Zollicoffer state that he "has a force sufficient, at his command and that he intends whenever [rebellion] shows its head to crush it out, let the cost be what it may."[17]

Increased Confederate vigilance partially negated the Unionist victory at the East Tennessee polls. Though all three Unionist representatives attempted to reach Washington, D.C., only one, Maynard, succeeded. George Bridges successfully escaped Tennessee before the election and waited for his family to join him in Kentucky. Confederate authorities sent word that his wife was ill, however, and arrested Bridges when he slipped back into Tennessee. Nelson, hoping to escape Confederate surveillance, rode into the mountains with a small escort immediately after the election. But on August 4 Confederate cavalry intercepted him in southwest Virginia, less than twenty miles from the Kentucky border. Secessionists wanted Nelson indicted for treason, and initially Zollicoffer, after consultation with district court judge West H. Humphreys, determined to send the Unionist leader secretly to Nashville to stand trial. Perhaps fearing the response that such a move would provoke, however, Zollicoffer reconsidered and instead sent Nelson to Richmond, leaving his fate to the government there.

Confederate pressure convinced both leaders to submit. Nelson was defiant at first, but President Davis gave him no choices other than recognition of Confederate authority or indefinite imprisonment. After several lengthy exchanges with the president, Nelson came to terms. In return for release from confinement and immunity from prosecution Nelson agreed to recognize the authority of the Confederate government, counsel Unionists to submit, and refrain from making public statements against the Confederacy. Nelson faithfully kept this agreement. Except for his law practice, which involved him in several war-related issues, he abandoned public life for the remainder of the Confederate occupation. Bridges likewise submitted to the Confederate government and agreed to remain quietly in East Tennessee, but in 1862 he secured a travel pass, ostensibly for business purposes, and fled East Tennessee.[18]

Though Confederate authorities managed to neutralize two powerful Unionist figures, two others eluded their grasp. Johnson had ridden out of East Tennessee in July, and Confederate troops had made no attempts to stop him. Maynard had spent election day in Scott County and had crossed the border into Kentucky as soon as the voting had ended. The Confederate failure to capture these two men was significant. Though Johnson and Maynard could no longer lead the resistance in person, they continuously pressured the Lincoln administration to rescue their loyal constituents and kept the cause of East Tennessee before the Northern public. After Federal forces captured much of Middle and West Tennessee in 1862, President Lincoln appointed Johnson military governor, and he and Maynard led attempts to create a loyal government in the state.

Confederate authorities soon moved against other resistance leaders. In early August Zollicoffer, in accordance with Benjamin's orders, began sending out expeditions to break up Unionist organizations and arrest their leaders. He also increased attempts to prevent Unionists from reaching Kentucky. At the same time, Confederate district attorney John Crozier Ramsey began arresting prominent Unionists. Robertson Topp estimated the number of Unionists detained at over one hundred, but it may have been higher, for in October the Confederate district court in Knoxville held a special three-week session to handle these cases. Topp concluded that many arrests were the result of personal grievances or past party conflicts, and he blamed not only Ramsey but also Postmaster C. W. Charleton and William Swan, all Democrats and old enemies of Brownlow, for their instigation. Secessionist hopes for stern measures were disappointed, however. District court judge Humphreys refused even to order trials for most of the defendants brought before him. He required only that Unionists take the oath of allegiance to the Confederate government and give bond for good behavior, and he freed even some who refused to meet these conditions. Humphreys, reflecting the conservatism of many Southern courts, rejected secessionist arguments that the war justified extreme measures and refused to set aside previous standards of individual rights and due process.[19]

But not all Unionists escaped punishment. In August the Confederate Congress passed two measures to eliminate the internal threat to the new nation. The Alien Enemies Act defined anyone refusing to recognize the authority of the Confederate government and retaining allegiance to another nation as an alien enemy. Such persons were given forty days either to swear allegiance to the Confederacy or take up residence elsewhere. Those who remained after this time were subject to arrest and expulsion. The Sequestration Act, in turn, stated that the property of alien enemies was subject to confiscation and sale at a public auction. East Tennessee secessionists energetically used these acts against their Unionist enemies. For the next two years the county courts were full of sequestration cases, and dozens, perhaps hundreds, of Unionists lost their homes and property. Sequestration actions created great bitterness against secessionists and led to retaliation when Federal forces seized control of the region.[20]

These measures, combined with the wave of arrests and the recent Federal defeat at Bull Run, caused some East Tennessee Unionists to waver. In October 1861 even Brownlow, the leading symbol of the Unionist revolt, apparently contemplated recognition of the Confederate government. But within a few weeks these fears passed. The attempted purge of Unionist leaders and the Sequestration Act damaged many Unionists, but they also confirmed Unionist fears about Confederate rule, and ultimately their effect was to stiffen loyalist resistance.[21]

By October it was clear to many that Confederate policies in East Tennessee were dangerously ineffective. Confederate attempts to convert Unionists had failed, while Zollicoffer and local authorities had proven unable to break up most Unionist organizations and establish Confederate authority. In part, Zollicoffer failed simply because he lacked sufficient troops to police all of East Tennessee. He had fewer than ten thousand men, most poorly armed and inadequately trained, and he had to concentrate them at major towns, railroad lines, and the passes on the Tennessee-Kentucky border. Thus many counties in East Tennessee remained untouched by Confederate authority. Further, the mountains and valleys, coves and forests of East Tennessee provided innumerable secret places that even the most vigilant Confederate surveillance would have missed. But Zollicoffer also misjudged where the true threat to his department lay. Though he, Harris, and Davis all continued to receive warnings that a loyalist revolt was imminent, an invasion from Kentucky also seemed certain, and Zollicoffer chose to give most of his attention to this danger. He moved six regiments to Jamestown, near the Kentucky border, and left the interior largely unguarded. Colonel William B. Wood, left in command at Knoxville, had at his disposal only two hundred infantry in Knoxville, one company of cavalry, and a few infantry companies scattered along the railroad line.[22]

Zollicoffer's dispatches in October reveal a harried man, distracted by repeated rumors of invasion and frustrated by the lack of reliable intelligence concerning his enemy's strength, position, or intentions. On October 25 he reported "reliable information" that ten thousand Union troops were advancing on Cumberland Gap. Five days later Zollicoffer estimated the Union force at nine thousand, placed it at London, Kentucky, and believed its aim to be Jacksborough or Jamestown. On November 4 he was still awaiting an attack on Jamestown by a Union force now estimated at six thousand, but the next day he received information that Union forces instead were fortifying London in expectation of an attack. Finally, on November 6 Zollicoffer reported that he was again expecting a Union invasion, this time from a force near Monticello. Each new report compelled Zollicoffer to shift his forces, and his uncertainty increased.[23]

Zollicoffer had not forgotten entirely about the loyalist menace, and on October 28 he sent cavalry to Jacksborough and Montgomery to cut off communications between Union troops in Kentucky and East Tennessee partisans. But he refused to give sufficient weight to the Unionist threat. From Knoxville, Wood repeatedly informed Zollicoffer that unrest among Unionists was increasing, and Wood became so worried that on November 4 he appealed directly to Richmond for reinforcements. But Zollicoffer believed that most Unionists were becoming reconciled to Confederate rule. He sympathized with Wood's fears, but in the end he largely dismissed the internal threat: "Watch the movements of the Lincoln men in East Tenn.—restrain our ultra-friends [hard-line secessionists] from acts of indiscretion—promptly meet and put down any attempted open hostility. But I have observed heretofore that a few of our friends about Knoxville are unnecessarily nervous—give their expressions of apprehension only their due weight." Eight days later his department erupted.[24]

While the East Tennessee Unionists mobilized, the Lincoln administration and Federal commanders formulated plans for the invasion of the region. In late June Lieutenant General Winfield Scott sent Lieutenant William Nelson to Kentucky to organize recruits from Kentucky and Tennessee and promised him sufficient arms and equipment. In July Nelson was joined by J. P. T. Carter, an influential Unionist from Carter County seeking arms for East Tennessee loyalists, and Samuel P. Carter, a lieutenant in the U.S. Navy whom Lincoln had recalled from duty, commissioned a colonel in the U.S. Army, and sent to Kentucky to organize Tennessee refugees. Informed by J. P. T. Carter that Confederate troops now blocked all routes into East Tennessee, Nelson abandoned any notion of attempting to smuggle arms into the region, but he continued organizing and training recruits at Camp Dick Robinson. In August Brigadier General William T. Sherman assumed command of the Department of the Cumberland, and in September Brigadier General George H. Thomas took over the organizing and training at Camp Dick Robinson. By that time two East Tennessee regiments had joined about five thousand other recruits. Thomas had the beginnings of an army, but his troops required considerable training and were poorly equipped. Andrew Johnson repeatedly lobbied the War Department for additional weapons, ammunition, and equipment, but with limited success. Part of a shipment of five thousand muskets intended for the Kentucky Home Guards was set aside for East Tennessee, and a group of Boston merchants headed by Amos Lawrence raised $1,750 to transport arms to the Unionists, but these efforts fell far short of what was required.[25]

Union officers were prodded into action in September, when the Reverend William B. Carter, a third member of the Carter clan, escaped from East Tennessee. Carter met with Sherman, Thomas, Johnson, and Maynard in Kentucky and then traveled to Washington, D.C., to present a brash plan to President Abraham Lincoln, Secretary of War Simon Cameron, and Major General George B. McClellan. Carter suggested that Unionists could assist a Northern move into East Tennessee by destroying nine key bridges on the railroads connecting East Tennessee with Georgia, Virginia, and Middle Tennessee. This sabotage would cut East Tennessee off from Confederate reinforcements, while an accompanying mass uprising would occupy the few forces in the region. Under these conditions Union troops could easily take and hold East Tennessee. McClellan favored the plan as a diversion for his impending Virginia campaign, and Lincoln, who still hoped to exploit Unionist sentiment in the South, was particularly interested in rescuing loyalist East Tennessee. In the last week of September the president ordered the Army of the Cumberland to seize and hold a strategic point on the East Tennessee and Virginia Railroad, and Carter left Washington with at least $2,500 for his operation and the belief that he had a firm commitment for an invasion.

Upon his return to Kentucky, Carter met with Thomas to finalize his plans. He then slipped back into East Tennessee, accompanied by two Union officers, Captain William Cross of Scott County and Captain David Fry of Greene. The three men formed several small groups of local volunteers. Carter assigned one or two bridges to each and set the operation for the night of November 8. Confederate authorities, though generally aware that Unionists had made threats against the railroads, apparently had no specific knowledge of Carter's plan and failed to provide adequate guards for all the bridges.[26]

On October 22 and 27 Carter sent messages to Thomas describing Unionist sufferings and urging Federal troops to move quickly. Thomas did not receive these notes until November 4, however, and apparently he sent no reply. Carter therefore was not informed of a change in Federal plans, though he may have guessed that fact. Sherman had initially approved the East Tennessee campaign with considerable reluctance, and his doubts had grown considerably since. Fearful of the possibility of a joint invasion of Kentucky by Zollicoffer and Confederate troops in Middle Tennessee, increasingly overwhelmed by his responsibilities, and close to a breakdown, Sherman could not face the risks that an invasion of East Tennessee entailed. All the regiments in eastern Kentucky were below strength, and all lacked weapons and equipment. Further, the territory in which Union forces would have to operate was extremely rugged, and the lack of water and rail transportation would make supplying even a small army difficult. There was no guarantee that, even if Union troops captured East Tennessee, they could hold it for long.[27]

Thomas was more resolute than Sherman. Accompanied by both Horace Maynard and Andrew Johnson, by late October he had marched six regiments to Crab Orchard, Kentucky, forty miles from Cumberland Gap, and had sent patrols almost to the border. But on November 5 Sherman's doubts won out, and he ordered Thomas to remain where he was. Thomas protested the order and urged Sherman to reconsider, while Johnson frantically implored Sherman to proceed and threatened to lead the East Tennessee troops himself. Sherman could not be moved, however, and on November 8, only a few hours before the bridges were scheduled to be burned, he ordered the invasion postponed indefinitely. Sherman rescinded this order a few days later, but by then it was too late for the East Tennessee Unionists.[28]

Despite the stalled Union advance, Carter carried out his part of the plan. The reasons for Carter's persistence are not clear. It is possible that he was unaware that Sherman had canceled the invasion and was relying on the arrangements made in Washington. It is equally likely that Carter suspected that Union plans had changed and was gambling that an uprising would force Federal troops to enter East Tennessee. Whatever the case, the results, though short of Carter's expectations, were impressive. Loyalist partisans destroyed five of nine bridges: the Hiwassee River Bridge in Bradley County, the Lick Creek Bridge near Greeneville, the Holston River Bridge in Sullivan County, and two spans over Chickamauga Creek near Chattanooga. Transportation on three different railroads, the East Tennessee and Virginia, the East Tennessee and Georgia, and the Western and Atlantic, was disrupted. Unionist bands also destroyed telegraph lines at numerous points, temporarily isolating the main Confederate force at Cumberland Gap and cutting Knoxville off from Nashville and Richmond.

Various mishaps preserved the remaining four bridges. Two Unionists rode to Bridgeport, Alabama, to break the Memphis and Charleston Bridge spanning the Tennessee River, but they could not penetrate the large guard detail there. Insurgents also found the Watauga River Bridge in Carter County and the Tennessee River Bridge near Loudon too heavily guarded to approach. Finally, the loyalists assigned to the Holston River Bridge near Strawberry Plains were plagued by poor planning and worse luck. Thirteen men got onto the bridge but were then surprised by a single guard. In the ensuing struggle two Unionists were wounded, and the group, having lost both their matches and their nerve, gave up the attempt. But considering the nature of the operation, attempting as it did the simultaneous destruction of bridges spread along 270 miles of track, even its partial success was remarkable.[29]

The news of the bridge burnings and the rumor that a Federal army had entered East Tennessee quickly sparked a mass revolt. At least three hundred men gathered at Clift's farm in Hamilton County, and one panicked Confederate reported that seventy-five Federal soldiers had also been seen. Four hundred Unionists assembled near Strawberry Plains to threaten the bridge there. Over

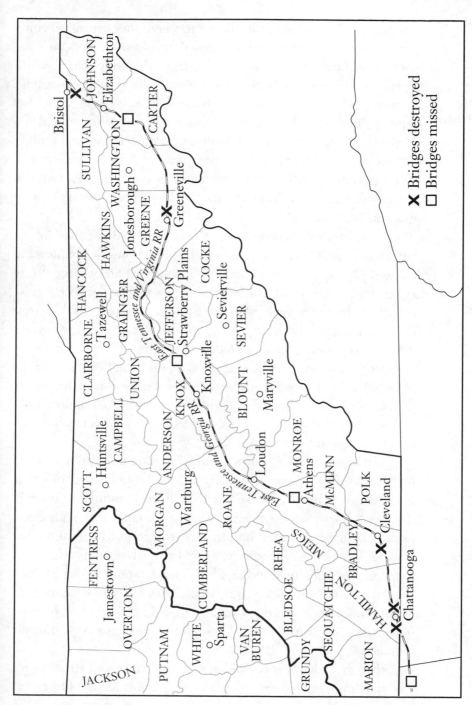

MAP 4. *Bridges Burned by Unionists, November 8, 1861*

one thousand gathered at Elizabethton, where they organized companies, elected officers, and stockpiled supplies. Confederate authorities at Loudon reported threats against the bridge there, while terrified secessionists in Greeneville pleaded for protection against Unionists gathering in that area. Large Unionist bands were also reported in Cocke, Washington, Hancock, Meigs, Sevier, Carter, McMinn, Bradley, Rhea, Knox, Johnson, Scott, Morgan, and Campbell Counties. Citizens in the border areas of North Carolina and Georgia, frightened by the uproar, asked for protection. As the post commander at Knoxville summarized, "The whole country is now in a state of rebellion."[30]

The November uprising revealed the magnitude of the Unionists' mobilization. But it also demonstrated their unpreparedness for combat. Although the four hundred Unionists at Strawberry Plains faced only a company of Confederate regulars and a few secessionist volunteers from Knoxville, they were unable to capture and destroy the bridge there. The insurgents at Elizabethton held out for over a week and repulsed several Confederate assaults, but they were eventually forced to flee, and dozens were captured and imprisoned. In other counties Unionists dispersed after exchanging a few shots with Confederate troops. The uprising was meant to support a Federal invasion, and when that invasion failed to materialize open rebellion collapsed.[31]

It will never be known how many Unionists were privy to Carter's plan. A Confederate officer from East Tennessee asserted that fewer than five hundred were involved in the conspiracy. Oliver P. Temple, who wrote the most complete account of this incident, placed the figure at three hundred. Most prominent loyalists, including Temple and Brownlow, denied any advance knowledge of the plot. The magnitude and rapidity of the Unionist uprising might suggest that the conspiracy was widespread, but Unionists had already proven their ability to mobilize quickly. Further, logic supports a low number, for any large plot would have been difficult to hide.[32]

Although Federal forces did not arrive, the Confederates did. The uprising jolted state authorities and Confederate officers out of their complacency, and within hours reinforcements were rolling toward East Tennessee. Brigadier General William H. Carroll brought two regiments from Memphis, and four additional regiments came from Middle Tennessee and Georgia. The continued threat of a Union invasion forced Zollicoffer to hold most of his forces on the border, but he sent one regiment to strengthen the defenses at Knoxville.

These forces moved quickly and energetically to crush the uprising. Carroll placed Knoxville under martial law, controlled all access into and out of the town, and sent his forces to conduct a house-to-house search for weapons. Movement into and out of Chattanooga was also restricted. Confederate forces, aided by secessionist volunteers, attacked and dispersed camps of Unionists in over a dozen counties. They then fanned out into the countryside, going farm to farm, arresting men reported as bridge burners or known to have been at a Unionist camp, and taking them to Knoxville. They entered homes to search for arms and ammunition, carried off food and possessions, and lay in wait for Unionist fugitives to emerge from their hiding places. Confederate troops had orders to limit arrests to men guilty of sabotage or those found "in arms" against the government, but they were not inclined to make fine distinctions, and anyone known to have voted against secession was at risk. There is also evidence that Confederate troops chose to shoot down or hang some loyalists on the spot, though the number of atrocities was probably not so great as Unionists later charged.[33]

Zollicoffer believed that Unionists had betrayed his trust, and he was bitter and vindictive. On November 12 he declared that "their leaders should be seized and held as prisoners. The leniency shown them has been unavailing. They have acted with base duplicity, and should no longer be trusted." Zollicoffer also ordered that those "fugitive traitors" still in rebellion "should now be pursued to extermination if possible," and asserted that "those that are yet hostile can only be cured of their folly by severity. They should be made to feel in their persons and their property that their hostile attitude promises to them nothing but destruction." Conciliation having failed, Zollicoffer now embraced repression.[34]

Zollicoffer's abrupt shift in approach had little significance, however, for his influence on policy in East Tennessee declined after the rebellion. Zollicoffer remained on the Kentucky border until December, sometimes out of contact with his subordinates, and most of the hard, dirty work of suppressing the uprising was left to Carroll, Wood, and Colonel Danville Leadbetter. Furthermore, the Confederate War Department no longer trusted Zollicoffer's leadership and directly intervened in East Tennessee. Wood had written

Richmond for guidance concerning the punishment of Unionist prisoners, and on November 25 Benjamin sent identical instructions to Zollicoffer, Wood, Leadbetter, and Carroll:

> 1st. All such as can be identified as having been engaged in bridgeburning are to be tried summarily by drum-head court-martial, and, if found guilty, executed on the spot by hanging. It would be well to leave their bodies hanging in the vicinity of the burned bridges.
> 2nd. All such as have not been so engaged are to be treated as prisoners of war, and sent with an armed guard to Tuscaloosa, Ala., there to be kept imprisoned at the depot selected by the Government for prisoners of war. Wherever you can discover that arms are concealed by these traitors you will send out detachments, search for and seize the arms. In no case is one of the men known to have been in arms against the Government to be released on any pledge or oath of allegiance. The time for such measures is past. They are all to be held as prisoners of war, and held in jail till the end of the war. Such as come in voluntarily, take the oath of allegiance, and surrender their arms are alone to be treated with leniency.
> P.S. Judge Patterson, Colonel Pickens, and other ringleaders of the same class must be sent at once to Tuscaloosa to jail as prisoners of war.[35]

After hasty trials, Confederate military tribunals at Greeneville and Knoxville convicted seven men of bridge burning. Three had their sentences commuted, but four were executed in the manner that Benjamin had prescribed. Over two hundred other loyalists, including state senators and representatives, local officials, and other influential figures accused of involvement in the conspiracy, were sent to military prisons in the Deep South. A few Unionists chose to enlist rather than face imprisonment, but the remainder, totaling around one thousand, languished for days or weeks in local jails. District court judge Humphreys attempted to issue writs for the release of some loyalists, but military officers spurned civilian interference.[36]

The most prominent figure arrested at this time was William G. Brownlow. Brownlow had published the last issue of the *Whig* on October 24, claiming that Confederate harassment had driven him to bankruptcy and accusing Confederate authorities of plotting to arrest him. According to Temple, Brownlow had then attempted to flee to Kentucky but had turned back when he learned that Confederate troops blocked all the mountain passes. On November 5 Brownlow had again disappeared from Knoxville, this time taking refuge with Unionists in Sevier County. The impending bridge burnings may have precipitated his flight, but this is not clear. Brownlow claimed that he left Knoxville to avoid arrest and to collect debts owed his paper, and he denied any knowledge of the conspiracy. After hiding for almost three weeks Brownlow secretly returned to Knoxville and sent a letter to Carroll offering to give himself up in return for a promise of safe passage out of Tennessee. Carroll agreed, and on December 5 Brownlow appeared at Carroll's headquarters for his passport. But the following day, before Brownlow could depart, Confederate district attorney John Crozier Ramsey obtained a warrant for his arrest and had him detained in the Knoxville jail. Brownlow protested to Carroll that their agreement had been violated, but the general pointed out that he had promised Brownlow protection only against military arrest, that he had no authority over Ramsey, and that Brownlow had in fact agreed if necessary to answer charges in civil court.

Brownlow remained in prison for more than three weeks. He then took sick and was allowed to return to his home, where he remained under house arrest. Lack of evidence eventually forced Ramsey to drop his charges against Brownlow, but military authorities then immediately rearrested him. Brownlow complained unceasingly of his treatment and repeatedly demanded that he be allowed to leave East Tennessee. Knoxville secessionists urged that Brownlow be tried for treason, but the manner in which Brownlow had been arrested proved an increasing embarrassment. In February even Benjamin concluded that Confederate authorities had shown bad faith in imprisoning the editor and urged that he be given safe passage out of Confederate territory. The new East Tennessee commander, Major General George B. Crittenden, agreed, and in early March Confederate cavalry escorted Brownlow to Union lines near Nashville.[37]

In addition to laying down new policy, the War Department also showed its displeasure with Zollicoffer by reorganizing the command structure in East Tennessee. On November 15 Benjamin gave Leadbetter responsibility for protecting the railroads and suppressing the insurrection, leaving Zollicoffer in command only of the troops on the border. Leadbetter had led the forces that had broken up the Unionist camp at Elizabethton. He had also adjudicated at the Greeneville tribunal and ordered three men hanged. Leadbetter's decisions were rumored to have been swift and ruthless, and his obvious zeal for the Confederate cause won Benjamin's trust. Then on December 13 the secretary of war ordered Crittenden to

Kentucky to take charge of forces there, thus completing his repudiation of Zollicoffer. Benjamin reminded Crittenden that "the policy of the Government [is] to show no further clemency to rebels in arms," and he repeated the orders he had sent to Wood on November 25. But Crittenden did not arrive until early January, by which time Zollicoffer had advanced into Kentucky. A few days later Zollicoffer died leading Confederate forces in the ill-fated battle of Mill Springs.[38]

By the middle of December Confederate commanders could report that the uprising had ended. They had dispersed all large groups of armed Unionists, arrested dozens of leaders, and detained hundreds of Unionist partisans. Nonetheless, the potential for resistance remained. In late November 1861 Major General Albert Sidney Johnston reported to Governor Harris that recruits from East Tennessee could not be transferred elsewhere until their families were secured against violence, a report echoed by a secessionist from Jonesborough. In December Leadbetter reported that the Confederate hold on the northern counties was tenuous and asserted that Confederate sympathizers remained in great danger. J. G. M. Ramsey also predicted that, despite their defeat, Unionists would revolt again if given a chance.[39]

As the repression dragged on into January the Richmond government again modified its policies. Some arrests, particularly that of the elderly state senator Levi Trewhitt, had caused even Confederate supporters to question Confederate harshness. Both Unionists and secessionists urged that Trewhitt be released and informed Benjamin that many other arrests had been unjustified. Tennessee congressmen also questioned the secretary of state concerning Confederate policy in the eastern counties. In response Benjamin instituted a review of the cases of all Unionists still confined in Knoxville and ordered that anyone arrested without cause be released.[40]

The cancellation of the Federal invasion doomed Unionist hopes for an early deliverance from Confederate rule. The bridge sabotage temporarily halted transportation on the railroads, but Leadbetter reported on November 13 that some trains were still running, and the lines were fully reopened in January 1862. Temple considered the bridge burnings a terrible mistake because of the repression they brought, and other Unionists were angry with Carter for attempting such a dangerous scheme. The outcome certainly did not benefit the Unionist population. The uprising created vast confusion and terrified Confederate authorities and East Tennessee secessionists, but rather than loosening the Confederate grip on East Tennessee it led to a hardening of Confederate policy.[41]

At the same time, it would be an error to overestimate the importance of the bridge burnings. Contrary to the claims of Unionists in 1861 and some historians since, conditions were not improving in East Tennessee in November 1861. Unionists were actively and openly resisting Confederate rule, Confederate troops were persecuting Unionists, and loyalists and secessionists had already come to blows. Confederate authorities were clearly losing patience with East Tennessee, and a less conciliatory policy would eventually have been implemented no matter what. The bridge burnings intensified the Unionist-secessionist conflict, but they did not create it.

East Tennessee Unionists suffered greatly from Confederate repression, and they would attempt no more massive uprisings. But Confederate oppression did not destroy the Unionist resistance. Loyalist defiance would ebb and flow in the remaining twenty months of Confederate occupation, but it would never dry up. After November 1861 Unionists would operate in smaller bands, seek limited objectives, and rely on the weapons of ambush, harassment, and intimidation to achieve their purposes. Increasingly, secessionists would respond in kind.

4 Hanging, Shooting, and Robbing

Control of East Tennessee would be determined by the struggle among four different forces. The Confederate and Union armies would shape the conflict in East Tennessee through both their occupation policies and their military operations. But the core of the East Tennessee war was the struggle between secessionist and loyalist partisans. Their war, which was fueled by both local grievances and the national conflict, began before Confederate forces ever set foot in East Tennessee and would continue after the last Union soldier had left. It was fought out in the economic, social, and intellectual arenas as well as the political and military, and it employed nonviolent as well as violent means. The editor who encouraged resistance to the occupying forces, the representative who pressured his government to adopt a harsher policy against dissent, the farmer who burned his neighbor's barn, and the bushwhacker who ambushed an enemy scout were all parts of the same war.

The violence in East Tennessee divided into three spheres, military, political, and criminal. The first included operations related to the conventional war, such as raids on enemy communications, assaults on enemy troops, and aid to friendly soldiers. The second sphere involved the harassment, intimidation, and murder of supporters of the enemy government. Unionist and secessionist guerrilla bands beat civilians holding the wrong political views, ambushed them on the road, shot them in their homes, and plundered and burned their houses, barns, and possessions. The third sphere, criminal, included actions such as theft and assault that did not always possess a military or political significance but that were nonetheless a common feature of guerrilla operations. Many bushwhacker bands lived partly or entirely by theft, and they routinely broke into houses, carried off horses and stock, and waylaid people on the roads.

These distinctions among the different types of partisan violence, though valid and important, are also somewhat artificial and distorting. Different guerrilla bands did possess different aims, and their operations did vary in character and purpose. At the same time, many guerrilla bands engaged in all three types of actions, depending on the circumstances, and all three kinds of violence shaped the outcome of the East Tennessee war. Most importantly, while the distinction between violence motivated by political ends and violence originating in personal grievances is not unimportant, the participants themselves did not always separate the two. The conflict in East Tennessee was inherently ambiguous, both militarily and morally, and the violence can therefore best be understood not as a set of clearly defined categories but rather as a spectrum, with much overlapping and much blurring.

By 1865 the violence in East Tennessee had reached frightening heights, and it appalled not only outsiders but also many inhabitants of this region, Unionist and secessionist alike. Yet the partisan violence was neither shapeless nor senseless. It reflected not only the tremendous passions that the war had generated but also a perceptive understanding of the implications of the conflict. East Tennesseans fought for control of their districts, their counties, and their homes, and the outcome of this struggle would be crucial no matter which side triumphed in the conventional war. The central issue was political domination, and the central aim was that "we," not "they," control this valley, this county, or ultimately this region that East Tennesseans called home. East Tennesseans did not always define "we" and "they" along strict Union-Confederate lines or in ways that made sense either to outside observers then or to historians today. Furthermore, many selfish motives, including greed, revenge, fear, and personal spite, also influenced this struggle. But that did not make it a senseless conflict. Rather, it simply means that the war must be understood from the perspective of Civil War East Tennessee. The guerrilla war was an ideological conflict, and the political motives, though sometimes blurred and smudged, were always visible.

Secessionist and Unionist guerrilla bands possessed a number of common features. As in other regions of the South, most were made up of men from the same community, a characteristic that reflected the political and military traditions of antebellum America. Like regular companies at the beginning of the war, guerrilla bands coalesced around prominent figures: state representatives, justices of the peace, lawyers, wealthy farmers, and county officials. A number of delegates to the Greeneville Convention, including Robert K. Byrd and Joseph A. Cooper, organized partisan units in the summer of 1861. Other Unionist leaders included Daniel Stover, the assistant marshal of Carter County, and William Clift, a large landowner and merchant in Hamilton County. But not all guerrilla leaders were prominent figures, and many, particularly in the latter years of the war, were marked only by their ruthlessness, cunning, and daring. "Tinker Dave" Beatty was a small farmer in Fentress County, while Daniel Ellis was a wagon maker. And Champ Ferguson, a secessionist bushwhacker from Sparta and perhaps the most successful partisan leader in the East Tennessee war, was known before the war primarily for his physical strength and his skill in stealing horses.[1]

A profile of about one hundred Unionist and secessionist guerrillas reveals important similarities. Partisans on both sides tended to be in their late thirties, though Unionists were slightly younger. The majority in both camps were married, had two or more children, and owned either a farm or a business. But Unionist and secessionist guerrillas were divided by occupation and wealth. The majority of Unionists were small farmers, but artisans and farm laborers were well represented. Conversely, almost all Confederate bushwhackers who could be clearly identified were farmers with substantial land holdings. Their average amount of real property was three times that of loyalists, and their average personal property holdings were twice as great. The sample is small enough that these conclusions should be used with caution, but they do suggest that Confederate partisans were more likely to come from the ranks of the wealthy.[2]

The bridge burnings and the failed uprising opened a new phase of the war in East Tennessee. A minority of loyalists, discouraged by the failure of the Union army to rescue them and stunned by the weight of the Confederate response, gave up the struggle. Others who did not submit nonetheless recognized the futility of open warfare and reverted to a campaign of harassment. And still others, who concluded that their only hope of salvation lay with the North, abandoned their homes and fled to Kentucky to join the Union army.

A network for smuggling recruits (and later escaped Federal prisoners) out of East Tennessee began to take shape almost immediately after Tennessee ratified the ordinance of secession. Initially it hardly constituted a system at all, but as the war progressed it became increasingly organized and complex. Eventually hundreds of persons participated in this network by providing shelter and supplies, pointing out safe roads and fords, ferrying escapees across rivers, and warning of Confederate patrols. Loyalist women, many of whom stayed in East Tennessee when their husbands fled, played a key role in this enterprise. Many Unionists died in the attempt to leave East Tennessee, while many who aided them were imprisoned for their disloyalty.[3]

At the center of the escape network were the pilots, the men who organized recruits and guided them out of East Tennessee. Piloting was an extraordinarily hazardous duty, and the price of failure was confinement in a Confederate prison or death. But the enterprise was also essential, for only persons with a detailed knowledge of the terrain and skill at evading Confederate patrols could lead recruits to Kentucky. Dozens of East Tennesseans, motivated by both patriotism and profit, took up this work. Many were colorful figures who attracted considerable attention, and a few became legends.

The most famous civilian pilot was Daniel Ellis. A farmer and wagon maker from Carter County, Ellis had helped burn the Holston River Bridge in Sullivan County, joined the Unionist encampment near Elizabethton, been captured by Confederate forces, and escaped after a few days confinement. Ellis began piloting in August 1862 and continued until early 1865. He claimed to have made at least fifteen trips to Kentucky and to have brought out several thousand men. Ellis also acted as a guerrilla captain, and he led several attacks on secessionists and Confederate troops in Carter and Johnson Counties. Shortly after the war Ellis published an account of his experiences, *Thrilling Adventures of Daniel Ellis*. Ellis inflated his accomplishments, but much of the work is corroborated by other sources, and it is by far the best account of the difficulties and dangers of piloting. Other famous civilian pilots included Thomas Spurgeon, a Bradley County Unionist nicknamed the "Red Fox," and Spencer Deaton, a Knox County loyalist who was captured and hanged in 1864.[4]

Union officers recognized the importance of the exodus from East Tennessee and aided fugitives in their flight. Several civilian pilots, including Ellis and Spurgeon, occasionally received transportation and supplies, and in March 1865 Ellis was commissioned a captain in the U.S. Army. Union officers also sent scouts across the border to escort Unionist escapees the last few miles into Kentucky. Finally, the Federal army provided additional pilots from Union ranks, typically East Tennessee or North Carolina loyalists who had escaped the Confederacy and joined the Union army. One of the most prominent of these was David Fry, an influential Unionist from Greene County. Fry had left East Tennessee in the summer of 1861, made his way to Camp Dick Robinson, and received a commission as a captain. He had then returned to East Tennessee with William B. Carter and led the band that destroyed the Lick Creek Bridge. After the uprising failed, Fry organized a group of followers, led a number of raids on secessionists in East Tennessee and western North Carolina, and recruited several men for Federal service. When Confederate troops pursued Fry to the Laurel Valley of North Carolina in April 1862 he attempted to lead his followers to Kentucky. But a Confederate patrol intercepted them, and Fry was incarcerated in a Confederate prison in Atlanta and sentenced to hang. Fry escaped and made his way back to Kentucky, and eventually he would join a second ill-fated venture, the Andrews Railroad Raid.[5]

Most escapes to Kentucky followed a common pattern. They began with the news that a pilot would soon arrive to lead an expedition. This information would be cautiously circulated among men who wished to leave, and they would establish a rendezvous, usually a remote site after sundown. If all went well, the pilot would appear at the appointed time and the loyalists would set out. In the first months of the war refugees commonly traveled in large groups, believing that their numbers would protect them from Confederate forces. This tactic often resulted in capture, however, and by 1862 most groups instead relied on secrecy and stealth. Whenever possible they traveled at night, and they chose the most deserted paths and the roughest terrain, where Confederate cavalry could not follow. In emergencies refugees might stop at loyalist houses for shelter and food, but this was a risky practice, for any house or farm might be watched by Confederate troops. After several days of hard traveling fugitives would cross the last Tennessee mountain range, step across the border into Kentucky, and make their way to Camp Dick Robinson to enroll in Federal service.[6]

Even with the aid of an experienced pilot a successful escape from East Tennessee was a dangerous and difficult task, for weather, terrain, and other factors combined to impede safe movement. Refugees had to cross several rivers and creeks before reaching safety, and though sometimes they employed ferries operated by loyalists, more often they avoided this risk and simply forded the streams, risking hypothermia. In winter they also had to fight ice, snow, and wind, and because lighting a fire was dangerous many refugees suffered from frostbite. Boots and clothes wore out quickly, and many escapees literally finished the journey on bare, bloody feet. And traveling at night sometimes meant marching in such darkness that men could not see each other and had to tie themselves together to avoid getting lost.

The worst impediment, though, was the Confederate blockade. Southern commanders began sealing off the border in the summer of 1861, and throughout 1862 and 1863 Confederate patrols steadily increased, particularly along established routes such as the Holston River and Powell River valleys. Pilots and refugees had to employ all their wits and skill to avoid discovery, and frequently the loyalists failed. In July 1861 Dr. J. W. Thornburgh, a physician from New Market, organized a company and attempted to lead it to Kentucky. But Confederate cavalry intercepted Thornburgh at Bull's Gap, and he and eight others were sent to prison. In January 1862 Southern troops trapped thirty-nine escapees in the mountains near Cumberland Gap, while in April Confederate cavalry intercepted 600 Unionists near Fincastle and captured 475 of them. And numerous stories told by Unionists and Confederate troops of stumbling across the bodies of refugees who had been shot or hanged indicate that a considerable number of other fugitives never completed the journey to Kentucky.[7]

Two accounts illustrate particularly well the difficulties that escapees faced. Thomas Doak Edington endured two serious mishaps before reaching Kentucky. The night scheduled for his first attempt was black and rainy, and the pilot, Spencer Deaton, did not appear. Nonetheless, about fifty men, of the two hundred expected, started out. But many soon lost their way and drifted away from the group, and the rest became discouraged and returned home. Two days later, when Deaton appeared, the Unionists tried again. The first night went by without incident, but the following day the escapees blundered into a small group of Confederate cavalry. Several

Unionists turned and ran, but the majority chose to fight. Counting on surprise, they charged the outnumbered patrol, scattered them, and escaped. The remainder of the trip went by without incident, and after a few days Edington and the others reached Union lines.[8]

Another escapee, Robert Allan Ragan, suffered even more misadventures. In 1862 Ragan traveled to Greene County to meet a pilot. He missed the rendezvous, but his disappointment was short lived, for Confederate cavalry overtook this group on their first day of travel and captured all but three. Ragan tried again to link up with a pilot in May 1863. He spent the day hiding at his father-in-law's farm, but that evening, just as he was setting out for the rendezvous, he saw Confederate soldiers coming up the lane. Ragan ran out the back door to escape, jumped a fence, and sliced his foot on a rock. The cut was so deep and painful that he could not walk and again had to stay behind. Ragan would not escape East Tennessee until July 1863, when George Kirk led 120 men out of Greene County. Even this trip nearly ended in disaster, as Ragan and the other recruits were almost betrayed by a hired guide and narrowly avoided capture by a Confederate patrol.[9]

In spite of numerous obstacles an astonishing number of Unionists arrived in Kentucky to serve in the Union army. Over a thousand East Tennesseans had reached Camp Dick Robinson by September 1861, and by March 1862 their numbers were sufficient to make up four regiments. The passage of the Confederate Conscription Act in March further accelerated this exodus. In late April 1862 Major General Edmund Kirby Smith estimated that seven thousand East Tennesseans had escaped within the last three weeks, and in August 1863 a Union private wrote from Camp Dick Robinson that 150 refugees were arriving every day. This hemorrhage of the loyalist male population continued until the eve of the Union invasion. In all, somewhere between 20,000 and 30,000 East Tennesseans wore the Union blue, far more than from any other region of the South and a remarkably large percentage of the Unionist vote in 1861.[10]

Not all loyalists chose to fight in uniform. As soon as Confederate authorities reduced the number of troops in East Tennessee, Unionists who remained at home resumed their war against secessionists and Confederate soldiers. In early 1862 loyalists in Scott and Morgan Counties killed a number of secessionists, issued death threats against others, and plundered and burned several Confederate homes. Loyalists also took over all county offices, reorganized their Home Guard units, and made clear their intent to drive out every Southern sympathizer in that region. Numbers of terrified secessionists fled to Kingston for safety, and reports of the violence soon reached Knoxville. In response Major General Edmund Kirby Smith sent almost one thousand men under Brigadier General Danville Leadbetter to restore order. Leadbetter's orders were to break up Unionist organizations, arrest their leaders, confiscate weapons, strip Scott County of supplies, and intimidate loyalists into submission. To emphasize Confederate resolve, Kirby Smith wrote Leadbetter, "I give you *carte blanche*, and will sustain you in any course you find necessary to adopt." But Unionists refused to be cowed. They lined the routes into Scott and Morgan, and Colonel John C. Vaughn reported that on the entire march from Kingston to Huntsville his men suffered guerrilla sniping "from inaccessible points." The Unionists then concentrated and attempted to block the Confederate march at Montgomery, an action that brought on a full-scale skirmish. Vaughn claimed to have killed fifteen partisans and taken seven prisoner, but he admitted that five of his soldiers were killed and twelve wounded. Confederate forces succeeded in scattering the guerrillas, but when they departed the Unionists simply reasserted control.[11]

Throughout East Tennessee, Unionist bands reemerged with remarkable speed and again began to intimidate secessionists. In April 1862 Kirby Smith reported that in twenty-five of East Tennessee's thirty-one counties there existed "organized armed bands that oppress men of Southern principles." Loyalists in Carter, Johnson, and Sevier Counties, sometimes in cooperation with North Carolina loyalists, robbed and threatened secessionists and drove many from their homes. In August Kirby Smith had to send a battalion to Clinton to eliminate "bushwhackers" who "have been hanging, shooting, and robbing men sympathetic to the cause of the South." And from many other counties came reports of beatings, shootings, and destruction.[12]

Unionist partisans also resumed their harassment of Confederate troops. Loyalists employed a variety of means for catching soldiers in a vulnerable position. A favorite tactic was to snipe at marching Confederate troops from the sides of narrow, wooded roads. When Kirby Smith returned to East Tennessee in October 1862 after his failed attempt to seize Kentucky, loyalists took the opportunity to harass his already demoralized troops. Tennessee and Kentucky bushwhackers dropped trees across roads to slow his retreat and shot at Confederate troops from the hills and trees that lined the route. Colonel Henry M. Doak remembered that Unionist guerrillas shot down a soldier riding next to him, and another Confederate cavalryman reported that his unit suffered four or five ambushes before reaching safety.[13]

Loyalists also hung on the fringes of Confederate camps, hoping to ambush soldiers coming in and out, and targeted soldiers who were traveling. In August 1862 Thomas Hall reported that a Tennessee soldier had been bushwhacked just outside their camp near Chattanooga. In June 1863 a Unionist band in Carter County discovered that two brothers, both Confederate recruiting officers, were home on leave. Seventeen bushwhackers came to the farm at night, lured the brothers out of the house with the report that Union forces had taken Carter's Depot, shot one in the yard, and carried the other off into the mountains. Neighbors assumed that the second officer also had been executed, but he eventually escaped his captors and returned.[14]

Loyalist bushwhackers thus acquired a formidable reputation, and Confederate soldiers sought safety in numbers. Captain William Stringfield, provost marshal of Carter County, admitted in 1862 that he "did not visit very much out—as the enforcement of *the conscript Law* made it a rather dangerous thing to do—unless with soldiers." Captain Stephen Whitaker wrote from Carter's Depot that "the people here they are nearly all Lincolnites or Toryes it is dangerous to go eny distance from camp." In August 1862 Colonel Alex Wallace warned his wife not to allow their son to attempt to follow the Confederate expedition into Kentucky, for "our rear will be harassed by Tories and bushwhackers making it unsafe for persons alone or small parties to follow us."[15]

The bridge burnings forced Confederate authorities greatly to increase their defenses on the East Tennessee railroads. Even so, scattered acts of sabotage continued throughout the war, and Confederate authorities remained extremely sensitive to threats to their communications. In July 1862 Kirby Smith received information that Unionists, in conjunction with Federal soldiers dressed as civilians, were preparing to burn the bridges at Loudon and Strawberry Plains. Kirby Smith believed the threat to be real, and he instructed his subordinates there to take precautions. In May 1863 Major General Simon B. Buckner warned the garrison at Mossy Creek that bushwhackers were assembling to destroy the bridge there. That same month Major General Dabney Maury predicted a second uprising in the event of a Union invasion: "As soon as the [Federal] Army enters they will doubtless become active allies; and our Rail Road and telegraph lines will cease to be of use to us." In July 1863 the presidents of the East Tennessee and Virginia and East Tennessee and Georgia Railroads sent an angry letter to President Jefferson Davis complaining of "the immense labors and privations we have undergone amidst a population of vindictive Tories" and demanded to know whether the government could protect their lines. And Davis attributed raids on the railroad in upper East Tennessee in September 1863 to "Tories and a few hundred of Burnside's cavalry."[16]

Acting alone, Unionist partisans killed and wounded numbers of Confederate troops and made their occupation duties hazardous. But they had no chance of actually driving out the Confederate army. Loyalists recognized that their only hope for deliverance lay with the North, and they devoted considerable energy to aiding Federal forces. One of their most effective roles was providing information concerning Confederate dispositions and movements to Union commanders in Kentucky. Brigadier General Felix K. Zollicoffer complained that no movement he made went unnoticed in East Tennessee, and Kirby Smith concluded that "East Tennessee is more difficult to operate in than the country of an acknowledged enemy." Many soldiers also complained of Unionist spying. One man serving with Zollicoffer blamed the general's futile attempts to locate the Union army in November 1861 on Unionist activity: "That is a great drawback on us, the people of this country are almost all of them at heart against us and our enemy is informed of all our movements and we deceived." Describing a march from southwest Virginia to Cumberland Gap, Franklin Gaillard worried that "the section through which the movement would be made is full of Tories who would quickly give information of our movements." Again, these complaints were justified, for when Federal cavalry raided East Tennessee in December 1862 Brigadier General Samuel P. Carter employed 150 loyalists, many of them Home Guards, to watch the roads and scout enemy movements.[17]

The Unionist communications network was extensive and effective. Not only did loyalists pass on information about Confederate movements, they also brought back newspapers from Kentucky and letters from soldiers in the Union army, warned communities of the approach of Confederate forces, and carried some of their own mail in order to bypass the suspect Confederate carriers. But the way in which that network functioned is unclear. Most contemporary descriptions of this system were vague, perhaps purposely so. William Randolph Carter, historian of the First Tennessee Cavalry (Union), stated only that "the secret means to escape to the Union lines was termed 'the Underground Railroad' and the secret network of communications, 'the Grapevine telegraph.'" Pilots apparently carried much information back and forth, but it appears that women played an equally critical role, serving as both spies and messengers. Humes asserted that most couriers to Kentucky were women, and Sarah Thompson, a Greeneville loyalist, claimed that on several occasions Unionist pilots brought packets of letters for her to distribute to her neighbors. Several Confederate soldiers also charged that loyalists employed women as couriers.[18]

Beyond these general descriptions little evidence reveals how messengers were able to travel unhindered, how they were able to spread news so quickly, or how many persons were engaged in these activities. It is likely, however, that East Tennesseans simply made use of skills and methods that they had already developed from living in this difficult region. The journalist Horace Kephart discovered a similar system of communication still operating in East Tennessee in the early twentieth century: "There is no telegraph, wired or wireless, but there is an effective substitute. It seemed as though, in one night, the news traveled from valley to cove, and from cove to nook, that I was investigating the moonshine business, and that I was apparently 'safe.'" Kephart also attempted to describe how the system might have worked:

Our mountaineers habitually note every track they pass, whether of beast or man, and "read the sign" with Indian-like facility. Often one of my companions would stop, as though shot, and point with his toe to the fresh imprint of a human foot in the dust or mud of a public road, exclaiming: "Now I wonder who *that* feller was. 'Twa'n't (so-and-so), for he hain't got no square-headed bobnails; twa'n't (such-a-one), cause he wouldn't be hyer at this time o'day"; and so he would go on, figuring by a process of elimination that is extremely cunning, until some such conclusion as this was reached, "That's some stranger goin on to Little River . . . and he's footin hit as if the devil was after him—I'll bet he's stabbed some bod and he's runnin' from the sheriff." Nor is the incident closed with that; our mountaineer will inquire from neighbors and passers by until he gets a description of the wayfarer, and then he will pass the word along.[19]

Some Federal officers believed that loyalist partisans could play an even larger role in Union strategy. In the spring of 1862 Union forces under Brigadier General George W. Morgan seized control of Cumberland Gap. Morgan was well acquainted with the Unionist resistance, and in May he gave William Clift a colonel's commission and sent him into Morgan and Scott Counties. Morgan authorized Clift to recruit a partisan unit, "annoy the enemy's rear," and interfere with Confederate communications and supply lines. Initially Clift enjoyed considerable success in his task. He established himself securely in Scott County and within a few months had organized at least four hundred recruits. But then Clift's operations went awry. In July and August his unit, now designated the Seventh Tennessee Infantry, made three attempts to ambush Confederate detachments in Morgan and Anderson Counties. Each time Clift failed to locate his target, but his movements attracted the attention of Confederate authorities. In mid-August a regiment of infantry and three hundred cavalry surprised Clift and scattered his partisans. Clift subsequently rebuilt his regiment, but while he won several victories over secessionist bushwhackers he had little impact on Confederate operations. Clift proved unable to accomplish the purposes that Morgan had envisioned, and in late 1862 or early 1863 he marched his regiment back to Kentucky and remained there until the August 1863 invasion.[20]

The role that African Americans played in partisan operations is uncertain. Scattered reports indicate that slaves and free blacks participated in both the escape network and communication system, serving as guides and messengers and supplying refugees with food and shelter. Some also escaped East Tennessee and served in the Federal army; in July 1863, for example, two black men were captured with a large group of Unionist refugees near Cumberland Gap. And some African Americans operated as guerrillas, for in November 1864 Colonel William Gibbs Allen was ambushed near Jonesborough and shot in the hand by a black bushwhacker. While it seems certain that blacks played the same roles as white Unionists in resisting Confederate rule, evidence concerning African American partisans is simply lacking. White East Tennesseans maintained their belief in black inferiority, and their accounts of partisan operations may have deliberately obscured the role of their black allies.[21]

The role of white Unionist women is clearer. There is ample evidence that loyalist women spied on Confederate troops, operated safe houses, brought supplies and information to men who were hiding out, and maintained farms when loyalist men left the region. Women also participated in the partisan violence and became its victims. In May 1862 a Southern soldier reported that a woman wielding an ax had wounded a Confederate officer. "Our boys did not kill the old woman, as has been reported. They only knocked her in the head with a gun and left her for dead." That same month Confederate officials arrested and imprisoned the wife of Robert K. Byrd, colonel of a regiment of East Tennessee recruits, as a "dangerous enemy." In October 1863 a Unionist near Bull's Gap claimed that Confederate soldiers had hanged several women who refused to reveal where their husbands were hiding and had shot another for "making a too free use of her tongue." In June 1864 a Union soldier claimed that secessionist guerrillas had shot a woman near Cleveland. There were also scattered reports of rape, by both regular soldiers and bushwhackers.[22]

Confederate troops repeatedly struck back at loyalist partisans, though with mixed success. In September 1862 Major General Sam Jones directed Colonel L. M. Allen to take 250 infantry and seventy-five cavalry into Sevier County to disperse a loyalist band, capture as many bushwhackers as possible, and arrest any citizens "aiding or abetting" the guerrillas. After defeating the bushwhackers Allen was to return to Knoxville with the infantry while leaving the cavalry in Sevier to "carry out certain instructions from the provost marshal." These instructions were not preserved, but it is likely that the cavalry's duties were to arrest Unionist leaders and confiscate weapons. That same month Jones ordered three companies to Johnson County to capture a group of North Carolina loyalists reported preparing to escape to Kentucky. In October 1862 the East Tennessee commander sent a detachment of the Thirty-first Alabama to Newport, Cocke County, to "break up and destroy all parties banded together in opposition to the laws of the Confederate Government and in defiance of its authority," and he again ordered troops into Johnson and Carter to deal with several bushwhacker bands there.[23]

Fighting guerrillas was a fatiguing, tedious, and dangerous task. One of the most revealing Confederate accounts was that of William Sloan, a soldier with the Third Tennessee Infantry. Sloan's narrative began on February 28, 1862, when his company was sent to the Holston River near Strawberry Plains to cut off "the various small bands of renegades who are almost daily crossing on the way to Kentucky." After five days of watching, the company commander secured information about a particular band of loyalist fugitives, and Sloan and a small group of men moved to McMillen's Station to waylay them. The Confederates lay out all night in a cold rain, but the fugitives never appeared. On March 17 the Third Tennessee marched to Clinton; then on March 27 it was sent to Kingston to join Leadbetter's expedition into Scott and Morgan Counties. On April 4 Sloan's regiment skirmished with bushwhackers in Scott County; four in the regiment were killed and seven wounded. For the rest of the spring and summer Sloan performed garrison duty and chased bushwhackers at Clinton, Knoxville, Tazewell, and Cumberland Gap.[24]

Confederate troops had great difficulty identifying and locating Unionist guerrillas and pinning them down to be captured or shot. Guerrillas possessed a number of advantages, particularly superior knowledge of the terrain, that enabled them to escape. Partisans could easily disappear to hiding places or disband and return to their homes. Unionists were particularly active in the mountain regions, and attempting to chase them through the woods or up steep trails was a daunting task. In late November 1861 Colonel Danville Leadbetter described for Adjutant and Inspector General Samuel Cooper his difficulties in suppressing rebellious Unionist bands: "At present they seem indisposed to fight, and the great difficulty is to reach them. Scattering in the mountain paths, they can scarcely be caught, and as their arms are hidden when not in use, it is almost impossible to disarm them." Two weeks later Leadbetter elaborated further on his troubles. He reported that he had pursued one loyalist band into the Newport area of Cocke County and had then devised a plan to trap them. He sent a regiment of his own troops toward Newport from the south and ordered up a second unit from Morristown to converge on the area from the opposite direction. Leadbetter admitted that after four days marching the total accomplishment of the expedition had been one wounded Unionist. As he concluded, "these people cannot be caught in this manner."[25]

William Sloan made the same complaints about the East Tennessee terrain: "I will say here that all of Scott County, and a great deal of contiguous territory, both in Tennessee and Kentucky, is a solid bed of rugged and precipitous mountains, cut and gashed in all directions, and deep ravines, and all having rough streams of water in them. . . . The roads alongside these steams are often mere trails, and the mountains bordering the streams are often so steep and craggy that bushwhackers can conceal themselves in good rifle range of a road and fire into a column of cavalry with perfect impunity, as it would often require an hour of hard climbing on foot to reach them." Sloan related one attempt to surprise a bushwhacker camp located high up on a ridge. His unit divided into two wings and attempted secretly to scale the ridge, but the guerrillas spotted them and fled long before they reached the top.[26]

In many cases, therefore, success against guerrillas depended not on clever tactics but on patience, hard work, and luck. An account by J. W. Gash, a trooper with the Seventh North Carolina Cavalry (Confederate), reveals the unpredictable nature of the counterguerrilla war. In late October 1862 Gash's unit was sent to Johnson County. On his first night Gash and twenty-five men went out to capture a group of North Carolina bushwhackers reported in the area. "They being thoroughly skilled in the art of dodging got wind of us being in the neighborhood and skedaddled." Gash's only accomplishment that night was the arrest of four men charged with harboring Unionist refugees. The next night Gash's luck turned, for his detachment captured seventeen Unionist bushwhackers and a Federal recruiting officer. By October 30 the Seventh North Carolina had collected thirty prisoners. But at other times Confederate efforts seemed futile. After a Unionist bushwhacker shot a Confederate soldier near Richmond, Kentucky, James Bennet McCrey went out with a detachment to track him down. "I started at about One P.M. with forty men to hunt the bushwhacker. Marched all evening, searched and ransacked every house for miles around, found some army equipment, consumed the whole night in the service and became much exhausted . . . but did not find the bushwhacker."[27]

Confederate soldiers quickly lost sight of the accepted laws of war in their conflict with loyalist guerrillas. A number of factors combined to poison their attitudes. First was the lack of reciprocity. Guerrillas did not follow the recognized rules of war, and their conduct was considered dishonorable. One Confederate cavalryman described bushwhacking as "a very annoying sort of warfare, that of the assassin—shooting you in the back and running off." When guerrillas failed to "fight fair," soldiers felt little obligation to do so. Many soldiers then transferred their anger into contempt. Unable to force bushwhackers to stand and fight, troops dismissed guerrillas as cowards lacking honor and manhood. Joel Haley, worn out by almost a month of chasing Unionist bands, concluded that "East Tennessee Tories will never fight if there is any avenue by which they can escape by *running*." Colonel William Gibbs Allen also dismissed all bushwhackers as cowards. And William Sloan, while conceding the effectiveness of guerrilla sniping, mocked loyalist partisans, stating that "the crack of a gun seems to inspire within them an irresistible inclination to run."[28]

The appearance of the bushwhackers added to this contempt. Weeks of lying out in the woods, constantly on the move and on guard, left them gaunt, dirty, and ill clothed, an appearance that hardly excited respect. Many soldiers viewed bushwhackers as not quite human and described operations against them as "hunting," transforming the guerrillas from human enemies into animals. These attitudes eroded moral restraints and justified treatment that would have been unacceptable if enacted upon real soldiers.

A second factor that corroded the attitudes of many soldiers was their belief that their service in East Tennessee was meaningless and unrewarding. After describing his regiment's attempts to disperse Unionist bands after the November uprising, Joel Haley concluded that "there is certainly no Laurels to be garnered by the conquest of such a force." Similarly, William Sloan complained that "our duties for the past two weeks have not been worth recording. We all spent the larger part of the holidays at home with our friends, and we might as well have spent all our time there, so far as any good we have done is concerned." Confederate soldiers had signed up to fight Yankees, not chase poor starved mountaineers around the wilds of East Tennessee, and many expressed a desire to transfer to Virginia where the real fighting was occurring. Adding to this sense of futility were the conditions in which soldiers lived. As in Missouri, many troops were posted in small units at remote garrisons, making their sense of identity and purpose difficult to maintain. As with other factors, this sense of meaninglessness produced frustrations that soldiers took out on their guerrilla enemies.[29]

As the partisan war progressed, Confederate soldiers became increasingly brutal. In October 1862 William Sloan's unit hanged two bushwhackers that they had captured and put a rope around the neck of a third Unionist to force him to admit that he was a guer-rilla. Sloan also suggested that summary executions were a common practice. J. C. Gruar was equally blunt in describing executions car-ried out by his unit: "Here is said to be 60 out *Lyers* in this country. The boys killed 4 or 5 since I came out. I did not see either I saw them put the rope around one fellows neck." And when a Georgia regiment made a raid into East Tennessee the men got drunk and executed a bushwhacker whom they had just captured.[30]

The most notorious Confederate atrocity was perpetrated in Jan-uary 1863 by members of the Sixty-fourth North Carolina. The in-cident's long history began in April 1862 when Major General Ed-mund Kirby Smith sent troops into the Laurel Valley of North Carolina to pursue Tennessee and North Carolina bushwhackers who had fled there for refuge. Kirby Smith's force endured three days of sniping and ambushes before reaching Laurel but managed to arrest only a few Unionists there. In January 1863 Unionists and deserters raided the town of Marshall and plundered several homes, including that of Colonel Lawrence M. Allen, former commander of the Sixty-fourth North Carolina. Lieutenant Colonel James Keith, who had taken over from Allen, marched the Sixty-fourth into Laurel Valley, arrested a number of those suspected of the raid, and started with them to Knoxville. But before reaching Confeder-ate headquarters Keith took the thirteen men and boys off the road into the woods, executed them, and buried the bodies.[31]

Confederate commanders almost certainly knew that their forces were committing atrocities, but unlike Union officers they kept their policies on this matter hidden. Kirby Smith, who followed Zollicoffer in command of East Tennessee, and Major General Sam Jones both routinely ordered expedition commanders to maintain strict discipline and prevent their troops from indiscriminately ha-rassing Unionists. But they also authorized Confederate troops to take whatever measures were necessary to break up Unionist organi-zations. Some Confederate officers interpreted these orders liber-ally, and department commanders did not pry too closely into their conduct.[32]

In September 1863 the Army of the Ohio invaded East Ten-nessee, and Union troops took control of about two-thirds of the re-gion. Their presence altered the balance of power in East Ten-nessee; it also intensified the partisan conflict. The loyalist scope of operations greatly increased, but at the same time secessionist parti-sans became more active and bold. Like Unionists, secessionist partisans sought to intimidate their loyalist enemies, kill them, or drive them out.

Loyalists provided extensive aid to Federal troops during the invasion. Major General Ambrose Burnside, commander of the Army of the Ohio, directed his subordinates to employ loyal citizens to scout the country and provide warning of enemy concentrations. Captain John Shrady noted that Union officers had no trouble acquiring information about the location of enemy forces, and another soldier reported that on a march near Tazewell "the people were all Union and warned us as to the most dangerous points, telling us of a road much safer than the main one." Burnside also commissioned bushwhacker leader "Tinker Dave" Beatty to "waylay the roads," harass Confederate communications, and hinder Confederate movements in White County and the surrounding area.[33]

Partisan assistance also helped the Army of the Ohio weather the Confederate assault on Knoxville in late 1863. Union forces had encountered little initial resistance to their invasion and had quickly seized Cumberland Gap, the Knoxville region, and the railroads as far north as Jonesborough and as far south as Loudon. But in late October a Confederate corps under Lieutenant General James Longstreet moved up from Chattanooga and besieged Federal forces in Knoxville. Union supplies quickly ran low, soldiers were reduced to quarter rations, and the ability of the Army of the Ohio to hold out appeared uncertain. Loyalists in Knox, Cocke, and Sevier Counties came to the army's assistance, however. Longstreet, misled by faulty maps, had failed to block navigation on the branch of the French Broad River that flowed into Knoxville, and night after night Unionists loaded rafts with provisions and floated them down to waiting troops. Longstreet eventually attempted to cut off these shipments, but a loyalist woman made her way into Knoxville and alerted Federal officers to this threat, enabling them to protect their supply line. The siege did not last long, as an advancing Union force under Major General William T. Sherman forced Longstreet to break it off. Unionist aid alleviated the suffering of Federal troops and demonstrated the advantages accruing to Federal forces from operating amid a friendly population.[34]

Secessionist guerrillas began to challenge the occupying troops in the winter of 1863. Like their Unionist counterparts, secessionist partisans preyed on small parties of troops caught away from their camps. In December 1863 Major General O. O. Howard wrote from Athens that "parties of guerrillas infest this whole country" and reported that they had become a considerable hazard. Secessionists shot two soldiers foraging near Motley's Ford in February 1864, and in the summer of that year twenty-five men sent to rescue an officer captured by guerrillas near Wilsonville were themselves ambushed. D. F. Beatty, stationed at Elk River, wrote that he and other soldiers only left camp in groups of ten or more because of Confederate guerrillas. In October 1864 guerrilla sniping forced two companies of the Fifteenth Pennsylvania Cavalry scouting a side road near Rogersville to give up their patrol and rejoin the full regiment. In January 1865 secessionist bushwhackers raided a small post near Dandridge and came away with six soldiers as prisoners, and in February secessionists twice attacked Union pickets near Greeneville.[35]

Just as Unionist bands targeted Confederate recruiting officers, secessionists also attacked symbols of Union authority. Federal deputy provost marshals, the officers primarily responsible for implementing occupation policies and enforcing the laws, were particular targets. The most devastating attack of this kind occurred in Athens in January 1865. McMinn County was a center of Confederate sentiment, and the deputy provost marshal there, Major John McGaughy, had recently banished several secessionist families and arrested a number of women accused of providing information to Confederate troops. In retaliation a combined force of guerrillas and Confederate cavalry, numbering perhaps three hundred, attacked Athens on the night of January 28. They engaged the garrison there for several hours and managed to take fifteen prisoners, including McGaughy. Southern guerrillas held the deputy provost marshal prisoner for several days and then deliberately executed him. Confederate forces also killed Joseph Divine, deputy provost marshal at nearby Madisonville, that same night. And in February 1864 secessionist guerrillas raided Washington and killed the provost marshal there.[36]

Federal officers committed large numbers of troops to the defense of their supply lines in East Tennessee. Nonetheless, Union communications suffered from frequent interruptions. Some of these raids may have been the work of Confederate cavalry, but others clearly were carried out by Southern partisans. In March 1864 Southern guerrillas tore up the track near Decherd and burned a train. In September an attack shut down the line between Knoxville and Chattanooga for several days. And in April 1865 bushwhackers derailed a train near Morristown and burnt the engine and thirteen cars. Confederate partisans did not limit their attacks to the railroads. Union soldiers in East Tennessee frequently complained that wagons carrying supplies were cut off and destroyed by guerrillas, and Captain Shrady concluded that it was not safe to send money by the Adams Express Company, for "guerrillas every once in a while make a dash upon the road."[37]

As the war progressed, an increasing number of guerrilla bands in East Tennessee came to be made up in part or in whole of deserters from the regular armies. Desertion had reached epidemic proportions in the Confederate Army by 1863, and many who abandoned their service fled to the more inaccessible regions of the South, including East Tennessee and western North Carolina. Their ranks were further swelled by men avoiding conscription. Union deserters, most of whom came from units stationed in East Tennessee, were fewer in number, but they also contributed to this problem. Most deserters were primarily interested in survival, but nonetheless they constituted a serious menace, for they plundered homes, fought with soldiers and militia, and were a danger to civilians and soldiers alike.[38]

Unionists dominated the majority of counties in East Tennessee. But they did not rule unopposed. Secessionists controlled a handful of counties outright, while in many others loyalists and secessionists continuously struggled for control. One center of Confederate activity was White County, which bordered Cumberland County in East Tennessee and was part of the Union District of East Tennessee. Partisan bands led by Champ Ferguson, William Bledsoe, John Hughes, and William Dunbar skirmished with Federal troops, captured and killed loyalists, and struggled with Unionist bands led by "Tinker Dave" Beatty and William Clift for control of territory and followers. Amanda McDowell, a young woman from Sparta, remembered that both Beatty's men and secessionist guerrillas visited her father and warned him against supporting the other side, and she chronicled continuous fighting between opposing guerrilla bands.[39]

Federal attempts to regain control of this area had the same disappointing results as Confederate operations in Scott and Morgan Counties. In late November 1863 Burnside sent the entire First Tennessee Cavalry and part of the Ninth Pennsylvania Cavalry to Sparta to break up secessionist bands there. The expedition commander, Colonel John Brownlow (son of William G. Brownlow), billeted his force in Sparta, set up fortifications, and sent out patrols, apparently in an attempt to flush the guerrillas out. Secessionists accepted this challenge, and on November 30 and December 1 they ambushed the Union scouts, killing four. Brownlow was unable to respond to the first attack, but he received immediate reports of the second and sent his entire force in pursuit. Union troops overtook the secessionists, and in the ensuing engagement Brownlow claimed to have killed ten and wounded perhaps twice that many bushwhackers. But Confederate guerrillas were apparently undeterred, for a few days later they ambushed a supply train and killed eight guards from the Ninth Pennsylvania Cavalry. Shortly thereafter Brownlow was called back to Knoxville, leaving the Confederate guerrillas free to resume their operations.[40]

In February 1864 Champ Ferguson's band raided the courier line between Washington and Sulphur Springs, killing two soldiers and taking a third prisoner. In response to this and other attacks, Major General George Thomas sent Colonel William B. Stokes, commander of the Fifth Tennessee Cavalry, to Sparta to try his hand. Stokes, a former state representative and a prominent opponent of secession in Middle Tennessee, was vain and ambitious, but he was inept, and his troops lacked training and discipline. Despite reports of brilliant victories over the guerrillas, Stokes proved no more able to break up these partisan bands than Brownlow. In May Thomas ordered him back to Nashville, and in July Major Thomas H. Reeve reported that Ferguson and other guerrillas were still hampering Federal operations in this area. That same month Ferguson's band raided two Union corrals near Kingston and made off with more than five hundred horses and mules. Reeve immediately went in pursuit, but he could not move quickly enough and managed to recover only a few mounts. Reeve then returned to Kingston, assembled reinforcements, and rode to Sparta, but again he located only a handful of horses and not a single bushwhacker. The discouraged major reported that the secessionists had likely dispersed into the mountains where they would never be found. Angry at his inability to pry any information from the people around Sparta, Reeve told his men to plunder every house in the town. Nonetheless, secessionist bands continued to control the Sparta area until the war's end.[41]

In early 1864 Confederate bands in the southern counties of East Tennessee also began to intimidate Unionists and harass Federal troops, with some success. Colonel Robert K. Byrd reported in May that secessionist bands in Rhea and Meigs Counties had become so threatening that if Federal troops were not sent Unionist families there would have to flee. In August Military Governor Andrew

Johnson asserted that the large number of East Tennesseans who had recently deserted the Federal army had done so because secessionist guerrillas were threatening their families. Daniel Ellis claimed that in September 1864 the Confederate Home Guard of Johnson County killed eleven men, burned a number of homes, and attempted to drive out all Unionist families in the county. In October secessionists in Blount County were reported to be "intimidating Union men," and in December Brigadier General Speed S. Fry reported that fourteen Unionists had died in Washington County within a few days. In March 1865 twenty loyalists, along with sixteen soldiers from the Seventh Tennessee Mounted Infantry, informed Brigadier General Davis Tillson that secessionist bands had taken over McMinn and Monroe Counties. They had beaten and killed a number of Unionists and forced a number of loyalists to abandon their farms. Secessionist partisans had become so threatening that Union soldiers from this area were now afraid to visit their families. And loyalists in Sequatchie County claimed that they had been unable to vote in the March elections because bushwhackers made it unsafe to go to the polls.[42]

In the last two years of the war secessionist guerrillas developed a new tactic that proved particularly effective. To elude Federal troops and Unionist home guards, they based themselves across the border in North Carolina and Georgia and raided into southern East Tennessee only at night. Guerrilla bands would sweep through a particular area, capture or kill a number of Union men, rob loyalist homes, and escape back to their hideouts before dawn. In some cases secessionist partisans were joined by renegade Confederate cavalry. Confederate bushwhackers, therefore, used Confederate territory as a sanctuary in the same way that the Viet Cong employed Laotian bases in the Vietnam War. Similarly, after 1863 Unionists used their base in East Tennessee to raid into western North Carolina.

The stories of these raids are numerous and terrifying. In August 1864 eighty secessionists under Bill Gibbs rode into Union County, killed three Unionists, and took nine civilians and three soldiers prisoner. In November Confederate partisans led by the notorious "Captain" John P. Gatewood, a Confederate deserter and reportedly a former member of Champ Ferguson's band, raided into both Polk and Bradley Counties, plundered more than twenty houses, drove off a herd of horses, and killed perhaps a dozen Unionists. In December Southern partisans rode into Monroe County and killed or captured twenty men. And in January 1865 Peter Smith wrote that Southern bushwhackers had recently been in Polk and killed at least five men. He claimed that many Unionist families were so frightened that they were sleeping in the woods, and he admitted that he was afraid to travel into either Polk or Rhea. The Unionist historian S. A. Hurlbut asserted that secessionist guerrillas raided Bradley County at least ten times in the last year of the war, and Polk, McMinn, and Meigs were also hit hard.[43]

All these attacks were meant to loosen the Unionist grip on East Tennessee and undermine Federal occupation policies. But in some cases the political purposes of secessionist attacks were particularly clear. In 1864 Confederate bands killed a number of East Tennesseans who had recently taken the oath of allegiance, attacks that were meant both as punishments and as deterrents to others. And in May 1865 secessionists threatened to disrupt the opening of the county court at Maryville, forcing Major General George Stoneman to send sixty men to guard the court officers.[44]

In response to secessionist violence, loyalists intensified their campaign to subdue and expel Confederate supporters. In January 1864 Unionist guerrillas captured a secessionist from Loudon and kept him prisoner one night. The next morning they started to take him to town but then changed their plans, dragged him off into the woods, shot him, and left him for dead. In March a Confederate soldier stationed at Greeneville wrote that secessionists were depressed at reports that Southern troops would soon be transferred, "for when we leave the Tories will make it very annoying to them. They are more vindictive than the Yankees." Eight secessionists from Johnson County petitioned Major General John C. Breckinridge for protection against several Unionist bands who were robbing and killing Southern supporters. And in the summer of 1864 Unionists in New Market began plundering secessionist homes and threatening their occupants. George F. Eagleton, a Presbyterian minister, was threatened and whipped, and he and his family eventually fled the town. None of their friends would help, for they also feared being beaten or killed.[45]

As both Unionist and secessionist bands intensified their operations, violence in East Tennessee became increasingly reciprocal. Attacks by one side led to retaliation by the other, and the result was an escalating cycle of violence that was difficult to halt. In April 1864 Daniel Ellis brought back to Johnson County a number of letters from soldiers as well as money for their families. When Confederate troops learned of Ellis's deliveries they swept through the county, broke into a number of Unionist homes, stole most of the money, and threatened the recipients. Ellis discovered that two local secessionists, Bill Waugh and Sam McQueen, had provided the soldiers with the names of the families, and he and other loyalists sought revenge. They were unable to find McQueen, but Ellis and his band broke into Waugh's home and killed him there. They then searched several secessionist houses for the money, and when they found none they stole several horses as compensation.[46]

Similar incidents occurred along the border area of Tennessee and North Carolina. North Carolina guerrillas regularly raided Cades Cove, a somewhat isolated settlement in Blount County, stripping the inhabitants of food and killing men caught out on the mountains. In response, Unionists formed a defensive network. Women and children watched routes leading into the cove and carried information, while the older men formed a militia. They were led by Russell Gregory, pastor of the Primitive Baptist Church, an institution that had been forced to close in 1862 because of its Unionist leanings. In the spring of 1864 secessionist guerrillas raided yet again and attempted to leave with stolen cattle and livestock and other supplies. Alerted by watchers, Unionists blocked the roads with trees, ambushed the raiders, and forced them to leave their plunder behind. This action forced secessionists to limit their subsequent attacks to the night hours. But Confederates had their revenge. Two weeks after their defeat, North Carolina guerrillas killed Gregory in his home.[47]

This internecine strife entered into almost all areas of East Tennessee life, and its effects were corrosive. The Unionist-secessionist conflict destroyed families, friendships, and institutions. It pitted family members against each other, split communities into factions, and erased former friendships. But perhaps no institution suffered more from the polarization of the population than the churches in East Tennessee. In July 1861 M. B. Ramsey wrote that one pastor was considering leaving Knoxville because the Unionist members of the church had stopped attending. A second Knoxville minister did resign because he supported the Union while most of the congregation was Southern. A pastor in Jonesborough confided to T. A. R. Nelson that his financial support had dropped considerably because he had "not prayed just as some people would like to have me." The Sunday after Horace Maynard fled to Washington in August 1861 the pastor of his former church prayed that the Unionist leader would never return to Tennessee, a prayer that delighted some but antagonized others. And a Unionist minister in Sullivan had his support cut off and was forced to flee to Indiana.[48]

The leadership of at least two denominations, Presbyterians and Methodists, deliberately turned their churches into battlegrounds in the Unionist-secessionist struggle. In May 1863 the secessionist-controlled East Tennessee Presbytery passed resolutions that forbade the licensing and ordination of any candidate who either opposed slavery or refused to support the Confederate government. In turn, in September 1864 loyalist Presbyterians voted to rejoin the Northern assembly. They were admitted in May 1865 and expelled all Confederate ministers. Confederate Presbyterians then formed their own assembly, and the two organizations were not reunited until the late 1870s.[49]

Similarly, in 1863 the Holston Methodist Conference, which was dominated by Bishop John Early, expelled more than a dozen pastors for their avowed Unionism, and in 1864 it instructed its ministers to refrain from taking the Federal oath of loyalty. When East Tennessee returned to Federal control, Unionists sought revenge. William G. Brownlow began advocating the formation of a loyal Methodist conference in 1863, and in 1864 Unionist ministers met in Knoxville and reunited the East Tennessee conference with the Northern organization. Aided by Northern bishops and Secretary of War Edwin M. Stanton, they then expelled a number of Southern ministers from their churches and took possession of most Methodist church property in East Tennessee. Unionist ministers were supported by loyalist partisans. A Unionist mob broke up a convention of secessionist Methodist ministers at Decatur in 1863, and over the next three years other mobs whipped secessionist pastors and disrupted Southern church meetings. But in the late 1860s the campaign to transform Methodist churches into loyalist organizations collapsed, and by the early 1870s most Methodist churches in East Tennessee had returned to Confederate hands.[50]

The presence of Federal troops freed loyalists in parts of East Tennessee from the fear of Confederate troops. But in other areas the war between Unionists and Southern soldiers continued unabated. In January 1864 a Confederate officer stationed near Bristol complained that he had to take six soldiers as an escort when delivering messages to Confederate foraging parties. That same month Unionist home guards in Sevier County dropped trees across roads to try to block the movement of troops from Sevierville to Madisonville. In March Unionist guerrillas near Blountville ambushed two small groups of soldiers. And in the fall of 1864 loyalists waylaid Confederate troops in Cocke County and stole their supplies.[51]

In February 1864 Major General John M. Schofield, newly appointed commander of the District of East Tennessee, repeated Morgan's experiment with Union-sponsored partisan units. Schofield believed that the tenuous Confederate hold on western North Carolina offered numerous opportunities for Union raids, and he authorized George Kirk, a Unionist leader from Greene County, to recruit men from the mountains of East Tennessee and North Carolina for partisan operations. Kirk, a delegate to the Knoxville and Greeneville Conventions, had already established a reputation as a skilled pilot, and he easily attracted followers. By July Kirk had enough men to make up a regiment, subsequently designated the Second North Carolina Mounted Infantry (Union). A second regiment, the Third North Carolina Mounted Infantry (Union), was later added.

Kirk's first operation, an attempt to disrupt the railroad between Salisbury and Greensboro, was a fiasco. Kirk failed even to reach Salisbury, and his only accomplishments were the dispersal of a camp of Confederate recruits and the destruction of a small train. Schofield then suggested to Kirk that he could "render more effective service by organizing the element of North Carolina hostile to Jeff Davis into a series of scouting companies that would protect each other, interrupt as much as possible the communications of the enemy, destroy his supply depots and bring in such information as may be useful to us." Kirk subsequently won several victories over secessionist guerrilla bands and harassed the weakened Confederate forces in North Carolina. But his men spent more of their time plundering and terrorizing secessionists. Overall, Kirk proved as much a disappointment as Clift, and again Federal officers discovered the limitations of their partisan allies.[52]

East Tennessee residents across the political spectrum suffered extensively from guerrilla violence, the flight of thousands of men into the Union and Confederate armies, economic dislocation, military confiscation, and widespread destruction. Their trials were further increased by an epidemic of crime, which developed in 1862 and did not subside until 1867. This epidemic had several causes. The breakdown of political and legal institutions left a vacuum of authority and law enforcement, while confiscation by the military made theft by civilians, particularly that carried out in retaliation, seem justified. There were also severe shortages of food and other necessities that drove many people to desperate measures. This was particularly true in the winter of 1863–64, when the demands of the Union army overburdened the already struggling economy. Finally, partisan bands on both sides supported themselves by plunder, and increasingly they began to use crime as a means to punish and intimidate their enemies.

Whatever the reasons, crime became a serious challenge to Confederate and Union officers. In July 1863 Confederate authorities had to send one hundred men into Sevier County to suppress "some bushwhackers and thieves" there. In late August, after Southern forces had left the Knoxville area, groups of robbers became particularly bold and active, even coming into Knoxville one night to steal horses. These bands became so dangerous that people in Knoxville formed self-defense companies to protect their property. In the winter of 1863–64 Federal Provost Marshal General Carter received several complaints from Anderson and Monroe Counties concerning "marauders" who came out of the mountains to rob people, and in January 1864 a band of thirty bushwhackers raided the town of Madisonville and robbed most of the homes there. Lieutenant Colonel William C. Bartlett reported from Cumberland Gap that "the place is much troubled by horse thieves and guerrillas who run in steal horses and then ride off." And reports of violent theft steadily came in from McMinn, Sequatchie, Hamilton, Grainger, Campbell, and other counties.[53]

Some of these crimes clearly possessed a political dimension. One loyalist robber band terrorized the Loudon area for several weeks in 1864, breaking into homes at night, stealing money and valuables, and threatening its victims. Union authorities eventually managed to arrest several of these men, but the deputy provost marshal soon released them, for the only witnesses against them were Confederate supporters. And in 1864 William Sloan complained of a Unionist band in the Benton area that was systematically robbing secessionist homes.[54]

These crimes demonstrate the blurred distinctions in the partisan war, for theft could result from hardship, greed, revenge, political calculation, or all these motives at once. But regardless of their motives criminal attacks could be as ruthless and terrifying as other partisan operations. Robbers strung up men by their necks, whipped them, or threatened to burn their homes until they revealed where their money and other valuables were hidden. Sometimes they also shot their victims after finishing their robbery. Neither women nor children were immune from this violence, and a number of women were hanged or tortured by robbers. Equally frightening was the practice of some robbers of pretending to be Union soldiers or actually wearing Federal uniforms and justifying their thefts as legal confiscation or retribution. In these cases victims could not be certain who was at their door or know whether resistance would bring them into conflict with the occupying authorities.[55]

Union troops experienced the same difficulties as their Confederate counterparts in attempting to locate and capture partisans. Brigadier General George Morgan reported in July 1862 that he had sent a regiment "on a four-nights circuitous march around another mountain ridge" to trap a guerrilla band that had been particularly troublesome to Union forces around Cumberland Gap, but stated "I am not sanguine of the success of the expedition." In the summer of 1864 Lieutenant Colonel Luther S. Trowbridge sent twenty-five men to rescue a Union officer captured by a secessionist band. The Union troopers followed the band into the mountains but were never able to overtake them, and after two days they gave up the chase and turned back. On their return the soldiers were ambushed by the same guerrilla band they had been pursuing and lost one man. The troopers drove off the bushwhackers and inflicted several casualties but again failed to catch them.[56]

To offset the partisan advantages in speed and stealth, Union officers devised a variety of tactics to bring guerrillas to bay. To trap one band camped on the bank of the Little Tennessee River near Chilhouee, Lieutenant Colonel Robert Klein of the Third Indiana Cavalry split his force, moved simultaneously down both banks of the river, and converged on the camp at dawn. Klein achieved surprise and claimed to have captured twenty-three guerrillas. Colonel Thomas J. Harrison of the Eighth Indiana Cavalry employed a similar tactic when he was sent to Sparta to suppress guerrilla activity there. Harrison divided his regiment into four groups, positioned them at different points around Sparta, and then converged simultaneously on the town. At the end of five days the Union commander reported four guerrillas killed, six wounded, and fifteen captured, as well as the recovery of stolen property from Champ Ferguson's farm. And Lieutenant Colonel George Gowin of the Sixth Tennessee Mounted Infantry (Federal) used a simpler, but equally effective, method. Sent into northern Georgia to track down a band of seventy-five guerrillas, Gowin simply ascertained the band's location, trailed them at a safe distance, waited until they had set up camp, and then surrounded them with his detachment. Gowin reported that his men killed several guerrillas and recovered a large supply of arms.[57]

Federal garrisons at strategic points in East Tennessee devoted a significant portion of their time to fighting bushwhackers. Confederate guerrillas were particularly active around Cumberland Gap, and Union troops there were constantly engaged. In October 1864 Captain W. P. Ammen reported that guerrillas under a secessionist named Litrell had been harassing Federal troops and asked for reinforcements. In early December Lieutenant Colonel William C. Bartlett stated that he had captured four bushwhackers and again asked for more troops. Later that month Bartlett reported that he had arrested Litrell and several of his bushwhackers, but he complained that his men had to "track them to their holes" and that it was almost impossible to capture them alive. In January 1865 the Union commander reported two more successful expeditions, one by the Second North Carolina Mounted Infantry (Union) that killed at least twelve guerrillas and captured ten, and another that killed an additional dozen. And in February Bartlett reported that he had captured a second guerrilla leader.[58]

Not all Federal officers were so enthusiastic about counter-guerrilla operations. In January 1864 Provost Marshal General Samuel P. Carter sent a detachment of the Second East Tennessee under Lieutenant William Estrada into Scott and Fentress Counties to destroy the numerous bands of bushwhackers and robbers that plagued that area. Instead of actively hunting for guerrillas, Estrada simply quartered his men in Wartburg, and Carter had to prod him into action: "This was not the design of sending you into that section. You are expected to scour the country, and arrest horse thieves and robbers who have so long infested that region and been a terror to the citizens. The General expects you to be vigilant and active, and do everything in your power to bring the villains . . . to justice." Similarly, even after loyalists near Cleveland made numerous pleas for protection against secessionist raids, the post commander there refused to pursue guerrillas, stating that he was there to guard the post and not to undertake field operations.[59]

From the beginning of the Federal occupation, numbers of officers and soldiers in East Tennessee adopted a policy of granting no quarter to bushwhackers. One Union soldier left this devious account of the killing of a prisoner:

The regiment had gone up the Railroad. They went up as far as Jonesborough, and then came back destroying the railroad as they came. On their way up there we had one man shot by a bush-whacker he belonged to our company his name was Isaac Rimer, They afterward captured a man in the woods who they think done it he was turned over to the Provost Guard of the Brigade, and as it consists of boys from *owr regiment* as well as some others a musket happened to go *accidentally* and the ball *happened to hit the bushwhacker*, of course the soldier who was so unfortunate as to have sutch an accident happen with his gun was *sevierly* repri-manded by his officer but I believe he was not arrested.

After guerrillas in the Cumberland Gap area attempted to hang a group of foragers whom they had captured, the commanding officer made it known that thereafter his men would take no prisoners. Union soldiers stationed near Sparta routinely gave no quarter when fighting bushwhackers or renegade cavalry. And other Union troops dealt with bushwhackers by performing summary executions, tor-turing bushwhackers to obtain information, or shooting guerrillas on sight. Like Confederate soldiers, Federal troops concluded that guerrillas were not legitimate combatants and did not deserve the honorable treatment accorded to enemy troops.[60]

These practices were similar to those followed in other theaters and were supported by General Orders 100, a document written by Francis Lieber and released by the War Department in 1863. Gen-eral Orders 100 established guidelines for the conduct of the war and covered such matters as the treatment of enemy civilians and property and the practice of military government. This document stated that combatants who did not wear a uniform or some insignia marking their combatant status and who were not enrolled in any military unit were not entitled to the protections accorded enemy soldiers. Persons caught engaging in guerrilla acts could be shot on sight, and soldiers were not obligated to give quarter to enemy bush-whackers. Guerrillas who were captured, however, were entitled to a trial by a military commission.[61]

Officers in East Tennessee implicitly or explicitly encouraged their men not to take guerrillas prisoner. In June 1864 the deputy provost marshal of Morgan County requested clarification of official policy toward bushwhacker bands. Provost Marshal General Carter replied that "with regard to guerrillas, they are, by the law of nature and Army Regulations, not to be treated as prisoners of war, but, if caught in arms, are *to be shot on the spot*." When Bartlett reported that he had captured a guerrilla from the notorious Litrell band and asked what should be done with him, Ammen sent this carefully worded response: "I reply that these men, if captured, must be sent to the Provost Marshal General of the District with charges, and a list of witnesses. In my opinion, it is best not to take such characters prisoners—to show them no quarter. If, unfortunately, they are taken, we will have to obey existing orders." Other officers went further and established tribunals to try guerrillas on the spot. The garrison at Tullahoma, which was constantly engaged in running down guerrilla bands in East and Middle Tennessee, tried men accused of bushwhacking and immediately executed those found guilty. But officers at Tullahoma acted with discretion; as one soldier explained, "when ordered to take our prisoners away, and not bring them back, we understood the meaning of the command."[62]

By 1865 Union commanders openly sanctioned the practice of giving no quarter. The order that guerrilla prisoners be given a fair trial remained in place, but officers simply encouraged their men not to take prisoners. In March 1865 Brigadier General Davis Tillson wrote Captain W. A. Cochran of the Seventh Tennessee Mounted Infantry: "I am exceedingly pleased with your success and especially with your not taking any prisoners." In April Major General George Stoneman instructed Colonel James Parsons of the Ninth Tennessee Cavalry that "the persons with whom you have to deal are outlaws, so long as they are at liberty, and as such should be treated. When taken prisoners, they must be treated as prisoners, and are entitled to trial, which takes time and entails trouble and expense. Give them to understand that . . . every man found in arms . . . will be treated as a public enemy and an outlaw, and killed like a mad dog." That same month the post commander at Jonesborough issued orders that "in the future no quarter will be shown guerrillas and robbers; they will be shot down whenever found."[63]

The significance of guerrilla operations in East Tennessee must be judged by the varying aims of the partisan forces. East Tennessee irregulars had little impact on either Confederate or Union strategy and operations, and the regular forces retained effective control of the rail lines, the major towns and cities, and other strategic points in East Tennessee. Guerrillas also had only a small effect on the number of troops committed to this theater. Southern commanders routinely stationed two to three regiments on the railroads, but these were as much a guarantee against Union cavalry raids as guer-

TABLE 3. *Confederate Troop Strengths, 1861–1863*

		Aggregate Present and Absent	Aggregate Present
1861	July	4,300	not available
	Sept.	11,457	10,194
	Dec.	16,183	12,128
1862	Mar.	8,000	not available
	May	20,731	14,446
	June	24,895	16,303
	Dec.	15,435	9,268
1863	Jan.	15,415	8,600
	Mar.	23,583	15,818
	May	27,598	18,752
	July	26,400	17,814

rilla attacks. The Confederacy required additional troops to control the loyalist population, but the number was smaller than some have asserted. During the November uprising Confederate commanders employed no more than nine regiments to restore control, and throughout 1862 and 1863 the number of troops stationed at garrisons in the interior of East Tennessee never exceeded eight thousand. (See Table 3.) The Confederate commitment to East Tennessee was small in comparison with the number of troops sent to other regions, and it is unlikely that the Unionist rebellion forced Confederate authorities to send more than five or six thousand more troops to this area than they would have if it had not been rebellious. Confederate guerrilla resistance had an equally small impact on the Federal commitment to East Tennessee. Though initially the North employed over 30,000 troops to conquer the region, this number declined significantly in the spring of 1864, when other campaigns took precedence. By December 1864 it had fallen to ten thousand, where it remained until the war's end. (See Table 4.) Again, most of these troops were positioned to defend East Tennessee against Confederate forces, not secessionist partisans.

But guerrillas greatly influenced the routine operations of both armies. Tasks such as transportation, communication, foraging, and scouting all became more difficult, more dangerous, and less efficient because of partisan harassment. Guerrillas derailed trains, burned wagons, stole supplies, and captured or killed pickets, couri-

TABLE 4. *Union Troop Strengths, 1863–1865*

			Aggregate Present and Absent	Aggregate Present
1863	Nov.		44,723	30,352
1864	Feb.		52,463	30,416
	Sept.		38,597	25,545
	Dec.		10,376	8,207
1865	Jan.		10,244	7,137
	Mar.		18,558	14,267

ers, and foragers. Both armies had to detail additional troops as railroad and wagon guards, and often foraging parties and scouts had to operate in larger groups than normal. The guerrillas had an equally powerful psychological impact on soldiers in East Tennessee. Troops on both sides made frequent references to guerrilla activity, took the bushwhacker threat seriously, and sought safety in large groups. For both Confederate and Union troops the guerrillas became an ever-present menace.

Loyalists made their greatest contribution to the Union victory by sending thousands of recruits to Kentucky. These soldiers represented a significant addition to Northern strength in the western theater and a corresponding drain on Confederate manpower. They also stood as powerful evidence of the failure of Confederate policy in East Tennessee. That men would leave their families and their homes to the mercy of their enemies and undertake a hazardous journey, rather than enter Confederate service, was an unequivocal rejection of the new government.

The success of Confederate and Union soldiers in fighting guerrillas was mixed. Regular troops clearly possessed superior discipline and tactical skills, and soldiers that were engaged in this service for any length of time developed effective tactics. Even allowing for exaggerated reports, Confederate and Union soldiers captured or killed hundreds of guerrillas. But soldiers also frequently spent days chasing bushwhackers to little effect. Further, neither the Confederacy nor the Union ever effectively controlled East Tennessee. Unionist guerrillas dominated the majority of counties, and though Confederate officers could disperse loyalist bands at will, Unionists simply resumed their operations when Confederate troops withdrew. Southern troops could neither impose Confederate authority nor protect Confederate supporters. Similarly, secessionist guerrillas dominated parts of southern East Tennessee, and Union troops failed to suppress dissent or guard loyalists in these areas. The Confederacy faced a large, highly organized loyalist population and simply lacked sufficient resources to fight loyalists effectively. The Union encountered a smaller, more localized threat, and effective suppression was a realistic aim. But East Tennessee was not a priority in Union strategy. Thus on neither side did the officers fighting this war have the numbers that they needed effectively to police East Tennessee.

Though both Confederate and Union officers carried out a number of large operations to break up partisan bands and intimidate the population, most of the effective counterguerrilla work in East Tennessee was small-scale and undramatic. It was an integral part of garrison duty, cavalry scouting, and the enforcement of conscription, and it acquired a routine like any other task. This work was dangerous and monotonous, and it entailed a seemingly endless number of marches, patrols, pickets, house-to-house searches, and missed encounters. The counterguerrilla war was fatiguing, tedious, frustrating, and brutalizing, and it is little wonder that the morale and discipline of troops in East Tennessee sagged. Although soldiers from both armies despised guerrillas, their mode of fighting them frequently descended to the same base level. The only barriers that separated the soldier from the guerrilla were a military code of conduct and military discipline, and when these eroded a uniform was not always sufficient to separate a soldier from a bushwhacker. In the field the issue frequently settled down to one factor, survival, and the war between the guerrillas and the soldiers became simple, primitive, and brutal.[64]

William G. Brownlow. A vitriolic editor who fought a personal war against the Confederacy, as governor, Brownlow led the unsuccessful attempt to bar Confederates from the political process and secure Unionist control of the entire state. McClung Historical Collection, Knoxville, Tennessee.

T. A. R. Nelson. Leader of the Unionist campaign against secession in 1861, Nelson came to symbolize the dilemma of conservative Southern Unionists, who opposed secession but were alienated by emancipation, disfranchisement, and other radical policies. McClung Historical Collection, Knoxville, Tennessee.

Horace Maynard. One of East Tennessee's most visible exiles, Maynard repeatedly pressed the Lincoln administration and Union generals to seize the region from Confederate control. He also aided Johnson's attempts to reconstruct the state government. Special Collections, Hoskins Library, University of Tennessee, Knoxville.

Oliver P. Temple. After having helped organize the Unionist campaign against seces-
sion, Temple submitted to Confederate authority and remained in East Tennessee. His
histories of Civil War East Tennessee portrayed Unionists as helpless victims of Confed-
erate oppression. McClung Historical Collection, Knoxville, Tennessee.

J. G. M. Ramsey. Physician, historian, and railroad promoter, Ramsey was one of East Tennessee's most prominent secessionists. The destruction of his home and library by Union troops in 1864 was a particularly notorious act of Unionist vengeance. McClung Historical Collection, Knoxville, Tennessee.

Landon Carter Haynes. A prewar enemy of Brownlow, Haynes represented Tennessee in the Confederate Senate, where he pressed the Confederate government for sterner measures against the Unionist resistance. Library of Congress.

5 An Enemy's Country

Confederate policy from May through November 1861 had been characterized by leniency and restraint. Rather than harshly suppressing dissent, Confederate authorities attempted to persuade Unionists voluntarily to accept Confederate rule. This policy was temporarily abandoned after the bridge burnings. Angered by the failure of leniency, Confederate authorities threw off most restraints. Employing military force, mass arrests, and confiscation, the Confederate government attempted to destroy Unionist organizations and terrorize the population into submission. A third phase in Confederate policy opened in February 1862, when the War Department sent Major General Edmund Kirby Smith to East Tennessee to restore order. The new commander sought to balance conciliation and coercion. He attempted to soothe loyalist fears, but he was also determined to force East Tennessee to function as a part of the Confederacy. The failure of Kirby Smith and his successor, Major General Sam Jones, to end loyalist dissent led to a final shift in policy. Beginning in late 1862, Confederate authorities more and more referred to East Tennessee loyalists not as Confederate citizens but as enemies, and they employed increasing force in an attempt to subdue, imprison, or drive out rebellious Unionists.

Where Zollicoffer had been a volunteer, Kirby Smith was a professional officer with a superior record. He had graduated from West Point in 1845 and had seen extensive service in the Mexican War, including action at Palo Alto, Resaca de la Palma, Monterey, Veracruz, and Mexico City. After the war he had taught mathematics at West Point for two years and then spent four years on the Texas frontier with the Fifth Infantry, skirmishing with Native Americans and Mexican raiders. In 1855 Captain Edmund Kirby

Smith had transferred to the newly formed Second United States Cavalry, Albert Sidney Johnston's famous regiment that included such Civil War notables as Robert E. Lee, George Thomas, and John Bell Hood.[1]

Politically Kirby Smith and Zollicoffer shared many traits. Both men were conservatives, both had denied the constitutionality and the wisdom of secession, and both had clung to the Union until the clash at Fort Sumter. Kirby Smith had remained with the Second Cavalry in Texas until that state ratified its ordinance of secession. He had ridden out with his regiment, but in March 1861 he had resigned his position in the U.S. Army and accepted a commission as a lieutenant colonel from the Confederate War Department.[2]

Perhaps no commander came to East Tennessee with more reluctance than Kirby Smith. After filling various posts in Virginia, in October 1861 he had been promoted to major general and attained the coveted post of division commander in the Army of Northern Virginia. Kirby Smith found his duties with this army gratifying, and he had recently settled his wife and children in nearby Lynchburg. His assignment to East Tennessee broke up this comfortable situation and placed him in an isolated region among a hostile population. Furthermore, his service there promised to be unrewarding, for East Tennessee afforded little opportunity to contribute to Southern victory or to prove himself as a commander.[3]

Kirby Smith's initial observations of East Tennessee confirmed his worst fears. To his wife he complained that "I find affairs here, as far as I am able to judge, in a much worse condition than represented." On March 13 he wrote that "no one can conceive the actual condition of East Tennessee, disloyal to the core, it is more dangerous and difficult to operate in than the country of an acknowledged enemy." Increasingly doubtful of his ability to restore East Tennessee to Confederate control, the following day he suggested to Major General Braxton Bragg that Confederate troops could be better used elsewhere: "East Tennessee is an Enemy's country, its people beyond the influence and control of our troops and in open rebellion. The force here at present is barely more than sufficient to guard the Pork Houses and the line of the Railroad—If under the circumstances you deem it advisable, I will turn over the defense of the Post to the Militia and willingly and gladly join you with such portion of my command, as you may direct." But the War Department was not yet willing to abandon East Tennessee, and Kirby Smith remained in Knoxville.[4]

In a series of more lucid dispatches Kirby Smith enumerated the deficiencies of his command. First, due to the reorganization ordered by Richmond the department had had no effective commander from December through February. Leadbetter had believed that he was responsible only for the defense of the rail lines, while Crittenden had been assigned command only of the forces on the Kentucky border. Confederate units had been left aimlessly scattered around the region, while administrative affairs were in disarray. Second, far too few troops were available. Defense of the rail lines and "porkeries" required one to two full regiments, which left only 2,300 men to cover Cumberland Cap and Knoxville. Chattanooga was almost entirely unprotected, and few troops were available to keep the Unionist population under control. Further, waves of disease had immobilized many men, and the terms of most of the regular regiments were due to expire soon. Most units in the department had never received proper arms and equipment, and most still lacked sufficient training. Finally, the East Tennessee militia was thoroughly disloyal and unreliable, and even some regular units raised in East Tennessee were "infected" with dissent.[5]

Events elsewhere in the western theater further contributed to Confederate difficulties in East Tennessee. In February Union forces under Brigadier General Ulysses S. Grant captured Forts Henry and Donelson and forced Confederate troops to abandon Nashville. A Confederate counterstroke at Shiloh battered Federal forces but failed to drive them back. By May the North had occupied much of Middle and West Tennessee and threatened the eastern region. Union victories forced the state government to flee, and President Lincoln appointed Andrew Johnson military governor. Confederates in East Tennessee, therefore, were isolated politically and threatened with invasion.[6]

These were daunting problems indeed. But Kirby Smith brought to East Tennessee an administrative and organizational ability that the department had previously lacked, and he worked hard to restore order. Within a few weeks he had made a number of reforms. Kirby Smith consolidated scattered units, assigned them to the most critical points, and created a small force for mobile operations. He increased training, secured more arms and equipment, and attempted to repair defects in the supply system. To make up for shortages of supplies, Kirby Smith gave officers greater latitude in foraging and instructed them to take food first from Unionists, while stipulating that loyalists as well as Confederate supporters be paid for all provisions acquired and left sufficient supplies for their own use. Finally, Kirby Smith attempted to improve Confederate discipline. He insisted that officers could not unilaterally seize abandoned property that was covered under Confederate state sequestration laws, reminded Confederate troops of the need to maintain a good reputation for discipline and order, and warned that he would personally hold officers responsible for the behavior of their men. Many defects remained, but the new commander brought order and purpose back to the East Tennessee command and eliminated some of the worst abuses that had grown up since the November uprising.[7]

Although much of Kirby Smith's energy in these first weeks went into administrative matters and strategic planning, by early April he had also developed a policy for winning back, or at least controlling, the rebellious population. Kirby Smith lacked Zollicoffer's empathy with Unionists, but he did believe that if approached properly much of the loyalist population might become reconciled to Confederate rule. Kirby Smith concluded that their resistance had been created by unscrupulous leaders who misrepresented the intentions of the Confederate government and frightened the population. Thus, if loyalists could be led into resistance, they might also be manipulated into accepting Confederate authority. On April 2 Kirby Smith summarized his observations for Adjutant and Inspector General Samuel Cooper: "The arrest of the leading men in every county, and their incarceration South, may bring these people right. They are an ignorant, primitive people, completely in the hands of, and under the guidance of, their leaders. . . . Remove these men, and a draft might soon be made, to which a portion of the population would respond."[8]

Confederate officials had already attempted to diminish the influence of Unionist leaders, particularly those who occupied county offices. In November 1861 the Confederate government had required that elected officials take a pledge to enforce Confederate laws, and in January 1862 Confederate officers administered an oath of allegiance to some officeholders in Knox and Sullivan Counties. Despite these pressures, many loyalist officials remained uncooperative. Kirby Smith thus proposed to bring all officeholders in East Tennessee under Confederate control. Newly elected county officers were scheduled to be sworn in on April 7. On April 2 Kirby Smith sent secret orders to subordinates at Clinton, Cleveland, Greeneville, Loudon, Morristown, Knoxville, and Cumberland Gap, instructing them, on the morning of April 7, to send parties of twenty-five men under discreet officers to observe the installation ceremonies in a number of counties. Confederate troops were to ensure that all elected officers took the oath of allegiance to the Confederate government and were to arrest and send to Knoxville anyone refusing to do so. This assertion of Southern authority was quite risky, for it brought the Confederate army directly into the local affairs of East Tennesseans. Kirby Smith recognized the possibility of resistance, and he instructed his subordinates not to communicate these instructions to their officers until just before their departure and reminded them to use "the utmost secrecy and precaution." But these fears proved largely unfounded. A few elected officials at Cleveland refused to take the oath and had to be arrested. But most Unionist officeholders, who had learned to accommodate Confederate demands, chose to submit, though they clearly did not alter their loyalties.[9]

Other arrests soon followed. On April 14 Kirby Smith ordered the commander at Morristown to detain Unionist leaders suspected of spreading "exaggerated" rumors concerning the Confederate draft and inciting men to flee to Kentucky. In May military officers and civilian authorities arrested other prominent loyalists suspected of encouraging continued resistance, including former state senator Montgomery Thornburgh, future Tennessee governor DeWitt Senter, and several delegates to the 1861 Knoxville and Greeneville Conventions. Once again these prisoners were held in Knoxville several days without charges, then notified that they were being sent to a military prison in Georgia. Their demands for a trial were rejected, and they eventually found themselves detained in Macon. Montgomery Thornburgh died in captivity, and his death became for Unionists a symbol of Confederate repression.[10]

Kirby Smith hoped that these arrests would demoralize the Unionist resistance. He recognized, however, that the courts in East Tennessee were too weak effectively to prosecute Unionists for disloyalty. Despite declarations of martial law in parts of East Tennessee in November and December 1861, civilian courts had continued to function and had provided considerable protection to Unionists. District court judge West H. Humphreys had freed dozens of Unionists arrested for rebellion, and other justices had issued writs of habeas corpus for persons held by the military. There were also charges that in most counties secessionists could not receive justice from Unionist judges and juries.[11]

Shortly after his arrival, therefore, Kirby Smith began pressing Richmond for a declaration of martial law. On April 8, 1862, President Jefferson Davis consented and suspended the writ of habeas corpus in the Department of East Tennessee. As amplified by the attorney general, Davis's proclamation suspended all civil jurisdictions except those exercising purely administrative functions. Criminal courts would continue to function, but the department commander was granted "super vision over the judicial tribunals of the Department" and possessed the power to establish military commissions to try criminal cases if civilian courts failed to do so efficiently and fairly. Potentially the entire judicial machinery of East Tennessee lay in the department commander's hands. Davis also authorized Kirby Smith to establish a "military police," institute stricter controls on travel, and prohibit the production and sale of all "spirituous liquors."[12]

Martial law gave Kirby Smith a powerful weapon against Unionist resistance. It allowed him to remove dangerous or influential loyalists from the population without fear of civilian interference. It greatly increased the risks and costs of dissent, and it reduced the ability of Unionist judges to use their power against secessionists. Though Kirby Smith did not make full use of his authority, martial law was a significant assertion of Confederate authority and revealed a hardening of Confederate attitudes.

Other repressive measures followed. In late April Confederate provost marshal Colonel William Churchwell expelled from East Tennessee the families of William G. Brownlow, Horace Maynard, and Andrew Johnson. He then threatened to banish the families of all Unionists who had escaped to Kentucky to join the Union army. Churchwell acted under the authority of the Alien Enemies Act and argued that the families of men living in the North and fighting against the Confederacy were not entitled to the resources and protection of the Confederacy. At the same time, state authorities continued to seize the property of Unionists who had fled to the North, including that of Johnson, Brownlow, and Maynard. These actions were legal but also unwise. Brownlow paraded Churchwell's expulsion order before the North as further evidence of Confederate cruelty and oppression, and the spectacle of women and children being forcibly removed from their homes embarrassed Confederate authorities.[13]

Finally, Kirby Smith continued Zollicoffer's attempts to stop the flight of East Tennessee manpower to Kentucky. On April 18 he ordered Colonel John C. Vaughn to employ all his available cavalry in patrolling the area between Clinton and "the north Valley of Powell's River," one of the major escape routes. Shortly thereafter Kirby Smith strengthened Southern forces in the Holston River Valley, another important crossing point. These increased Confederate patrols made the trip to Kentucky increasingly hazardous.[14]

Kirby Smith recognized that coercion alone would prove ineffective, and shortly after the declaration of martial law he launched a campaign to convince East Tennessee Unionists of the goodwill of the Confederate government. On April 18 he issued an offer of general amnesty, stating that any person who abandoned resistance to Confederate rule and took an oath of loyalty to the new government would be exempt from prosecution and protected from harassment. This offer of forgiveness extended even to East Tennesseans in the Union army, provided that they returned to the state within thirty days. In conjunction with the amnesty offer Kirby Smith published a circular that attempted to quiet Unionist fears of the Confederate government. He promised to protect "the lives and property" of East Tennesseans from all marauders, including his own troops, and to suspend the state militia draft. He also guaranteed that farmers raising and harvesting crops, and all other East Tennesseans engaged in productive activities, would not be disturbed by Confederate authorities. On April 23 Churchwell repeated the amnesty offer to Unionists in the Federal ranks, and on August 13 Kirby Smith issued a third proclamation "To the East Tennesseans in the United States Army," this time promising not only forgiveness but also compensation for arms and equipment brought back. Like Zollicoffer, Kirby Smith had concluded that neutrality was preferable to resistance and that the Confederate government would have to grant some latitude to loyalists. Though his proclamations were formal and stilted and revealed his contempt for the East Tennessee population, the amnesty offers represented a sincere attempt to heal some of the damage caused by Confederate excesses in November and December 1861 and to offer terms that East Tennesseans might accept, while still preserving Confederate authority.[15]

Kirby Smith further attempted to prove Confederate goodwill by suspending the draft in East Tennessee. He argued that given the "excited condition of the public mind" conscription would only drive Unionists into inaccessible hideouts or out of the state and would add little to Confederate manpower. As an alternative, Kirby Smith suggested using the existing East Tennessee regiments as a base for building loyalty. In keeping with his general assessment of East Tennessee Unionism, he argued that if these regiments, which were suspected of disloyalty, were sent out of the region into a "pure political atmosphere, and removed from their present associations," they might become reliable. New recruits could then be placed in these units, and their ties with the population might eventually foster a greater attachment to the Confederate cause. On April 7 Major General Robert E. Lee agreed that the East Tennessee regiments might be exchanged for units from other states if they enlisted for three years, and on May 11 Kirby Smith ordered the Fourth Tennessee, one of the most suspect units, to Georgia. On the same grounds, he attempted to prevent the disbandment of an East Tennessee "company of sappers and miners," a noncombat unit that Zollicoffer had created as an option for Unionists who were willing to serve in the army but would not enlist in regular units. Some Confederate officers and East Tennessee secessionists charged that the unit had become a refuge for conscript evaders and should be eliminated. Kirby Smith argued, however, that the company had done good service and that it was better to have the men in some sort of service than defying the draft law.[16]

Kirby Smith's campaign to win back the Unionist population was intense but short lived. After May the East Tennessee commander was increasingly forced to give his attention to the defense of his department against invasion, and his interest in political affairs declined. Following the Union victory at Shiloh and the occupation of Corinth, Mississippi, Major General Henry Halleck ordered Major General Don Carlos Buell and the Army of the Cumberland to march across Tennessee and seize the rail connections at Chattanooga. At about the same time, 12,000 men under Brigadier General George W. Morgan moved south from Kentucky and threatened Cumberland Gap, apparently in preparation for a larger invasion. Kirby Smith's 12,000 men were insufficient to defend all points at once, and he was forced to shuttle his forces up and down the valley in response to each real or imagined Federal advance. In spite of these efforts, Confederate troops had to evacuate Cumberland Gap, and twice advance Union forces came within artillery range of Chattanooga. By June Kirby Smith was exhausted and near despair: "I am so sad, distressed, and anxious. . . . The Enemy have now crossed the Cumberland Mountains, their name is legion and they come from every quarter—no sooner disposed of in one direction than they appear in another." Under such circumstances Kirby

Smith could give little thought to internal affairs, and his pacification campaign suffered.[17]

Fortunately for the Confederate cause, both Union threats dissipated. Federal commanders still feared the logistical difficulties of invading East Tennessee, and despite pressure from Johnson and Horace Maynard Union troops remained in Kentucky. Further, Buell was forced to make extensive repairs to the railroad lines, and he made slow progress toward Chattanooga. Union dispositions thus left Kentucky largely unguarded and invited a Confederate invasion. In mid-August, after supposedly coordinating their plans, Bragg and Kirby Smith marched north with dreams of bringing the Bluegrass state into the Confederacy.[18]

Before Kirby Smith left Knoxville he requested that Major General John P. McCown be appointed his temporary successor. McCown, a native of Sevier County, radiated confidence, declaring that "I am one of these people, and think I know them. I shall pursue such policy as my knowledge of the people and the interests of the country, dictates." But McCown floundered almost immediately. On September 17 he sent a dispatch to Richmond asking for guidance on a whole range of issues, many of which had already been settled, prompting Secretary of War George Randolph to conclude that "General McCown seems to have no policy of his own and recommends nothing." Further stating that "the treatment of the Union men in East Tennessee cannot be prescribed here, but must be determined on by some one thoroughly acquainted with the state of things in that region," Randolph replaced McCown with Major General Sam Jones, an officer with a troubled career. Jones had served as chief of artillery for Major General P. G. T. Beauregard and had fought at First Manassas. He had then served under Bragg and Major General Earl Van Dorn but had quarreled with both men and had eventually been assigned post commander at Chattanooga. Jones, thus, intended to make the most of his new assignment.[19]

Jones's diagnosis of the ills of his command and the prescriptions he offered differed little from Kirby Smith's. But Jones was far more dedicated to his duty of pacifying East Tennessee and far more sympathetic to the loyalist population. In late September Randolph recommended that Jones shift his headquarters and most of his forces to Murfreesboro in support of Bragg, an offer that Kirby Smith would have grasped eagerly. Jones refused, however, explaining that "I have no one who I could leave here with any feeling of confidence that the affairs of the Dept. would be managed as I think they should be."[20]

But Jones would not have an easy task. His initial instructions from Randolph revealed yet another shift in Confederate policy:

"Your chief duty, however, will be the execution of the conscript law in East Tenn. It will require great judgement, and we rely upon your firmness and prudence to carry out the law without exciting revolt. Confer with Gov. Harris, act in concert with him, and be on your guard in listening to the advice of persons exasperated by contact with the disaffected." As Randolph revealed, Confederate authorities were increasingly reluctant to continue to grant further concessions to a rebellious population. Richmond could not continue to make allowances to East Tennessee without exciting resentment elsewhere, and President Davis was determined to force the region to contribute to the military effort. The Confederate government was not yet willing to undertake the sweeping measures urged by East Tennessee secessionists, such as mass arrests and deportations, but it had decided to carry out conscription in East Tennessee, even at a very high cost.[21]

Conscription would in fact become the Confederacy's chief weapon against dissent in the last year of occupation. It would force potential conscripts in East Tennessee to declare their loyalties and separate friend from enemy, for Unionists eligible for the draft would have only three choices: submit, flee to Kentucky, or attempt to avoid conscription officers. The first would bring them under Confederate control and perhaps send them out of East Tennessee. The second would reduce the strength of the insurgent forces and reduce the internal threat to Confederate rule. And the third would force loyalists into open enmity and expose them to arrest and imprisonment. Some Confederate officers serving in the department argued that it was better to have Unionists as open enemies in the Union army than secret foes at home, and conscription may in fact have been a deliberate means of forcing the male population of East Tennessee into exile. Whatever the case, it is clear that during the last year of Confederate rule the main duty of the occupying force was to enforce the draft. The physical and moral costs of such a policy were high, but it reflected the growing frustration and anger of Confederate authorities.[22]

Like Kirby Smith, Jones found the depth and extent of resistance to Confederate rule in East Tennessee startling. He also identified the Unionist elite as the key to influencing the population, and he agreed that some of the most hostile leaders might have to be removed. But Jones also believed that Unionist leaders might be coopted and used for Confederate purposes. One of his first steps upon taking command was to initiate contact with a number of important Unionist figures. On September 25 Jones requested that T. A. R. Nelson visit his headquarters to discuss affairs in East Tennessee and, as a gesture of goodwill, lifted the restrictions that had been placed on Nelson's movements. In subsequent days Jones also met with Oliver P. Temple, John Baxter, Andrew Fleming, R. H. Hodges, and other Unionists who had been delegates to the Knoxville and Greeneville Conventions.[23]

On October 4 Jones reported success. Nelson had willingly written an "Address to the People of East Tennessee," a lengthy and essentially pro-Confederate discussion of the conflict, and given Jones permission to use it as he desired. The commanding general immediately arranged for the document to be published in the *Knoxville Register*, the *Athens Post*, and other papers, attempting, as he explained to Randolph, to pass Nelson's document off as a voluntary production. He refrained from tampering with the address's "Union tone" in the belief that this would make it more authentic and effective, and he wrote the editor of the *Athens Post* that "of course I do not want my name to appear in connection with it." Jones also received statements from three other influential figures, John Netherland, the Reverend Nathaniel G. Taylor, and Judge Seth Lucky, that appeared to promise submission and the use of their influence for the Confederate government. Encouraged by these seeming conversions, Jones then attempted to persuade Nelson and Netherland to stump East Tennessee in support of the Confederacy.[24]

Jones's timing in this campaign was fortunate, for the announcement of Lincoln's Preliminary Emancipation Proclamation on September 22 had created great consternation among Southern Unionists. They could support a war to restore the nation, but could they acquiesce in the destruction of a fundamental Southern institution? For Nelson, as for others, the answer was no. Nelson still denied the legality and wisdom of secession, and he accused Southern troops of committing numerous atrocities in East Tennessee. Nonetheless, Nelson insisted that the Lincoln administration now posed a greater threat to Southern rights than the Confederacy. He dwelt at length on Lincoln's unconstitutional acts: suspension of the writ of habeas corpus, imprisonment of civilians opposed to the conflict, calling up troops without a congressional declaration of war, and now the unlawful attempt to deprive Southerners of their slaves. A sense of betrayal marked Nelson's address. East Tennesseans had suffered for the Union and the constitution, and now Lincoln seemed determined to destroy those very things. Admitting that the experience of the last eighteen months would make any change in loyalties difficult, Nelson nonetheless concluded that East Tennessee must now join the rest of the South. He called on Unionists not only to submit to Confederate rule but also to enlist voluntarily in the Confederate forces:

> If you would save yourselves from a species of carnage unexampled in the history of North America, but unequivocally invited in Mr. Lincoln's proclamation, let every man who is able to fight buckle on his armor, and without awaiting the slow and tedious process of conscription, at once volunteer in the struggle against him [Lincoln]. The race is not always to the swift nor the battle to the strong, and it cannot in the nature of things be possible that a just God will prosper the efforts of a man or a Government which has hypocritically pretended to wage war in behalf of the Constitution, but now throws off the mask and sets it utterly at defiance.[25]

Jones was convinced that other Unionists had reached similar conclusions and that the Emancipation Proclamation could be used for Confederate purposes. In part he was correct. Nelson never became reconciled to emancipation, and his address stated the position that he himself had adopted and practiced, which was that the Confederacy was de facto a legitimate government to which Unionists might reasonably submit. After the publication of his address Nelson received petitions from Greeneville, Morristown, Bristol, Athens, Jonesborough, and Knoxville, some with fifty or more names, that expressed confusion concerning Lincoln's proclamation and asked him to come and give them guidance. Many Unionists did find it difficult to accept emancipation, even as a war measure, and this and other radical war policies would eventually split the Unionist party.[26]

But Jones's attempts to coopt the Unionist leadership ultimately failed. By the general's own admission, many East Tennesseans denounced the Emancipation Proclamation, or Nelson's address, or both, as forgeries perpetrated by the *Knoxville Register*. Others concluded that Nelson had agreed to write the address only in return for the release of his son from a Confederate prison. Further, while he called on Unionists to volunteer, Nelson himself avoided service, even when Kirby Smith offered him a commission in November 1862 if he would raise a regiment. Neither he nor John Netherland nor any other Unionist granted Jones's repeated requests to make speeches in support of the Confederacy. Nathaniel G. Taylor stated only that he professed to be "thoroughly Southern in heart and soul," a statement open to multiple interpretations, and other leaders whom Jones contacted appear to have been similarly disingenuous. Unionist leaders had become adept at accommodating themselves to Confederate rule, and they cooperated with Jones only enough to avoid prosecution. Jones had been deceived by the Unionist leaders, and he had perhaps deceived himself.[27]

Jones's efforts were admirable but misdirected. By October 1862 Unionist leadership had largely passed out of the hands of men such as Nelson and now rested with local leaders, bushwhackers, Union officers, and exiles such as Brownlow. Furthermore, the rebellious Unionists had suffered far too much to embrace the Confederacy, and it is unlikely that anyone could have persuaded them to submit. Why should they fear a far-off despotism in Washington when, every day, they experienced Confederate repression in person? Why should they be angered by Lincoln's unconstitutional acts when they had in their midst Confederate authorities who confiscated their property, drove them into military service, killed their friends, and burned their homes? Nelson and Jones were asking them to join forces with a real, live enemy to repel a far-off, imaginary one, a request that was clearly absurd.

Jones made equally high-minded attempts to end the partisan violence that was convulsing East Tennessee. Like his predecessors, Jones recognized that the conflict was fed by old party feuds and jealousies: "I believe there are Southern men in East Tennessee, small politicians generally, who do not desire that influential men who have heretofore been Union men should change their course and come out in support of the Government, men who if let alone would gladly have abandoned their hostility and opposition. They are actuated by petty party Jealousy, and have done much mischief by denunciatory articles in the public press." Kirby Smith had deliberately held himself aloof from the constant skirmishing between Unionist and secessionist leaders, disdaining, as a professional soldier, to soil himself with the dirt of politics. But Jones recognized that his position as commander in East Tennessee was inherently political, and he plunged directly into the conflict. Jones met with influential men on both sides, urged them to stop their agitation, and suggested that they use their influence to end the partisan feuding. He also asked the editors of the *Knoxville Register* and the *Athens Post* to publish not only Nelson's address but also editorials holding out the hand of friendship to Unionists and calling for an end to partisan conflict. Both papers complied, though Jones probably found their attempts at conciliation disappointing. James Sperry, editor of the *Register*, refused to apologize for secessionist attempts to silence Unionists, and he blamed the conflict on Brownlow's inflammatory statements. The *Register* did, however, deplore the terrible violence of the last year and call on all East Tennesseans, Unionist and secessionist, to end the destruction of their own society. Sperry also urged secessionists to befriend Unionists who joined the Confederate side.[28]

Hand in hand with Jones's wooing of the Unionist population went attempts to remove the greatest irritant in Confederate policy, conscription. On October 18 Jones requested that Richmond again suspend the draft and in its stead accept two volunteer regiments recently organized in East Tennessee. Like Kirby Smith, Jones argued that voluntary enlistment would bring in all reliable recruits now available in the department. The draft, conversely, would require more troops to chase down evaders, guard them in camps, and bring them to the front than it would ever net. Jones also asserted that conscription increased hostility to the government and undercut his attempts at reconciliation. He proposed instead a return to the same policy of neutrality that Zollicoffer had favored, arguing that "men who are so averse to entering the military service as to flee from their homes and conceal themselves in the mountains to avoid it would be far more serviceable to the Government in the corn and wheat fields and iron mines than in the ranks."[29]

The War Department was cold to Jones's proposals. The Confederacy had just suffered serious losses at the battles of Antietam and Perryville and needed every soldier it could get. It also faced increasing unhappiness with conscription throughout the Confederacy and could not afford to grant special exemptions to one region. Further, Jones's request that the government suspend conscription for only two weeks until the end of harvest and that the enrolling process continue during that time was illogical, and his overall scheme directly contradicted Confederate policy. Randolph pointed out that the previous suspension under Kirby Smith had had no discernible effect on the rebellious population and that it was unlikely that a second halt would have any better results. Randolph asserted that "the issue must be made with these people whether they will submit to the laws or not" and ordered Jones to take whatever measures were necessary to carry out conscription.[30]

Other orders similarly indicated Richmond's decreasing patience with East Tennessee. On September 23 Randolph permanently lifted the ban on the export of supplies from East Tennessee to other departments. This prohibition had been established under Kirby Smith in order to protect the region's dwindling resources, but the War Department now signaled its intention to give other theaters precedence over East Tennessee. Second, Randolph not only rejected Jones's requests for reinforcements but also ordered him to send some of his own troops to Bragg. Finally, the Confederate government took away martial law, one of the department commander's most effective weapons. Davis's original proclamation expired on October 4, and Jones immediately requested that the measure be reinstated, explaining on October 18 that "I have continued to enforce Martial Law, but the lawyers are meddling in the matter, and will produce some trouble and confusion *if the writ is no longer suspended.*" But martial law, along with other restrictions on civil liberties, had become an increasingly sensitive issue, and for the time Davis declined to seek congressional authorization for a second suspension.[31]

Several Confederate policies, including conscription, sequestration, and heavy taxes, undercut efforts to conciliate loyalists. But even more damaging was the behavior of Confederate troops. Zollicoffer, Kirby Smith, and Jones had sought to reassure loyalists of the goodwill of the Confederate government. They had ordered troops to maintain good discipline, avoid plundering, and treat the population with respect. But too often Confederate soldiers, motivated by contempt, anger, or apathy, ignored these orders, and Confederate officers either failed to control their men or willingly tolerated their behavior.

Well before the Civil War, East Tennessee possessed a reputation in the South as a backward, impoverished region inhabited by ignorant mountaineers. Many Southern troops brought these stereotypes with them, and while a few eventually changed their views many did not, for the intransigent Unionism and the palpable hostility of the population further strengthened the prejudice of Southern troops. The result was that many Southern soldiers hated their service in East Tennessee and responded with hatred and violence.

Southern soldiers conveyed their impressions of East Tennessee in stark but frequently humorous terms. Fuller Manly dismissed the region's inhabitants as unworthy of the soldiers' efforts: "As to the people, they have less refinement and cultivation about them than any set of people I ever did see; the men are an idle, worthless set of fellows who look to, and compel, the women to do all of the work that is done. . . . What I have seen of East Tennessee, the Yankees are perfectly welcome to it." G. W. Hunt, an officer with Brigadier General John Hunt Morgan's cavalry, similarly characterized East Tennesseans as degraded: "Did I stay long in this country, I should fear losing that respect and regard for the female sex, which I have been raised to have—here they unsex themselves, and by their conduct, lose all claim to be respected and regarded as ladies. . . . Was I in authority here, I should treat them as men." And Paul Turner Vaughn complained that he was "thoroughly sick of East Tennessee, where we are . . . surrounded by a poor ignorant and hostile people."[32]

Like many Northern and Southern troops in other theaters, Confederate soldiers stationed in East Tennessee engaged in petty theft, irregular foraging, and random destruction. In November 1861 Alexander Coffee admitted that his unit's "depredations" were causing considerable discontent and concluded, "We will cause a famine in a county where we stay long." A second soldier, Oliver Paine, conceded that Southern troops carried away all the chickens, hogs, and corn they could find, while Knoxville secessionist William G. McAdoo complained in October 1862 that passing soldiers had completely stripped his mother's farm near Clinton. Captain William Stringfield, an East Tennessee native and provost marshal of Carter County, charged that numerous Confederate soldiers, particularly those in the so-called scouting companies, carried off slaves, horses, and property and sold these goods in Georgia and South Carolina. Horse theft was a particular problem. In October 1862 Jones ordered McCown to investigate a number of charges of "confiscations" of horses by cavalry units, and Amanda McDowell, a young woman in Sparta, complained that "the people cannot keep a nag fit for anything even if they had anything to feed on. The soldiers steal them so."[33]

But many Confederate offenses in East Tennessee went far beyond the ordinary depredations of Civil War soldiers. In December

1861 Colonel Danville Leadbetter, failing in his attempts to capture bands of Unionists in Cocke County, compensated by sending
troops into Parrotsville and Warrensburg to arrest "troublemakers"
and impress horses, provisions, and weapons. "The whole country is
given to understand that this course will be pursued until quiet shall
be restored." William Sloan admitted that after an unsuccessful attempt to trap a guerrilla band on top of a ridge he and his men
burned down the house the guerrillas had been using. In 1862 Confederate forces burned at least twenty houses in the town of Tazewell, apparently in retaliation for Unionist resistance. In early 1864
renegade Confederate cavalry in Cocke County supposedly plundered and burned Unionist homes, tortured and killed loyalists, and
raped several women. In July 1864 Morgan's men reportedly burned
thirty-seven homes in Johnson County, drove the inhabitants out of
the region, and killed several men. Confederate officers themselves
admitted that their men forced Unionists into the Confederate
army, illegally seized wagons and teams for their own use, and ap-
propriated property that Unionists had abandoned when they fled to
Kentucky. Unionist historians recorded dozens of similar atrocities,
and while many of these were exaggerated or fabricated outright,
others were true. These depredations and crimes had a far greater
effect on loyalist perceptions of the Confederate government than
any proclamations by the department commander.[34]

In late October 1862 Union forces fought Confederate troops
under Bragg and Kirby Smith to a draw at Perryville, Kentucky.
Discouraged at the lack of support for the Confederacy in Kentucky,
Kirby Smith retreated back into East Tennessee and resumed command of the department, while Jones was transferred to the Department of West Virginia. Then in December 1862 Kirby Smith took
over the Department of the Trans-Mississippi. After their departure
Confederate policy became increasingly harsh. Kirby Smith's successor, Brigadier General Daniel S. Donelson, proposed conscript-
ing every single man of military age, including those who had been
given exemptions to work in the iron foundries, and sending them
to the Deep South. He also urged the arrest of prominent Unionists
as hostages for secessionists confined in Middle Tennessee and the
reestablishment of military courts. President Davis, who favored a
policy of "precaution and repression," conditionally approved these
suggestions, though he directed Donelson to confer with Governor Harris before taking any drastic steps. But Donelson did not remain long enough to attempt these stern measures. Major General

Simon B. Buckner, who followed Donelson, continued to enforce martial law, even though his authority to do so had passed, and refused to release Unionist prisoners, even when a justice issued writs of habeas corpus. Buckner's chief of staff also recommended that the commander send influential Unionists out of the state until the war's end and begin taking hostages in retaliation for Unionist bushwhacking, though again the commander did not implement these policies. By the summer of 1863 both conciliatory and repressive policies had clearly failed, and military and political leaders searched fruitlessly for a means to restore some measure of authority.[35]

A number of common themes ran through Confederate policy toward East Tennessee. The first was a dangerous misperception of the nature of East Tennessee Unionism. Few Confederate officers, even conservatives such as Zollicoffer and Kirby Smith, believed that any reasonable Southerner could cling to the Union after the fighting had begun. Thus they argued that Unionism was the product of demagogic and unprincipled leaders, who deliberately, and for their own gain, misled their followers concerning the causes of the war, the purposes of secession, and the intentions of the Confederate government. This belief appears again and again, not only in the proclamations and reports of commanders but also in the statements of lower-ranking officers and ordinary soldiers. Confederate officers also concluded that if these unprincipled leaders could be removed the people of East Tennessee would eventually come to their senses and embrace Confederate rule, and they therefore repeatedly attempted to silence or expel Unionist spokesmen.

A second constant was disagreement between the government in Richmond and commanders in East Tennessee over policy. Such conflicts were not surprising, for the two had different interests and different perspectives. The primary concern of the Confederate government was the defense of the nation's vital points, and its primary interest in East Tennessee was the contributions the region could make to the war effort, particularly transportation, foodstuffs, and men. Richmond never fully grasped the depth of the resistance in East Tennessee or the difficulties that officers there faced. Department commanders, conversely, were primarily interested in trying to defend East Tennessee from invasion, control a hostile population, and gain sufficient resources for their needs. The ongoing debate over conscription illustrates this clash particularly well. Both Kirby Smith and Jones quickly concluded that attempting to enforce the draft in the face of such fierce opposition was counterproductive and requested its suspension. The Davis administration gave in once but would not do so again, for it needed every available soldier and could not afford to jeopardize the war effort.

East Tennessee commanders also faced pressure from local secessionists to institute harsher policies. District Attorney John Crozier Ramsey, Postmaster C. W. Charleton, Colonel William Churchwell, Senator Landon Carter Haynes, John Crozier, J. G. M. Ramsey, and *Register* editor James Sperry all sent reports on conditions in the region to Richmond and pressured East Tennessee commanders to institute harsher policies. Their attempts to influence Confederate policies never fully succeeded, but officers could not completely disregard their scrutiny. Further, local officials seized Unionist property and attempted to arrest and try prominent loyalists on their own, actions that contradicted efforts at conciliation.[36]

A final problem was the tension between conciliation and coercion. On the one hand, Confederate authorities repeatedly voiced a commitment to restraint. They distinguished between dissenting actions and dissenting beliefs, and while they punished the first, they promised to tolerate the second. Zollicoffer proclaimed in 1861 that Unionists need not fear Confederate authorities as long as their beliefs did not spill over into actions. Kirby Smith made similar promises in 1862 and, in an exchange with Union brigadier general George Morgan, expressed his "earnest desire to allay the horrors of war and to conduct the campaign with as little severity as is consistent with the interests of my Government." Department commanders also repeatedly stipulated that mere Unionist beliefs were not sufficient grounds for arrest, a policy that held up under the greatest stresses. Even in the days following the November rebellion Brigadier General William H. Carroll announced that Unionist beliefs would be respected, and Secretary of War Judah P. Benjamin limited arrests to men involved with the bridge burnings or actually found in arms. Officers did not always follow these policies, of course, but it is significant that when Union forces entered East Tennessee they quickly abandoned attempts to distinguish between disloyal actions and disloyal beliefs.[37]

Despite these pronouncements, too often the behavior of Confederate troops was brutal and destructive. Confederate officers and soldiers, almost certainly with the knowledge of their commanders, ignored orders for restraint and frequently arrested persons simply on the basis of their Unionist sentiments. They recklessly seized supplies, plundered and burned homes, harassed Unionists indis-

criminately, and committed numerous atrocities. Their behavior worsened as the war went on and left deep scars on East Tennessee. This was evidenced by the widespread devastation of the region, a fact noted by numerous Union soldiers entering the region in 1863.
William Franklin Draper wrote that he would know that he was in East Tennessee "by the number of houses destroyed or abandoned." Similarly, R. E. Jameson concluded that while "the rebellion has left its devastating mark upon every Southern town . . . there are few places that have suffered more than Knoxville," while Marshall Miller asserted that "I have never been in a place yet where so much property or where so many lives have been destroyed." The war between Unionists and Confederate troops was ruthless and unyielding, and both sides used every available measure. Whether the region would fare any better under Federal control remained to be seen.[38]

6 Real or Supposed Danger

From the beginning of the war President Lincoln had taken a particular interest in East Tennessee. Retaining some belief in the potential of Southern Unionism, he was anxious to secure this loyalist region and employ it as a base for rebuilding a loyal state government. Lincoln was also impressed with the importance of the rail line linking Virginia to Tennessee, Georgia, Alabama, and Mississippi, and his orders for the Union invasion in November 1861 had stressed the advantages of cutting this line of communications. But Lincoln was never able to bring his commanders to share these views. Union officers conceded the importance of the East Tennessee railroads, but they were even more impressed with the logistical difficulties of supplying an army over mountain roads. Union commanders were also more concerned with the South's large population and industrial centers than with this remote region, regardless of how loyal it was. Lincoln, therefore, faced repeated frustrations in his attempts to rescue East Tennessee. Deeply disappointed with Sherman's cancellation of the invasion in November 1861, in December and January he repeatedly pressured Sherman's successor, Major Don General Carlos Buell, to make East Tennessee his primary target. But Buell considered an invasion of the region nearly impossible, and he was far more interested in Nashville. Buell first put Lincoln off, then bluntly rejected the president's plans for East Tennessee.[1]

Unionist refugees had not been silent during the Confederate occupation. Andrew Johnson, Horace Maynard, William G. Brownlow, Andrew Jackson Fletcher, and others repeatedly urged the Lincoln administration to occupy East Tennessee, worked to create public sympathy for the Unionist population, and attempted to convey to Union officers the desperation of the East Tennessee loyalists. Throughout December 1861 and January 1862 Johnson and Maynard joined Lincoln in pressuring Buell to move immediately into East Tennessee, and Johnson's disgust with Buell's caution helped poison relations between the two after Johnson was appointed military governor of Tennessee. Unionist hopes rose in the spring of 1862, however, when Federal forces under Brigadier General George W. Morgan occupied Cumberland Gap and Major General Henry W. Halleck, after specifically promising Johnson that "East Tennessee will very soon be attended to," sent Buell marching toward Chattanooga. But again disappointment waited. Morgan was forced to abandon Cumberland Gap, Buell's advance toward Chattanooga stalled, Confederate forces invaded Kentucky, and for a second time the campaign to liberate East Tennessee was postponed.[2]

As each opportunity passed, Maynard and Johnson became more desperate. After Federal forces threatened Chattanooga and then withdrew, Johnson lamented that "the demonstrations which have been made upon lower East Tennessee, causing the people to manifest their Union feelings and sentiments and then to be abandoned, have been crushing, ruinous to thousands." In August Johnson complained to Major General George Thomas that "the redemption of East Tennessee seems almost to be as remote as it was when I was with you at Camp Dick Robinson. I have almost despaired of the people ever being relieved from their oppressors. . . . Can you send me no word that will inspire hope." The following month, when it was clear that no invasion would occur in 1862, Johnson concluded that "East Tennessee seems doomed, there is scarcely a hope left." By 1863 Johnson's patience was nearly gone. Reminding Lincoln of "the oppression and inhumanity daily inflicted" in East Tennessee, he insisted that "if the Government do not give that protection guaranteed by the Constitution the Tennessee forces should be massed and permitted to enter East Tennessee. . . . This summer should not pass without protection being extended."[3]

The Unionist lobbying campaign was not confined to Washington, for Brownlow took the cause of East Tennessee directly to the Northern public. Brownlow had been released from captivity and escorted out of East Tennessee in March 1862. After a brief stay in Nashville, where he met with Maynard and addressed Union troops, he traveled to Cincinnati, where local Republican leaders prevailed upon him to give several public addresses on the evils of the Confederacy. Brownlow agreed, and for several nights he amused, outraged, and inspired his audiences with tales of the degeneracy of Southern society, the duplicity of the Confederate government, the brutality of Southern troops, and the courage of Tennessee Unionists. Republican Party leaders and War Department officials recognized the potential benefits of similar lectures elsewhere, and from Cincinnati Brownlow went on to Indianapolis, Cleveland, Chicago, Pittsburgh, Harrisburg, Philadelphia, Baltimore, New York City, and numerous smaller cities in between, giving the same rousing performance. The Republican Party provided lodging, travel arrangements, and funds, and the War Department sent recruiting officers to enroll men inspired by Brownlow's oratory. By the time Brownlow reached the East Coast several newspapers were picking up his speeches and printing them in full.[4]

Brownlow reveled in the attention, but in May 1862 exhaustion forced him to end his tour. Returning to his former medium, he retired to a house in New Jersey to write an account of his battles with the Confederacy. The result, titled *Sketches of the Rise, Progress, and Decline of Secession* but more commonly known as "Brownlow's Book," consisted largely of *Whig* editorials haphazardly arranged and loosely strung together with narrative. The result was a tedious and confusing tale, but despite its lack of literary merit "Brownlow's Book" sold over 100,000 copies. Brownlow portrayed in graphic detail the supposed atrocities of Confederate troops in East Tennessee, and he begged the government to act: "In God's name, I call upon President Lincoln, and upon his Cabinet and army-officers, to say how long they will suffer a loyal people, true to the Union and to the Government of their fathers, to suffer in this way. . . . Let the Government, if it have any regard for its obligations, redeem that country at once, and liberate these people, no matter at what cost of blood and treasure."[5]

Brownlow's efforts ensured that not only much of the Northern public, but also numbers of Union officers and soldiers, were familiar with the loyalist resistance in East Tennessee. On the eve of the invasion Burnside reminded his troops that "the present campaign takes them through a friendly territory, and that humanity, and the best interests of the service, require that the loyal inhabitants be treated with kindness." On September 10 Burnside wrote Lincoln, "I look upon East Tennessee as one of the most loyal sections of the United States," and on September 17 he again reminded his men that "it is the mission of this Army to rescue East Tennessee from rebel despotism." This perception influenced not only Burnside's

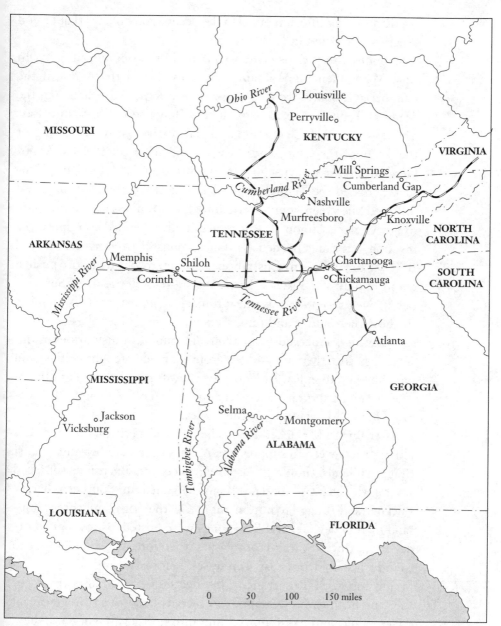

MAP 5. *Western Theater, 1863*

conduct of the campaign but also the occupation policies that he and others would adopt in East Tennessee.[6]

Unionist frustrations came to an end in the summer of 1863. In June Major General William Rosecrans moved the Army of the Cumberland south from Murfreesboro. Repeatedly flanking the Army of Tennessee, Rosecrans forced Bragg to fall back into East Tennessee toward Chattanooga. Then in the last week of August the Army of the Ohio, under the command of the ill-fated Major General Ambrose Burnside, moved south from Crab Orchard, Kentucky, crossed the Tennessee border west of Cumberland Gap, and followed the steep trails down into East Tennessee. Confederate Major General Simon B. Buckner initially intended to oppose the invasion, but Bragg needed assistance against Rosecrans and ordered Buckner to fall back to Chattanooga. Union troops therefore pushed ahead rapidly and reached Knoxville by the afternoon of September 2. Their reception was extraordinary. Unionists came from miles to cheer the soldiers and offer food and drink. Guerrillas and conscript evaders emerged from their hideouts. Loyalists brought out U.S. flags that they had hidden from Confederate authorities, and men lined up to enlist. In Knoxville crowds paraded through Burnside's headquarters and celebrated the return of William G. Brownlow, Horace Maynard, and other exiles.[7]

After Burnside reached Knoxville he faced a critical decision. His initial orders were to support the Army of the Cumberland against Bragg while also holding East Tennessee. But Burnside still faced several threats. Cumberland Gap remained in Southern hands, Buckner and Bragg lay not far off in Chattanooga, and three thousand men under General Sam Jones were posted just over the border in southwest Virginia. Burnside, therefore, determined first to solidify his hold on East Tennessee before shifting forces south to link up with Rosecrans. This decision proved disastrous for the Union. In early September Rosecrans had driven Bragg out of Chattanooga and had followed him into northern Georgia. Believing that Bragg was still retreating, Rosecrans sent his three corps on different roads to move through the mountain passes south of Chattanooga. Seeing an opportunity to catch Rosecrans at a disadvantage, Bragg attempted unsuccessfully to concentrate his forces against one of the Union corps. Rosecrans realized his danger in time and managed to regroup. Nonetheless, on September 18–19 the Army of Tennessee, reinforced by troops that Major General James Longstreet had brought from Virginia, smashed into Rosecrans's hasty dispositions. Repeatedly assaulting the right wing, they eventually found a gap and began to roll up the Union line. Major General George Thomas led a stand that eventually halted the Confederate advance and earned him the title "the Rock of Chickamauga." Union troops were forced to retreat into Chattanooga, however, and Bragg soon cut off their supply routes.[8]

Burnside was not fully aware of the threat that Rosecrans faced, and he continued with his own operations. Two forces, one moving south from Kentucky and one north from Knoxville, trapped Confederate forces at Cumberland Gap and forced their surrender on September 10. Six days later Union troops marched up the East Tennessee and Virginia Railroad and began skirmishing with Jones's troops, who had crossed the border and begun moving down the valley. These operations were interrupted, however, on September 22, when Burnside received orders to take his entire force south to Rosecrans's aid. Burnside complied, but he was slow in concentrating his troops, and by the time he was ready to march Rosecrans had already suffered defeat at the battle of Chickamauga. Burnside's failure to support Rosecrans brought severe criticism and further tarnished his image, but Burnside insisted that he had followed Halleck's orders as best as he could.[9]

Burnside resumed his operations in upper East Tennessee in early October, and Union forces soon routed Jones at Bull's Gap and chased the Confederates all the way back to Blountville, near the Virginia line. But they failed to trap and destroy Jones's entire force as Burnside had planned. Burnside's staff attributed this failure to the previous delay in their operations and the absence of the units sent south to assist Rosecrans. In fact, geography made the elimination of Confederate forces from upper East Tennessee an almost impossible task, for Confederate forces could simply fall back into Virginia and then return to East Tennessee at will.[10]

Even greater setbacks were to come. In early October Bragg, who still had Rosecrans locked up in Chattanooga, sent 15,000 men under Longstreet to retake East Tennessee. This was a remarkable risk, for Halleck had sent Union forces from both Virginia and Mississippi to rescue the Army of the Cumberland and ordered Major General Ulysses S. Grant to take charge. But Bragg was quite anxious to be rid of Longstreet. Since the battle of Chickamauga the Army of Tennessee had been wracked with infighting, and several division commanders had petitioned for Bragg's removal. Longstreet had supported them, and Bragg suspected him of scheming to take over command of the army. Longstreet, in turn, was ready to be free of Bragg. Further, retaking Knoxville would restore Confederate rail connections with Virginia and eliminate all Union gains in East Tennessee.

Burnside learned of Longstreet's advance on November 12 and, after consulting with Grant, decided to withdraw to Knoxville. Burnside's intent was to draw Longstreet as far from Chattanooga as possible and aid Grant's attempt to break the Confederate stranglehold. The plan succeeded, but at some cost. Burnside barely beat Longstreet back to Knoxville, and he had to sacrifice most of three regiments to buy the extra day his engineers needed to complete the city's defenses. But Burnside detailed most of his forces for fatigue duty and called out the entire male population of Knoxville, and by November 20 Federal engineers had constructed defenses formidable enough to force Longstreet into a siege.

For two weeks the fate of the Army of the Ohio was uncertain. Despite provisions rafted into Knoxville by loyalists upriver, Union supplies quickly ran low, and troops were reduced to quarter rations. Federal officers advised a number of prominent Unionists to escape to Kentucky to avoid being captured when the city fell. But then Burnside's fortunes turned. Under Grant's energetic leadership, Union forces reopened the supply lines to Chattanooga. In two days' battles they then broke Confederate lines and forced Bragg to fall back into Georgia. Grant then sent Major General William T. Sherman with 20,000 men to break the siege at Knoxville. Longstreet soon learned of Bragg's defeat and the approach of a Union relief force, but, unwilling to give up his enterprise, he attempted a direct assault on Union fortifications. The results were disastrous. Obstructions had prevented Confederate officers from fully observing Union defenses, and when fourteen Confederate regiments opened the attack at dawn on November 29 they tumbled down the eleven-foot walls of a moat and came directly under Union fire. Prepositioned Union artillery raked the attackers, while Union infantry shot down those Confederates who managed to work their way out. By the time Longstreet called off the attack he had suffered six hundred casualties. Burnside's losses were slight in comparison.[11]

This short battle of Knoxville ended Longstreet's campaign to recapture East Tennessee, and Confederate forces retreated north of Knoxville. The Union force sent in relief reached Maryville on December 5, and Sherman went ahead into Knoxville to confer with Burnside. Their discussion was not pleasant. Sherman had driven his men to exhaustion, but when he reached the city he found Burnside and his staff eating a Thanksgiving dinner. Nonetheless, Sherman offered to bring up the entire Fourth Corps and assist Burnside in driving Longstreet out of East Tennessee. But Burnside was fearful of overburdening his fragile supply system, and he decided to take only two divisions.[12]

Burnside's refusal to accept aid proved to be his second major blunder. On December 7 he marched north out of Knoxville and followed Longstreet as far as Rogersville. After a week of skirmishing, however, Longstreet counterattacked in force and drove the Federals back to Blaine's Cross Roads. This setback ended Union attempts to clear East Tennessee. Burnside resigned his command in late December, and his successor, Major General John G. Foster, soon became too ill to take the field. Foster was followed by Major General John Schofield, but by the time Schofield arrived in February 1864 other Union aims took precedence over East Tennessee. Sherman, who wanted no distractions from preparations for his Atlanta campaign, instructed Schofield not to challenge Longstreet, and he refused to alter this decision even at the urging of President Lincoln. Grant also saw East Tennessee as a low priority, and in early February he abandoned his plans to send fourteen thousand men under Thomas to drive Longstreet out.

These decisions were based on both practical considerations and strategic priorities. As Grant noted, the lack of transportation and the scarcity of forage made it difficult to sustain a large force in East Tennessee. Further, if threatened, Longstreet could simply fall back into Virginia and then return to East Tennessee as soon as Union forces departed. Both Grant and Sherman believed that when spring came Longstreet would voluntarily rejoin Lee in Virginia, and they concluded that the costs of driving him out were not justified. Union commanders were in no hurry for Confederate forces to leave East Tennessee, for as long as Longstreet remained isolated in this theater he could not contribute to Confederate operations in Virginia or Georgia, the two areas now central in Union planning.[13]

The Union decision to abandon northern East Tennessee to Confederate control was strategically defensible, but the consequences for East Tennessee loyalists were grave. Longstreet remained in the area of Bull's Gap until early April 1864. He subsisted his forces entirely on the countryside, and before returning to the Army of Northern Virginia he stripped the region of as many supplies as he could carry. Even after Longstreet's departure three to four thousand Confederate troops remained in upper East Tennessee, mostly cavalry under the command of Brigadier General John Hunt Morgan. By all accounts, both Union and Confederate, these forces were frightfully undisciplined, and they continued to plunder Unionists and secessionists alike.[14]

In mid-1864 Union authorities made one final attempt to secure northern East Tennessee. Johnson's attempts as military governor to restore a loyal government in Tennessee had made little progress, and he increasingly looked to East Tennessee as a political base. Johnson was also increasingly distressed by the continued Confederate occupation of upper East Tennessee and by reports of Confederate depredations. In 1863 he secured authority from Secretary of War Edwin M. Stanton to recruit several regiments of infantry and cavalry for operations in Tennessee, and in July 1864 he persuaded Stanton to transfer a brigade of cavalry under Brigadier General Alvin C. Gillem to East Tennessee. Gillem, a Unionist from Middle Tennessee and one of Johnson's political associates, was competent and aggressive, and Johnson had high hopes for his success. Gillem's orders were simply to "kill or drive out all bands of lawless persons who now infest that part of the state." Gillem arrived in East Tennessee in August, and in September he defeated Confederate forces at Russellville and Blue Springs, victories that raised Unionist hopes. But Gillem's insistence on remaining independent of the authority of department commander Brigadier General Jacob Ammen created tensions that hampered Union operations. In November Major General John C. Breckinridge, commander of the Confederate Department of East Tennessee and Southwest Virginia, threw together a force of about 2,500 men and surprised Gillem at Russellville. Gillem could get no reinforcements from Ammen, and Breckinridge shattered the Union force and drove the remnants back almost to Knoxville. In December Gillem rebounded, and he and Major General George Stoneman counterattacked and chased Breckinridge back out of East Tennessee. But the end did not come until March, when Stoneman, raiding into North Carolina, drove up the East Tennessee Valley and scattered the remaining Confederate cavalry and guerrilla units. Thus northern East Tennessee remained in Confederate hands until almost the end of the war.[15]

While Burnside attempted to secure East Tennessee, he also developed policies to reassert Federal control. The situation that he faced was sobering. More than two years of war had left deep scars on the region. Military demands had overburdened the economy while the disappearance of much of the male population had disrupted normal production. The partisan conflict had become bitter and widespread, and violence had become integral to politics. Further, the perceived illegitimacy of Confederate rule had created a general mistrust of and contempt for authority. The task of restoring order to East Tennessee would prove more difficult than the occupation itself.

Burnside already possessed considerable experience in governing a divided region. In March 1863 he had taken over the Department of the Ohio, an area that included not only divided Kentucky but also Indiana, Illinois, and Ohio, states with sizable minorities sympathetic to the Confederacy. There Burnside had faced a number of perplexing problems, including secret pro-Confederate organizations, armed resistance to conscription, and overzealous officers who magnified the internal threat. The centerpiece of Burnside's policy had been General Orders No. 38. This document was based partly on guidelines furnished by Halleck and partly on President Lincoln's December 1862 proclamation suspending the writ of habeas corpus and applying martial law to persons who were openly disloyal. General Orders No. 38 stated that anyone committing "acts for the benefit of the enemies of our country," such as carrying on a secret correspondence or harboring escaped enemy prisoners, was subject to execution. Anyone openly declaring sympathy for the enemy might be tried by a military court and face imprisonment, banishment, or even death. These orders, as well as the suspension of two Chicago newspapers and the arrest of Clement L. Vallandigham, a prominent Democratic opponent of the war, had aroused considerable protest, and Burnside had been forced to soften his policies. He had succeeded in suppressing the most open acts of disloyalty, but parts of the Midwest remained volatile.[16]

Burnside could also draw on the policies developed by Union commanders in other regions. In Missouri, for example, Halleck had placed levies on wealthy St. Louis secessionists to support Unionist refugees and pay for damages caused by guerrilla attacks. Later commanders, including Schofield, had confiscated property, arrested the families of known guerrillas, and sent dozens of families south of Union lines. In West Tennessee Grant and his corps commanders had banished prominent Confederates, destroyed property in retaliation for guerrilla attacks, and taxed secessionists for damages. In Middle Tennessee Johnson had arrested Confederate editors and ministers, taken control of municipal governments, and disfranchised Confederate supporters. And in most occupied areas Union forces strictly controlled trade, foraged heavily from Confederate supporters, required loyalty oaths and bonds for good behavior, held communities responsible for guerrilla attacks, and imprisoned influential secessionists.[17]

Burnside believed that East Tennessee loyalists could prove valuable allies, and he attempted to make full use of them. Burnside established three organizations for restoring Federal control of East Tennessee. The first was the office of provost marshal general for the District of East Tennessee, an office, significantly, that was completely independent of the provost marshal of the Army of the Ohio. The provost marshal's role was to assist the department commander in governing East Tennessee, and Burnside granted him broad powers: "The Provost Marshal General will have jurisdiction in all civil matters—will take cognizance of arrests, and of all violations of civil or military law, and will have the general supervision and direction of the District in all cases that pertain to his Department." Until the establishment of civilian government the provost marshal's office would be the chief political and legal institution in East Tennessee, and it would have primary responsibility for implementing Union occupation policies, suppressing dissent, and restoring and maintaining order.[18]

Burnside's choice to head this office was Brigadier General Samuel P. Carter, the naval lieutenant whom Lincoln had sent to Kentucky in July 1861 to help organize East Tennessee refugees. Carter was a cousin of the Reverend William B. Carter, organizer of the 1861 bridge burnings. After the failed uprising Samuel P. Carter had commanded a brigade in the Army of the Cumberland and seen action in Kentucky and Tennessee. In December 1862 he had led the first large-scale raid into East Tennessee and had burned three railroad bridges, torn up ten miles of track, wrecked a small train, and returned to Kentucky with few losses. Carter proved an excellent choice for provost marshal. He was politically shrewd and generally fair, and he established a powerful and efficient organization. In December 1864 exhaustion forced him to resign his office, and Lieutenant Colonel Luther S. Trowbridge of the Tenth Michigan Cavalry took his place.[19]

The provost marshal's office was well stocked with loyalists. Carter had the authority to appoint one or more deputy provost marshals for each county. Of the thirty-two men who filled these posts, thirteen were East Tennessee civilians, four were officers from East Tennessee units, and the remainder were Northern officers. Thus, over half of the officials responsible for implementing occupation policies, determining loyalty and disloyalty, and punishing opposition were East Tennessee Unionists. Carter's appointments had a certain logic, for native deputies possessed a far greater knowledge of the local population than Northern officers ever could. Nonetheless, the makeup of the provost marshal general's office jeopardized its ability to govern the region impartially and justly. Some provost marshals shared Carter's sense of justice, but others used their position to harass secessionists indiscriminately and take revenge for wrongs suffered under the Confederate occupation.[20]

The second organization that Burnside established in East Tennessee was a "secret police," headed by Robert A. Crawford of Greene County. Burnside directed Crawford to report on enemy movements, send agents into Confederate lines to gather intelligence, and provide information on disloyal citizens. Crawford was also authorized to recruit assistants; make requisitions for supplies, arms, and weapons; arrest persons suspected of giving aid to the enemy; and seize their property for the use of his organization. Crawford's military value is unknown, but he provided information on a number of East Tennessee secessionists and received at least $1,000 for his work. Burnside also established small mounted units of local Unionists to supplement the activities of regular cavalry.[21]

Finally, Burnside, on Carter's recommendation, created the "National Guard of Tennessee," an organization of self-defense units that would replace the old Tennessee militia. Guard companies were organized in accordance with army regulations, and in an emergency the district commander could call them into service. In turn, guard members received muskets, ammunition, and equipment, which they were allowed to keep and use even when not in Federal service.[22]

This last point was highly significant. Burnside's initial orders authorizing the formation of guard units stated only that their purpose was the "defense of their homes" and "securing their several counties from invasion." But their powers soon expanded. On November 4, 1863, Burnside authorized National Guard members to arrest stragglers from the regular forces, "such citizens as are known to have been guilty of acts of oppression and cruelty to Union men, and generally any suspicious characters who may not be able to give a satisfactory account of themselves." In June 1864, in response to a request from Grainger County for permission to organize a National Guard company, Carter went further than Burnside, stating that "self defense is a law of nature and every guerrilla and horse thief should be shot on sight by any and every citizen who may meet them. Assure the citizens who are loyal in Grainger that they do not need an order to protect themselves against thieves and robbers." Carter later recorded that guard companies had been established to put down guerrillas and robber bands and assist the provost marshal general in enforcing the laws and suppressing disloyalty. Guard units, therefore, were given considerable latitude in their operations.[23]

Federal assistance to East Tennessee guard units was extremely generous. On September 17, 1863, Burnside ordered post commanders in East Tennessee to distribute surplus arms and ammunition to loyal citizens. On October 4 he made arrangements to transport weapons "to the upper counties of East Tennessee," and in July 1864 Schofield, Burnside's successor, again authorized the distribution of arms to guard units. Union officers displayed no hesitation in following these orders. Between November 1864 and May 1865 they issued at least 27,000 rounds of musket and pistol ammunition, as well as a large number of muskets, to guard units in Hancock, Knox, Grainger, Claiborne, Greene, Hawkins, Cocke, and Blount Counties. This figure, large as it is, covers fewer than half the counties in which guard units were organized and does not include the first thirteen months of the Union occupation. The total weaponry that the Union command put into the hands of National Guardsmen was remarkable.[24]

The Tennessee National Guard played a significant role in the Union occupation, both by assisting the regular forces and by acting as a police force. In January 1864, after Confederate cavalry had raided into Sevier County and captured a Union wagon train, the Home Guard there guided the Fifteenth Pennsylvania Cavalry along back roads to the Confederate camp and enabled them to surprise the enemy troopers and recapture the wagons. Guardsmen also apparently fought alongside the Federal troops, for Foster noted that "the remains of the rebel party broke and fled to the mountains closely pursued by the Union home guards." In January 1865 Lieutenant Colonel William C. Bartlett reported that he was employing two guard companies for operations against guerrillas, and in February 1865 Brigadier General Jacob Ammen detached fifty regulars from the Second Ohio Heavy Artillery and sent them to Blaine's Cross Roads "to cooperate with Capt G. S. White of the Home Guard in an expedition after bushwhackers." Guard units also assisted deputy provost marshals in arresting and guarding prisoners, and they defended their communities against guerrillas, deserter bands, and horse thieves.[25]

Federal officers also employed the services of the most influential Unionist in East Tennessee. On October 16, 1863, the Reverend William G. Brownlow, accompanied by Representative Horace Maynard, returned to Knoxville. The editor would have come home with or without Federal assistance, but Union officers did all they could to speed his return. Burnside provided Brownlow with a printing press that Union forces had captured in Alexandria, Tennessee, loads of paper and supplies, and $1,500 for his initial expenses. Burnside also sent an army ambulance to transport Brownlow and his family, five army wagons to haul his possessions, and a cavalry company to escort them from Cincinnati. Through his paper, Brownlow quickly reestablished himself as the chief spokesman of the Unionists. But his powers did not end there. Brownlow also brought with him an appointment as special treasury agent for East Tennessee, a post that gave him the authority to issue or withhold licenses to trade, seize goods traded without a license, and confiscate and dispose of property abandoned by disloyal persons. Brownlow energetically used his office to reward his friends, punish his enemies, and increase his political power.[26]

Burnside and Carter began to define occupation policy almost immediately after the invasion. The foundation of their policies was Lincoln's December 1863 Proclamation of Amnesty and Reconstruction, and their central mechanisms were the loyalty oath and the arrest of persons who resisted Federal authority. Lincoln's proclamation offered a pardon to all Southerners except high-ranking officials, provided that they took an oath of loyalty and agreed to accept the abolition of slavery, and stated that when a number of voters equal to 10 percent of the state's vote in 1860 took an oath they would be able to establish a new state government. Emphasizing his hopes for reconciliation, on September 12, 1863, Carter authorized all post commanders in East Tennessee to administer the oath of allegiance to any citizen willing to swear to its provisions, including deserters and paroled prisoners from the Confederate army if the commander had sufficient proof of their sincerity. When

Lincoln released his amnesty proclamation in December, Carter printed and distributed hundreds of copies of this document and exhorted secessionists promptly to accept its terms.[27]

The loyalty oath would quickly become the centerpiece of Union policy. It was the primary means not only for bringing East Tennessee Confederates back into the Union but also for sifting the loyal from the disloyal. The oath exposed the disloyal to punishment, for those who refused to take it and those who took it but then violated its provisions were immediately liable to arrest and imprisonment. Loyalty oaths served the same purpose for Federal officers that conscription had for the Confederate officials. But they also gave Union authorities a greater reach into the population, for officers could, and did, employ them against not only men of military age but also women and old men.

Though Federal authorities had some hopes for reconciliation, they were equally ready to punish dissent. From the beginning of their occupation, Union officers determined that rather than attempting to conciliate persons who resisted Federal authority they would place them in positions where they could not threaten the occupation government. Thus the most common Federal responses to resistance were imprisonment and banishment.

In the first months of the war Union officers targeted primarily three groups: influential secessionists who might encourage resistance and attempt to undermine Federal authority; former Confederate officials, particularly conscript officers; and persons engaged in active resistance, including guerrillas, spies, and persons giving aid to the enemy. These persons were either confined in military prisons until the war's end, sent south of Union lines, or exiled north of the Ohio River until the war's end. In October 1863, for example, Federal officers arrested and imprisoned Robert McNelley, editor of the pro-Confederate *Cleveland Banner*, and closed down his paper. The following month Burnside sent some of Knoxville's most prominent secessionists, including William H. Sneed, John Crozier, and Charles McGhee, to Kentucky. And in 1864 Carter, perhaps at the urging of Brownlow, arrested *Register* editor James Sperry and former Confederate district attorney John Crozier Ramsey and sent them to the Federal officer's prison on Johnson's Island.[28]

Union authorities particularly favored arrest and imprisonment as a means of controlling and punishing resistance. But there existed other, less drastic means of drawing a line between the loyal and the disloyal. Unionists were entitled to various privileges denied secessionists. They could receive licenses to sell goods and conduct other kinds of business, while disloyal persons might be denied the right even to purchase basic goods. Prominent Unionists received protection from foraging as well as rent for property used by the military, while Confederates were exposed to impressment and confiscation. When secessionists fled East Tennessee, Union authorities took control of their property, and the original owners often had great difficulty regaining their titles after the war. Unionists were also allowed to retain firearms and distill brandy, rights withheld persons considered disloyal. Finally, loyalists sometimes received special favors. For example, Lieutenant Colonel John Brownlow (William G. Brownlow's son) impressed a dozen wagons and teams from secessionists and turned them over to Oliver P. Temple so that the Unionist leader could haul his tobacco to market. In all these ways Federal authorities stigmatized dissent, singling out disloyal persons and denying them the opportunity to lead a normal existence.[29]

Initially the majority of secessionists, though they might suffer harassment and the denial of certain privileges, were not prosecuted, for most Union officers drew a distinction between disloyal acts and disloyal sentiments. But as Union frustrations with secessionist resistance in East Tennessee increased, Federal officers became far more willing to punish any manifestation of dissent, whether action, word, or even supposed thought. Anyone refusing to take the amnesty oath, violating the oath's provisions, or expressing "disloyal sentiments" might be incarcerated. On June 25 Major Thomas H. Reeve, commander of U.S. forces at Kingston, ordered that no person, male or female, who had not yet taken the oath be allowed to pass through Union lines or purchase goods from sutlers or merchants. He also directed that "all noted disloyal persons will be arrested at once, and either subscribe to the oath at once or be sent to Knoxville as prisoners, and turned over to the Provost Marshal General." Similarly, in early August, in a directive intended as a statement of policy for all East Tennessee, Carter sent these instructions to the deputy provost marshal of Union County: "All persons, man or woman, if they aver their sympathy for the rebellion or its supporters openly in any shape or manner or who use language or act in such manner as to show contempt for the U.S. Government or the officers and supporters thereof you will arrest and send to this office, to be sent out of the United States forever in accordance with Genl Sherman's orders."[30]

Much of this increased Federal belligerence was directed against women. As in other parts of the South, Federal officers in East Tennessee found white secessionist women particularly troublesome. They snubbed Union officers, harassed the occupying troops, displayed Confederate flags, carried medicine and supplies across Union lines, spied for Confederate authorities, and forcefully defended their homes against plundering. Within a few months Federal authorities lost their reluctance to punish women. On January 10, 1864, Carter requested the names of several women in Strawberry Plains who had cheered for President Jefferson Davis when a line of Confederate prisoners passed their house. In April Union officers at Loudon arrested Julie Lenoir, a young woman from a prominent secessionist family, for remarking in a store that "she wished she could get to Morgan and tell him how few soldiers there were." The deputy provost marshal detained Lenoir in jail one night and required her, two of her friends, and all the women in two other families to take the oath. In June authorities threatened to arrest three other Loudon women for supposedly mocking a Union funeral procession. On April 26 Schofield tersely telegraphed his chief of staff, "I do not want any more rebel women in Knoxville," and in August Carter asked Major John McGaughy, deputy provost marshal of McMinn County, to send the names of all the women "who are still open in their expression of disloyalty." In December 1864 Carter arrested and sent south a woman named Kline who had come to Knoxville from Montgomery, Alabama. Carter explained her arrest this way: "She refuses absolutely to take the amnesty oath and used . . . language both disloyal and unladylike. She is smart and far too dangerous a person to remain within our lines."[31]

A second change in Union policy was more careful provisions for the administration of the loyalty oath. Initially the provost marshal general, deputy provost marshals, and numerous "special commissioners" were all authorized to administer the oath. Union authorities discovered, however, that this broad grant of authority created numerous opportunities for fraud and led to confusion concerning what constituted a valid oath. In October 1864, therefore, Carter instructed commanders to refuse to administer the oath to persons they suspected of desiring only to protect themselves or their property. This warning proved insufficient, and in January 1865 the new provost marshal general, Lieutenant Colonel Luther S. Trowbridge, ordered that hereafter only the provost marshal general himself, or special commissioners appointed by the district commander, would have the authority to administer the loyalty oath. He also warned that he would arrest anyone illegally administering the oath, and he instructed Union officers and deputy provost marshals to confiscate certificates for illegally issued oaths.[32]

Not only were the mechanisms for administering the oath tightened, but the oaths themselves became more comprehensive and restrictive. The first oath employed in East Tennessee required its adherents to swear only to support the constitution and laws of the United States, refrain from taking up arms against the Federal government, and avoid giving aid or information to Confederate forces. But by mid-1864 numerous provisions had been added to this simple formula. Adherents now had to swear to uphold the supremacy of the Federal government and to support all Federal actions to defeat the Confederacy:

> I will maintain the National Sovereignty paramount to that of all state, county, and corporate powers; that I will support to the utmost of my ability all proclamations in regard to slaves, issued by the President of the United States as Commander in Chief of the U.S. Army; that I will forever discountenance, discourage, and oppose secession, rebellion, and the disintegration of the Federal Union; that I will disclaim and denounce all faith and fellowship with the so-called Confederate armies, and pledge my property and my life to the sacred performance of this my solemn Oath of Allegiance to the Government of the United States.
>
> I furthermore swear that I will not disclose anything that I may have seen or heard within the Federal lines to the enemies of the United States, that may in any way be detrimental to the United States or be beneficial to the enemies thereof. So help me God. The violation of this oath is death.[33]

In part, this transformation of Union policy simply reflected the growing harshness of the war everywhere. But more particular factors were also at work. First, Federal officers became increasingly frustrated at the continued rebelliousness of the small but determined secessionist population in East Tennessee. Second, Confederate guerrilla activity increased significantly in East Tennessee in the spring and summer of 1864, angering Union authorities and driving them to more extreme measures. Third, Sherman was just beginning his campaign against Atlanta, and he was determined to protect his communications, which ran from Nashville to Chattanooga and south into Georgia. Sherman insisted that any dissent in his rear, including that in East Tennessee, be quashed.[34]

The final factor was a pronouncement issued by Sherman on Southern guerrilla operations. On June 21, 1864, Sherman wrote a long directive to Brigadier General Stephen G. Burbridge in Kentucky and sent copies to all his district commanders, including Schofield in East Tennessee, as a guide to future policies toward disaffection. Sherman dismissed guerrilla activities as "simple murder, horse-stealing, arson and other well-defined crimes" and insisted that "all Govts and Communities have a right to guard against real or even supposed danger." In his usual extreme manner, Sherman then provided specific instructions for the treatment of bushwhackers:

1st. You may order all your Post and District Commanders that guerrillas are not soldiers but wild beasts unknown to the usages of war.

2d. The civil power being insufficient to protect life and property, "in necessitate re" to prevent Anarchy "which nature abhors" the Military steps in and is rightful, constitutional, and lawful. Under this law everybody can be made to "Stay at home and mind his and her own business" and if they wont do that can be sent away where they wont keep their honest neighbors in fear of danger, robbery, and insult.

3d. Your Military Commanders, Provost Marshals, and other agents may arrest all males and females, who have encouraged or harbored guerrillas and robbers, and you may cause them to be collected in Louisville and when you have enough say 300 or 400 I will cause them to be sent down the Mississippi through their guerrilla gauntlets and by a sailing ship send them to a land where they may take their negroes and make a colony with laws and a future of their own. I wish you to be careful that no personalities are mixed up in this, nor does a full and generous love of country, "of the South," or their State or county form a cause of banishment, but that devilish spirit which will not be satisfied and thus makes war the pretext for murder, arson, theft in all its guises, perjury, and all the crimes of human nature.

I do not object to Southern men and women having what they call "Southern feelings" if confined to love of country and of peace, honor and security and even of little family pride but these become "crimes" when enlarged to mean love of murder, of wars desolation famine and all the horrid attendants of anarchy.

Sherman probably had no intention of carrying out the last threat, but his ruthless tone encouraged East Tennessee commanders to take stern measures.[35]

As policies against dissent hardened, Federal officers faced an increasing problem of determining the fate of hundreds of secessionist prisoners. Burnside had viewed dissent as primarily a legal issue, and on September 15 he had established legal machinery for trying civilian prisoners. Following guidelines provided by the War Department in 1862, Burnside authorized "Commanders of Army Corps, Districts, Divisions, and Separate Brigades" to establish military commissions to try "offenses against the laws of war, which are not triable by a General Court Martial." These commissions had the authority both to adjudicate cases against civilians charged with criminal or political offenses and handle minor offenses by Union soldiers. Burnside was determined to be just, and he established strict procedural guidelines for the commissions. All arrests had to be accompanied by a written statement of the charges and a list of witnesses, and defendants had the right to answer all charges and present evidence on their behalf. In addition, any sentence imposing "loss of life, confiscation of property, or imprisonment exceeding the term of thirty days" had to be reviewed by the district commander. These safeguards were meant to prevent arbitrary proceedings, and in the cases that actually went before commissions Union justice was quite discriminating. Over half the prisoners tried by military courts were either found not guilty or had their convictions overturned by the district commander.[36]

But most cases were never tried, and the result was that Union justice was arbitrary, erratic, and harsh. Prison records reveal that Union officers were careless in preferring charges, for about two-thirds of the prisoners confined in Knoxville had no offense listed against them. This may have partially reflected lapses in record keeping, but it also resulted from the common failure of local commanders and deputy provost marshals to send written charges with their prisoners. Furthermore, of those prisoners against whom offenses were listed, about a third constituted ill-defined trespasses such as being an "active and dangerous rebel."[37]

Even worse, Union justice was frequently delayed or abandoned altogether. Many defendants sat in jail three to six months before their cases were decided, while many others never received a trial at all. This situation grew worse as the war progressed, and in January

1865 Carter had to urge the district commander to appoint commissions to try the dozens of prisoners who had been detained in Knoxville for so long. In part, this neglect occurred because military commissions were slow, lengthy proceedings that could handle only a few cases at a time, and the number of prisoners simply overwhelmed the judicial mechanisms. It was easier, therefore, to leave disloyalty cases to the provost marshal general or not try them at all. But in part the neglect was also deliberate. The indefinite imprisonment of persons accused of disloyalty kept them from threatening Federal control and was a simple policy to implement.[38]

The increasing tendency to punish any hint of disloyalty encountered a particular problem in East Tennessee. Many Unionists, including prominent leaders, had in various ways accommodated themselves to Confederate rule and had committed acts that might now be deemed disloyal. John Baxter had run for the Confederate House of Representatives. Seth Lucky and Andrew Johnson's son-in-law, David T. Patterson, had served as Confederate justices. T. A. R. Nelson, Oliver P. Temple, John Netherland, John Fleming, and other Unionist lawyers had taken an oath of loyalty to the Confederacy in order to practice law in Confederate courts. And Temple and his brother, Major, had even had a contract with the Confederate government to produce salt. Legally all these men fell outside the provisions of President Lincoln's proclamation, for that document had excluded "civil or diplomatic officers or agents of the so called confederate government; all who have left judicial stations under the United States to aid the rebellion." To deny them amnesty, however, would have been a clear injustice and a heavy blow to loyal Southerners.[39]

In January 1864 Carter brought this problem to Lincoln's attention. As he pointed out, many East Tennesseans whose loyalty was beyond question had served in state and local offices during the Confederation occupation. They had done so, Carter asserted, primarily to keep secessionists out of these offices. In addition, Carter pointed out that such offices were "considered as belonging to the state organization or being separate and distinct from those who received their appointment and commissions from the so-called Confederate Govt." Lincoln accepted Carter's arguments and granted special pardons to East Tennessee Unionists who fell in this category.[40]

Lincoln's graceful action avoided the alienation of important Unionist figures. But special pardons were only an expedient. These cases were indicative of the trials and confusions of a population caught between competing governments, and the question of exactly what defined loyalty remained unanswered. What should be the fate of a person such as T. A. R. Nelson, who had bowed to circumstances and recognized the Confederacy as de facto a legitimate government? Or men who had "volunteered" for Confederate service to avoid imprisonment? Or others who had been forcibly conscripted? What would constitute justice to persons who had accommodated themselves to Confederate rule to be able to travel, or conduct business, or buy salt? How did authorities distinguish between real and circumstantial disloyalty, and where did they draw the line between survival and treason? All these and similar perplexing questions were the unhappy legacy of a region of conflicting loyalties and divided government and would continue to plague East Tennessee long after the war.

The policy of granting extensive powers to native Unionists and making them partners in the occupation of East Tennessee aimed at restoring a loyal government as quickly as possible. But that policy, combined with increasingly harsh Federal policies, carried serious risks. It provided further opportunities for Unionists to take revenge on secessionists, and it encouraged, rather than constrained, partisan violence and disorder. Unionists had their own agenda, an agenda that did not always mesh with Federal aims, and this difference frequently created complications for the Union command.

Provost Marshal General Carter generally attempted to balance radical demands for vengeance with moderate desires for reconciliation. One of Carter's first acts was to issue a proclamation asking for help in identifying and locating persons guilty of persecuting Unionists: "All persons who have any knowledge of the murder of Union people in East Tennessee within the past two years, or of other outrages committed upon them, on account of their loyalty to the United States Government, are requested to furnish this office with all such information, together with the names and residences of witnesses by whom the facts can be substantiated in order that measures may be adopted to bring the guilty parties to justice." Samuel W. Scott and Samuel P. Angel, officers of the Thirteenth Tennessee Cavalry, claim that Carter also considered the possibility of offering rewards for evidence against secessionists who had committed violence against Unionists, though he eventually abandoned the idea for fear of retaliation. But Carter was also determined that justice be executed only by the state. In September 1863 he reminded Unionists that the time for vigilante justice had passed and urged loyalists instead to bring their grievances to his office or to the courts. A few months later he warned Unionists that Federal officers would arrest anyone, Unionist or secessionist, who engaged in unlawful acts, and he ordered his deputies to jail all vigilantes and robbers that they captured regardless of political beliefs. Carter could be vindictive, but generally he favored reconciliation and the restoration of order.[41]

Brownlow's views were quite different. Maynard claimed that one of the purposes of Brownlow's new paper, maliciously renamed the *Knoxville Whig and Rebel Ventilator*, was to prevent Carter and other Union officers from adopting policies that were too lenient toward secessionists, and Brownlow in fact exerted all his influence toward that end. He repeatedly stated that Unionists and secessionists could not live together in East Tennessee, and he called on secessionists to leave the region permanently. Brownlow also encouraged Unionists to ruin their enemies by initiating costly damage suits against them. Finally, he asserted that secessionist guerrillas should be shot on sight, and he explicitly called for vengeance against the men who had executed the Unionist bridge burners in 1861: "Keep it before the people that it is proper and right for Union men to shoot down upon sight, each and all of those murderers and that it is the duty that East Tennessee union men owe to their country, to their God, and to their abused relatives to see that these men, each, anyone of them, or all, die violent deaths, if they shall dare to show themselves in East Tennessee during the present century."[42]

Difficulties with the Tennessee National Guard also illustrate the dangers of the alliance with East Tennessee loyalists. Numerous guard units took advantage of their power to persecute their secessionist enemies, and several committed so many thefts and assaults that Federal authorities had to discipline some or all the members. In June 1864 Carter investigated two guard members in Sevier County for stealing horses and money. That same month Schofield disbanded the entire guard company of Cocke County for numerous thefts. In October 1864 Carter ordered three guard members detained for horse theft, and in May 1865 he arrested the commander of the Maryville Home Guards for misconduct. Such criminal activity by Unionist guardsmen was probably inevitable. It is likely that many guard members were guerrillas and that the new guard units duplicated the Home Guard units that Unionists had established on their own in 1861 and 1862. Further, the vague grant of authority to guardsmen to defend themselves, arrest suspicious persons, and impress horses and supplies was an invitation to abuse. After being harassed by Confederate authorities and having their property confiscated, it was easy for guardsmen to justify treating their secessionist neighbors in the same way. In the distorted moral atmosphere of East Tennessee, the line between confiscation and theft, and between criminal acts and acts of war, was often blurred.[43]

Federal authorities did not deliberately foment violence in East Tennessee, and in fact they made some efforts to control it. Carter sought to restrain Unionist partisans, and Federal officers attempted to monitor guard units and ensure that they did not abuse their powers. Each guard company had to be properly enrolled and officered and when in service had to make regular reports to Knoxville. When guardsmen made an arrest they were instructed to turn over the prisoner, as well as a written statement of the charges and a description of the circumstances of the arrest, to the nearest deputy provost marshal or military post. They were also ordered to keep records of any supplies they confiscated for their operations. The district commander personally authorized most issues of ammunition, and he, as well as the provost marshal general, possessed the authority to disband undisciplined guard companies.[44]

Nonetheless, the thrust of Union policy encouraged continued partisan violence. Union authorities could not afford to alienate their allies by restraining or prosecuting them too severely, and the incitements of Unionist spokesmen such as Brownlow far outweighed the pronouncements of Union officers. Furthermore, at the same time that Union authorities were disarming secessionists, they were placing thousands of weapons into the hands of loyalists and encouraging them to enforce the laws on their own. The results were predictable. But Union authorities required the aid of local loyalists if they were to secure effective control of East Tennessee. Unionist cooperation was also essential to the establishment of a reliable loyal government in the postwar period, and whether they wished to or not, Union authorities had no choice but to work with and aid men such as Brownlow, the captains of local guard units, and other vengeful Unionists, regardless of their faults.

A final factor that damaged Union efforts to restore order in East Tennessee was the behavior of Federal troops. Despite officers' attempts to maintain discipline, Union soldiers indiscriminately plundered loyalists and secessionists alike and pushed East Tennessee to the brink of economic collapse. Their rampant foraging and other crimes angered secessionists and forced even many loyalists to question the intentions of the Federal government.

Burnside took a conservative view of property rights in wartime, and he established strict orders on foraging. In September 1863 he announced that officers would be held responsible for depredations committed by their units and spelled out the punishment that soldiers guilty of theft would receive: "The Commanding General directs that any person found guilty of such disgraceful conduct be stripped of his uniform, his head shaved, then branded on the left cheek with the letter 'T' as a thief, and drummed out of the service." Burnside also established a board of claims and staffed it mostly with prominent East Tennessee Unionists. But these measures proved insufficient, and the department commander soon had to take sterner measures against illegal foraging. Burnside increased the number of guards placed around camps, stiffened the penalties for soldiers found outside lines without a pass, ordered that officers of units that tore up fence rails for firewood be assessed three times the value of the fence, and began fining soldiers the value of the stock they killed.[45]

Sadly, these measures proved largely futile. Throughout December 1863 and January 1864 Provost Marshal General Carter, whose office bore the brunt of civilian complaints, sent increasingly anguished pleas to Union commanders to control the depredations of Union troops. Carter claimed that foraging regulations and safeguards were ignored and loyal citizens insulted, and he forwarded a number of letters from loyalist civilians, including this eloquent appeal from T. A. R. Nelson:

> The Union Army is more destructive to Union men than the rebel army ever was. Our fences are burned, our horses are taken, our people are stripped in many instances of the very last vestige of subsistence, our means to make a crop next year are rapidly being destroyed, and when the best Union men in the country make appeals to the soldiers, they are heartlessly cursed as rebels; or when certificates are given as to property taken, they are generally for much less than the true amount, and a citizen in attempting to enforce a claim against the government has to run the gauntlet of "the circumlocution office," until, discouraged and disheartened, he turns away, feeling that the government which

he loved and honored and trusted, and which never did him any harm before the war, has at last become cruel and unjust, and cares nothing for his sorrows and sufferings.

In January 1864 Brigadier General Samuel D. Sturgis agreed with Nelson's grim portrait, complaining that he was "forced to listen hourly to the complaints of loyal citizens, of the cruel treatments they receive at the hands of many of the troops of this command. Soldiers, it appears, are permitted to wander away from their camps alone or in squads, with no intent but to plunder and rob helpless families, whose male members are bearing arms in the cause of their country." Many of these robberies were accompanied by violence, including beatings, torture, and occasionally rape.[46]

The epidemic of plundering in East Tennessee resulted partly from habits developed in other theaters and the exceptionally harsh winter of 1863–64. But it also stemmed from defects in the supply system. Owing to the peculiarities of the Southern railroad network, supplies could reach central and northern East Tennessee only through a long indirect haul: Louisville to Nashville to Chattanooga and finally up to Knoxville. The difficulties of rail transportation into East Tennessee were further complicated by Union strategy. After November 1863 rail lines from Nashville were monopolized by the Army of the Tennessee and the Army of the Cumberland in preparation for their campaign against Atlanta. The solution to East Tennessee's supply problems was to construct a line directly from Louisville to Knoxville, but though Union engineers made surveys the railroad was not built during the war. Thus, most supplies for East Tennessee were hauled by wagons from Kentucky over astonishingly poor roads. William F. Draper asserted, "I have seen and written of bad roads before but the road down the East Tennessee side of the mountain was the worst of all," and another Union soldier claimed that each wagon had to pulled up the steepest hills by sixty men.[47]

The supply arm of the Army of the Ohio was also defective and preparations for the East Tennessee campaign inadequate. On August 27, 1863, W. H. Bradbury, a clerk to one of the commissaries in the Twenty-third Army Corps, concluded that "things are badly arranged and I am afraid we shall suffer for want of supplies." Bradbury proved correct, and within a few weeks after entering East Tennessee Federal troops ran short on supplies and began to live off the country. A lieutenant from the Seventy-fourth Indiana attributed depredations by his company to the fact that his men had received no supplies except crackers for many days. He asserted that conditions were the same in other units and stated that irregular foraging was already so common that he believed no one would take notice of his unit's activities. Chauncey Welton complained that "we have been marching about 25 miles a day with nothing but two crackers for 3 days, no coffee meal or any thing else, except what little we could steal from secesh." A soldier stationed near Tazewell described a typical day's ration as a pint of cornmeal and a small portion of "blue, skinny beef, killed before it had a chance to drop dead of starvation," while an officer admitted that on some days the only ration that could be issued was an ear of corn: "I never saw the army in worse condition for rations before." Major General Gordon Granger admitted that he had "issued . . . the most stringent orders and done everything in my power to prevent marauding, but hungry men are difficult to control after fasting for five months on half and quarter rations. Nothing has pained me so much as being compelled to strip the country; friend and foe must fare alike, or the army must starve." And Sturgis conceded that "no laws, nor orders, nor regulations, nor activity on the part of a commander, can prevent the demoralization . . . of an Army compelled, by the necessity of the case, to subsist on the country in which it may be operating." The number of Federal troops in East Tennessee simply exceeded the capacity of the supply lines, and plundering was the inevitable result.[48]

A final, particularly tragic Union policy was the taking of hostages in an attempt to prevent, or in retaliation for, arrests by Confederate forces. This policy resulted largely from the continuation of divided control in East Tennessee and the inability of Union forces to protect loyalists in northeastern East Tennessee. The first steps toward hostage taking in East Tennessee were actually taken well before the invasion. In June 1862 Johnson arrested seventy Middle Tennessee secessionists and attempted to exchange them for a similar number of East Tennessee Unionists detained in the Confederate military prison at Mobile. He failed, but in August Johnson again proposed an exchange of Unionists and secessionist political prisoners. Similarly, in June 1862 Brigadier General George Morgan, commanding Union forces at Cumberland Gap, arrested a number of secessionists in retaliation for the reported confinement of large numbers of Unionist political prisoners. Morgan soon had to evacuate the Gap, however, and thus his attempt to secure the release of loyalist prisoners proved as futile as Johnson's.[49]

It is not clear exactly when Union authorities again began to take hostages in East Tennessee, but it was not long after the invasion. The first vague reference to a hostage prisoner appeared in November 1863, and the practice accelerated thereafter. In all, from November 1863 through April 1865 Union authorities arrested at least thirty secessionists as hostages. Some were taken in response to recent arrests by Confederate officers, while others were seized in retaliation for Unionists who had been taken months ago. In January 1864, for example, Carter detained Judge T. Nixon van Dyke and two other McMinn County secessionists in retaliation for the confinement of Jesse Blackburn, a Unionist captured in November 1863. In August 1864 Carter ordered the arrest and confinement of two Grainger County secessionists in response to the imprisonment of a Unionist named Brooke, and on October 28 he requested Gillem to detain three secessionists in exchange for two Unionists recently seized at Dandridge. Union authorities also attempted to use hostages to protect loyalists and Federal troops from attacks by guerrillas and Confederate cavalry. After Southern partisans raided Athens and executed Deputy Provost Marshal John McGaughy, Union officers published a list of prominent secessionists who would be imprisoned and their property confiscated or destroyed if further attacks occurred. Likewise, after a series of guerrilla strikes into Union County, Carter sought permission to arrest a number of influential secessionists there and banish them in the event of another raid.[50]

Confederate forces responded in kind. In July 1864 Brigadier General John Hunt Morgan requested permission from Adjutant and Inspector General Samuel Cooper to arrest the families of several influential Unionists in upper East Tennessee in retaliation for the recent banishment of several Knoxville secessionists. Cooper did not consent, but in August Morgan, after allowing several loyalist families to leave Confederate-held territory, informed Carter that if the mistreatment of secessionists continued he would instead begin imprisoning loyalists. And in September Brigadier General John C. Vaughn warned that if Union authorities refused to exchange civilian prisoners he would "arrest and confine every Union man I can get hold of in E Tenn as Hostages for our friends." The actual number of hostages taken by Confederate authorities is uncertain, but it was probably close to the Federal total.[51]

Though it was a terrible practice, hostage taking was a logical outcome of the conflict in East Tennessee. From the beginning, political control had been the real issue in this struggle, and the population itself had been the real battleground. Both Confederate and Union authorities had for a time attempted to mask this reality and limit the impact of the war on the people of East Tennessee, but divided control brought this struggle completely into the open. Divided control meant that neither government could directly protect all its supporters, and thus each side, angered by the growing number of arrests by the other, resorted to desperate attempts at deterrence. The immediate result was just the opposite of what was intended. Arrests led to counterarrests, the number of prisoners grew, and increasingly the people of East Tennessee, caught between competing forces, suffered.

At the same time, both sides recognized the evil and the essential futility of hostage taking, and both desired to bring it to an end. In November 1863 Confederate and Union authorities began exchanging prisoners on an informal, reciprocal basis, and in February 1864 they also began allowing dissenting families to move to territory controlled by the other side. Then in August 1864 Brigadier General John Hunt Morgan suggested that he and Carter negotiate an agreement for the release of all noncriminal, nonmilitary prisoners and henceforth ban the taking of both political prisoners and hostages. Carter quickly accepted the proposal, appointed three commissioners to conduct the negotiations, and issued a circular soliciting information concerning all Unionists thought to be held in Confederate prisons. Fighting delayed the first meeting by more than a month, but in September Union and Confederate commissioners finally met at Greeneville. They made rapid progress and within a few weeks were apparently near an agreement, for on October 26 Vaughn, who had succeeded Morgan, requested that Major General John C. Breckinridge, commander of the District of East Tennessee and Southwest Virginia, send all East Tennessee civilians confined in Confederate prisons to Bristol and place them under his control.[52]

But higher authorities intervened and jeopardized these negotiations. On November 9 Breckinridge notified Vaughn that any agreement must include all civilian prisoners held by both sides. The fate of J. B. Heiskell, an East Tennessee secessionist indicted for treason in the U.S. District Court at Nashville, seems to have been the primary Confederate concern. Breckinridge, unfortunately, had raised an intractable issue. Carter had already turned over several other secessionists to the state or Federal courts, and authorities in

Washington ruled that these prisoners had to remain in civilian hands. The East Tennessee commissioners met twice to discuss this point, but they failed to find a workable compromise, and the negotiations appeared doomed.[53]

Shortly thereafter, for reasons that remain unclear, events took a new turn. On November 20 Vaughn notified Carter that he had again received authorization from Breckinridge to conclude an agreement, and on December 1 Carter and Vaughn signed formal terms of exchange. The agreement contained four simple provisions. First, Confederate authorities would send all East Tennessee civilian prisoners to Union lines. Second, the Union command in turn would release all the hostages it had taken in retaliation for Confederate arrests. Third, Carter would attempt to gain the release of secessionists formally charged with political offenses. And fourth, both sides would allow all citizens who had fled their homes to return and live unmolested as long as they remained quiet and violated no laws. The two commanders also made a separate verbal agreement that Carter would again press for the release of the men indicted for treason, while Vaughn would be allowed to detain five hostages until they were freed.[54]

Confederate and Union officers in East Tennessee began to implement this agreement immediately. In early December Vaughn notified Carter that twenty-nine prisoners had been sent to his lines to be exchanged. Carter in turn released several hostages and sent Vaughn a list of their names. He also forwarded a copy of the agreement to Major General Ethan Allan Hitchcock, Union commissioner for exchange, and requested that Hitchcock send all East Tennessee civilian prisoners at Camp Chase and Johnson's Island to Knoxville. On December 23 Hitchcock approved the agreement on the condition that it was understood to be a local arrangement only, and by February 8 Union authorities had released nineteen secessionist prisoners and had made preparations to free several more.[55]

Yet again the process foundered, partly on the objections of higher authorities and partly on bad faith on both sides. Confederate secretary of war James A. Seddon had actually rejected the agreement on December 15, again because it did not guarantee that all secessionists, including those now in the hands of civil authorities, would be released and was therefore "inequitable." Though Vaughn had reported to Carter that twenty-nine Unionist hostages had been turned over to him, Richmond had in fact refused to release any civilian prisoners. Thus Vaughn had apparently lied to

Carter, and he had also failed to inform Carter that Seddon had nullified the agreement. It is possible that Vaughn was unaware of, or did not understand, Seddon's action, for he continued to press Breckinridge to send the East Tennessee prisoners to his headquarters. But it is equally possible that he had deliberately misled Carter in an attempt to gain the release of the secessionist prisoners. On the other side, Carter led Vaughn to believe that he could gain the release of the Confederate prisoners indicted for treason, even though he had made no progress at all in that direction.[56]

Grievances on both sides boiled over in early 1865. On February 8 Trowbridge notified Vaughn that Union authorities had now released fifteen Confederate prisoners, while no Unionists had been freed in turn, and he urged Vaughn to fulfill Confederate obligations. Six days later Trowbridge sent Vaughn the names of three additional men whom he had freed and this time warned that if the Confederates did not now release their Unionist prisoners "immediate and full retaliation will be visited upon general officers of the Confederate Army now in our hands." Vaughn, in turn, forwarded Trowbridge's February 8 letter and a list of secessionist prisoners who had been freed to Breckinridge and demanded that his superiors send him eighteen Unionists to release in turn. But Vaughn also sent Trowbridge a belligerent letter that called into question the good faith of Union authorities. Vaughn claimed that some men reported as released were still detained, asserted that other prisoners whom Trowbridge reported as having died in captivity were in fact still alive, and again brought up the dispute about which prisoners were covered under the agreement. Vaughn also accused Trowbridge of violating the Union promise to make no further political arrests and notified him that Confederate authorities were prepared to retaliate in kind.[57]

The final blow to the hoped-for exchange came on March 2, when Seddon informed Vaughn that a national, comprehensive agreement for the release of all citizen prisoners had been concluded. Tennessee prisoners, therefore, would not be sent to him, but would be exchanged elsewhere. Thus seven months of effort by the East Tennessee authorities had resulted in the release of only a handful of prisoners, while greatly increasing the rancor between the two sides. Part of the blame for this failure lay with authorities in Washington and Richmond for their refusal to make concessions to the peculiarities of the East Tennessee situation. Part also falls on Carter and Vaughn for their errors in conducting the negotiations and bad faith in carrying out the exchange. But ultimately their failure simply reflected the harsh and distorted environment in which they operated. The pressures to take hostages were stronger than the desire to end this cruel practice, and the continued struggle for control of the population eroded the little trust that Carter and Vaughn had established.[58]

Several factors account for the Union failure to restore order to East Tennessee. One was the partisan nature of Union policy, which encouraged the reestablishment of a loyal government at the expense of ending guerrilla violence. Federal officers gave considerable responsibility to Unionists, and while some loyalists demonstrated fairness, others seized the opportunity to take revenge. A second factor was Federal policy, which stressed control over conciliation and which led to recklessness in pursuing Confederate supporters. The third difficulty was a lack of resources. The initial Union commitment to East Tennessee was generous, but in the spring and summer of 1864 most of these units were either returned to the East Coast or transferred south for Sherman's campaign against Atlanta. By 1865 fewer than ten thousand men garrisoned East Tennessee, far too few to control dissent and enforce law and order. The final, most important factor, though, was the nature of the conflict itself. Many of the causes of the fighting in East Tennessee were long standing and deeply rooted in the region's history. No outside force could hope to intervene in such a conflict and eliminate all the grievances and passions that drove it. At most, Union authorities could limit the level of violence and prevent the worst abuses. The result was that East Tennessee entered the postwar period in a perilous state.

7 Separation Is Best

On April 9, 1865, General Robert E. Lee, his army weakened by lack of supplies, disease, desertion, and months of constant fighting, surrendered to Grant and ordered the Army of Northern Virginia to disband. General Joe Johnston continued for a few more days to oppose Sherman's advance through North Carolina, but in late April, after some confusion about the surrender terms, his forces laid down their arms. On May 10 Union cavalry captured President Jefferson Davis in Georgia, and shortly thereafter the remaining Confederate forces, including those in the Trans-Mississippi, went home. By late spring, therefore, the conventional war was over, though Union troops continued to occupy the South and Confederate and Union partisans in Missouri, Kentucky, and other states fought on.

Despite the formal peace, the war in East Tennessee went on unabated. The Unionist-secessionist conflict for control of this region was not yet fully resolved, and for more than two years life in East Tennessee continued to be characterized by beatings, killings, theft, and legal and political battles. By 1868 Unionists had achieved many of their aims, but their victory was not so complete as they had hoped, and the costs of their triumph were high.

The skirmishing between secessionist guerrillas and Union troops continued into the summer. On April 13 Major General David S. Stanley reported that only a few Confederate bushwhackers had been seen recently near Greeneville and claimed that Unionist bands were killing or chasing away those who remained. On May 5 Brigadier General Davis Tillson stated that guerrilla bands in the mountains of northern East Tennessee were disbanding, and on May 16 Colonel James Parsons asserted that the area north of the Clinch Mountains was quiet except for a few robber bands. But in other areas Southern guerrilla bands remained defiant. On April 17 B. W. Howard, a Unionist in Sevier County, reported that secessionists from Cocke County had recently killed several Unionists and threatened to shoot anyone participating in the restoration of the courts and the government. He claimed that many Unionists were hiding in the woods or leaving the county, while farmers were afraid to work their fields. On April 20 a guerrilla band destroyed a train at Talbott Station, and one week later a military courier was waylaid near Warm Springs. On April 30 Captain James Harrington reported that Unionist citizens at Rutledge had petitioned his company not to leave that area, for many loyalists, especially those who had given testimony against "rebels," feared retaliation. And in other areas Confederate guerrillas continued to fight until May or even June.[1]

With the conventional war over, Union officers intensified their efforts to stamp out partisan resistance. In late April Stoneman ordered the Ninth Tennessee Cavalry to pacify the Clinch River area, "scour" the entire region between the Holston River and the Cumberland Mountains, and protect the court at Rutledge. A few weeks later, Stoneman sent a force of cavalry north of Knoxville to restore order in Knox, Anderson, Campbell, and Montgomery Counties, while Thomas ordered the Fourth Tennessee Mounted Infantry to pacify White, Overton, Fentress, Montgomery, and Morgan. After a rendezvous in Morgan, Stoneman's cavalry moved to disperse guerrilla bands in Roane, Rhea, and Hamilton, while the mounted infantry cleared the area between the Little River and the Holston. These operations were apparently effective. On April 30 Captain Harrington of the Ninth Tennessee Cavalry reported that he had arrested nine men suspected of bushwhacking and chased away most of the remaining guerrillas in the Rutledge area. Colonel James Parsons stated that he had encountered little resistance around Rogersville. And Amanda McDowell claimed that by late May most guerrillas in the Sparta area had surrendered.[2]

Union officers extended little mercy to guerrillas in the postwar period. In line with General Orders 100 and established Federal practices, Stoneman informed Thomas that he had authorized his troopers "to take no prisoners" when fighting guerrillas, an order with which his officers fully complied. On May 1 Thomas instructed commanders in Tennessee, Kentucky, and Mississippi to offer all bushwhackers the same surrender terms that Grant had given the Army of Northern Virginia. Any who refused to give themselves up would "hereafter be regarded as outlaws, and be proceeded against, pursued, and when captured, treated as outlaws."[3]

Civil authorities took an equally harsh stance. Officials at Sweetwater advised citizens to shoot bushwhackers on sight and summarily executed at least one suspected guerrilla. In May the newly established Tennessee legislature made bushwhacking, house burning, housebreaking, bridge burning, and other typical guerrilla acts capital crimes. Several bushwhackers were also tried in various county courts for murder, theft, or other crimes. The most sensational of these cases was that of Champ Ferguson, who was arrested in late May, tried by a military commission in Nashville, and executed.[4]

In the first months after the war Federal officers also aided Unionist authorities in restoring order and implementing reconstruction policies. In May 1865 seventy-five men were sent to Jonesborough to assist the U.S. marshal in arresting men indicted for treason. In June ten soldiers were detailed to apprehend horse thieves in Sullivan County, and in September Major General Alvin C. Gillem ordered twenty-five men to Cleveland to investigate the destruction of a Freedmen's Bureau School. Stoneman also threatened to arrest anyone wearing the uniform or insignia of a Confederate officer and required returning veterans to take a loyalty oath or be sent to Georgia. But in most areas Federal units were mustered out or transferred within a few months, and the influence of the Federal army in East Tennessee quickly declined.[5]

Continued violence by Unionist bands posed a far greater threat to peace in East Tennessee than the operations of Confederate bushwhackers. For a number of reasons the Unionist intimidation of secessionists actually increased after the Confederate surrender. The end of the war sent both Confederate and Union veterans back to East Tennessee, and the peculiar proximity of these two groups inevitably increased tensions in the region, particularly when many Federal soldiers came home ready to avenge the wrongs that they and their families had suffered at Confederate hands. Unionists were also determined to control postwar East Tennessee, and they attempted to expel as many secessionists as possible from the region. Finally, the collapse of the Confederacy meant that Unionists no longer had to fear Confederate retribution, and for this reason they may have acted more boldly than during the war.

The first group to suffer Unionist vengeance were returning Confederate soldiers. On May 1, 1865, a Federal soldier stationed in Knoxville stated that Unionists had already killed three or four veterans from the Army of Northern Virginia and had sworn revenge against a group of Confederate cavalry who had ridden in to surrender. Elizabeth Caswell wrote that Confederate veterans in Knoxville were repeatedly threatened, and David Anderson Deaderick remembered that numbers of Confederate troops fled the town after several Unionist attacks. This violence was not confined to Knoxville. Shortly after his return to Blount County James Harris was waylaid by fourteen Unionists, threatened with a pistol, and "given 34 licks with a two-handed brush." Two Confederates in Grainger County were similarly ambushed and beaten, and several soldiers in Dandridge were also assaulted. Colonel William Gibbs Allen reported the deaths of four soldiers in Rhea and Washington Counties and claimed that he knew many others who had been severely beaten. In May 1865 Union officers had to send a detachment of troops to Concord to halt fighting between Federal and Confederate veterans, and in September one man wrote President Andrew Johnson from Greeneville that many Confederate soldiers had been "beaten severely and ordered to leave in five days."[6]

Confederate veterans were not the only victims of Unionist vengeance. Any East Tennessean known to have supported the Confederacy was at risk. In May 1865 one secessionist attempting to flee East Tennessee was waylaid near Loudon and killed. In July a band of Unionists broke into the house of a secessionist in Morristown, shot him, and attempted to kill his brother. In Washington County a group of veterans killed a man whom they suspected of mistreating Unionists during the Confederate occupation. Secessionists in Jonesborough claimed that two men had been killed and two women raped. And David Key reported that at the opening day of court in Harrison Unionist mobs badly beat a number of secessionists.[7]

Knoxville was the site of some of the worst violence. In June 1865 one Knoxville woman recited a grim litany of attacks carried out by returning Federal soldiers: "Dr. Massengill was terribly cowhided—Bob West had his skull broken—Epps was beaten all most to death—and a good many more—a man by the name of Beard was severely beaten by Shade Harris." Another group of Federals broke into the county jail, took out a man accused of shooting a Unionist, and hanged him. And one night in August five Unionists surrounded the home of a Knoxville secessionist named Cox, fired several shots into the house, and eventually killed him. This violence had a profound impact on secessionists. Many fled Knoxville and did not return for months, while others who had been summoned to answer charges in district court refused to appear, even at the risk of a contempt charge. John G. King reported to Nelson that "many of your clients feel some apprehension in going to Knoxville for fear of violence from the mob." W. W. Wallace, who claimed to have been threatened by the same men who killed Cox, stated that "I don't think duty requires me to appear there to be shot down like a dog without provocation as Cox was." A. L. Mims, whose brother was killed at Morristown, also refused to return to Knoxville, as did Hugh Bogle and Joseph Tucker, both of whom had received threats. The secessionist fear of violence was so great that district court judge Connelly F. Trigg had to postpone many proceedings until the next term.[8]

Of course not all areas of East Tennessee suffered partisan violence, and not all secessionists were assaulted. Chattanooga was relatively quiet, and several prominent Confederates returned there and settled down quietly. Robert A. Ragan claimed that in Cocke County returning Confederate veterans suffered no harm, for "these boys went into the rebel army at the beginning of the war in 1861, and did not stay to rob and kill Union men." Even so, Unionist violence against secessionists was frighteningly widespread. In June 1865 a Morristown man concluded sadly that "not a day passes but what some 'rebel' receives his 400 lashes or its equivalent—the contents of a minnie rifle—Even persons whose names have not been associated with the armies of this or any adjacent department share the same brutal fate." Father Abraham Ryan asserted that Knoxville was "worse in scenes of blood and acts of violence than even Nashville was. Scarcely a day passes that is not signalized by some murder or other crime." Samuel Milligan wrote Johnson from Greeneville that "not a day passes but some man or family is either beaten almost to death, or driven from the county." Secessionists in Greeneville, Rogersville, and other towns begged for protection. And in September Thomas reported to Johnson that he received "almost daily" complaints of loyalist violence.[9]

Secessionists in East Tennessee apparently made few attempts to fight back against this persecution. Though the Ku Klux Klan originated in Tennessee in 1867 and controlled many counties in Middle and West Tennessee by 1868, the organization made no headway in the eastern counties. In 1868 a few Klansmen posted pamphlets in Knoxville and Chattanooga and made threats against Unionist leaders, but they were quickly suppressed. Confederates in Sullivan County, which had a secessionist majority, assaulted a justice of the peace for attempting to prosecute Confederate supporters, and a small group of Klansmen there fought with members of the Loyal League during the August 1868 elections. But these were scattered incidents, for in most counties secessionists were outnumbered and were more likely to flee than resort to violence.[10]

East Tennessee Unionists clearly intended not only to punish secessionists but also to drive them permanently out of East Tennessee. In May 1865 Robert Johnson wrote his father, now President Johnson, that "the Union men will not permit the leaders, and others that persecuted their families to live in this section." Three Union veterans asked their father to relay the following message to secessionists in Carter and Washington Counties: "They was for separation and we a posed it all we cold they said when they got thear independence that the Union famelyes cold not stay hear no how now we expect to come hear shortly and we have concluded that separation is Best and they must leave thear before we come." Federal veterans posted a similar notice in New Market. Brownlow himself, both in articles in the *Knoxville Whig* and in proclamations as governor, explicitly encouraged revenge against Confederates. Mrs. Horace Maynard attributed violence by Unionists to their determination not to live with secessionists: "You know they used to say that the Union men and 'Southern' men could not live together, and the former have taken them at their word and sent them away, rather hurriedly."[11]

The Unionists' campaign to remove their enemies from East Tennessee was systematic and ruthless. In Washington County Unionists regularly issued notices to secessionists to leave and threatened violence against any who refused. A Rogersville woman claimed that a Unionist "mob" had conspired to deny Confederates access to schools, churches, and employment. O. R. Broyles concluded that "the Union party of the border states" had "united as one man to drive the friends of the Southern cause from their homes, confiscate their real estates, and shoot them down as wild beasts." And in Knoxville Father Ryan asserted that "no one can live here safe and secure that does not swear by Brownlow."[12]

While some Unionists pursued their enemies with violence, others turned to the newly opened courts for revenge. Dozens of loyalists entered damage suits against secessionists for losses supposedly suffered during the war, while Unionist officials charged hundreds of secessionists with treason. Like partisan violence during the war, a variety of motives drove these suits, including compensation for actual losses, a desire to punish supporters of the Confederacy, greed, and a deliberate attempt to make it impossible for Confederates to live in East Tennessee.

Confederate officers who had enforced the draft and other occupation policies were particularly likely to suffer damage suits. James A. Rhea was sued by two different men whom he had imprisoned while post commander at Jonesborough. A second Confederate officer faced three different suits, totaling more than $60,000, for the arrests of several Unionists, while a third lost his lands in Hamilton and Bradley Counties for capturing draft evaders. Captain William W. Stringfield, provost marshal in Carter County, was sued for burning a field in 1862. William Brecht pursued four different soldiers for supposedly arresting, imprisoning, and attempting to hang him, and Levi Lynes requested T. A. R. Nelson to enter a suit against a Confederate captain, Frank Phipps, for allegedly beating him with a club, blinding him in one eye, and driving him out of Tennessee. Two other officers with reputations for harshness against Unionists, Colonel William Brazelton and Colonel William Gibbs Allen, were also pursued in court.[13]

Prominent secessionists accused of encouraging the arrests of Unionists or supplying information to Confederate authorities were also vulnerable to legal harassment. The heirs of Levi Pickens entered a damage suit against several influential Confederates, including John Crozier, William Sneed, and Confederate commissioner D. B. Reynolds, for Pickens's death while in Confederate custody in December 1861. Pickens had been arrested on suspicion of involvement in or knowledge of the bridge burnings, briefly confined in Knoxville, and sent to the Confederate military prison at Tuscaloosa. He was sixty years old, and he had died on the way to Alabama. In a similar case, James W. Trewhitt sued three prominent secessionists for the arrest, imprisonment, and subsequent death of his father, Levi Trewhitt. Like Pickens, Trewhitt was a prominent Unionist who had been arrested in the wake of the bridge burnings and who had not survived conditions in a Confederate prison. And in 1865 Brownlow sued Sneed, Crozier, Reynolds, and Confederate district attorney John Crozier Ramsey for his arrest in 1861.[14]

The county courts of East Tennessee were full of similar cases in the first years of reconstruction. In January 1866 David Key reported from Chattanooga that "every rebel of prominence or property is sued for damages and the dockets of the courts are groaning under this class of suits." In late 1867 a Unionist wrote Nelson from

Jonesborough that several of Nelson's clients were waiting to pursue their cases and that "the times are quite favorable for trying damages." And in June 1868 Tom Brabson wrote that the county court at Greeneville was "trying damage cases they are giving the rebs HELL." [15]

The results of these damage suits were mixed. Juries in most county courts tended to be sympathetic, and many Unionists initially won large settlements. James Trewhitt was awarded $35,000, while the representatives of Levi Pickens received a judgment for $100,000. Brownlow likewise won his suit in Knox County Court and was awarded $25,000. But several factors prevented many Unionists from actually collecting most of the damages awarded. The first was that frequently there was little of value for the plaintiffs to secure, for many secessionists had suffered great losses during the war or had had their lands confiscated by the Federal government. The second difficulty was the changing legal and political climate in Tennessee. By the late 1860s the view that Confederate officers and civil officials had been acting as agents of a de facto government and were therefore immune from prosecution for all actions except actual violations of military or criminal laws had prevailed in both the state supreme court and many county courts. A number of secessionists, therefore, were successful in appealing adverse verdicts once this more favorable legal climate had emerged. The defendants in Brownlow's suit, for example, appealed the case to the Tennessee Supreme Court and got the judgment overturned. A final factor that undercut the Unionist legal campaign, and one that Unionists in East Tennessee found particularly hard to accept, was President Johnson's conciliatory policies toward the South. Despite Johnson's stern measures against Confederates while military governor, the president was now determined to restore the Southern states to the Union as quickly as possible, and he opposed any attempts to remake the South's political system. Johnson therefore opposed attempts to punish Confederates, and he generously pardoned hundreds of Confederate officials who fell outside President Lincoln's 1863 Proclamation of Amnesty and Reconstruction. Many secessionists, therefore, were able to use their special pardons as a defense against prosecution. [16]

Private damage suits offered Unionists the opportunity to impoverish their enemies and gain compensation for themselves. But loyalist officials also attempted to exploit the powers of the Federal district court. In 1861 Brownlow, Temple, Nelson, and other Unionist spokesmen had insisted that secession was illegal and unconstitutional. Four years later, having won their war and gained control of the district court, loyalists now intended to prosecute every secessionist they could identify. Unionists intended not only to punish their enemies but also to enforce their claim that secession was treason, thereby denying the legitimacy of their enemies' cause.

The U.S. District Court of the Eastern Division of Tennessee (Knoxville) reopened on May 16, 1864. Connelly F. Trigg, a successful lawyer, delegate to the Knoxville and Greeneville Conventions, and member of the secret Unionist Executive Committee, was appointed district court judge, and by May 28 a grand jury composed of some of the most uncompromising loyalists in East Tennessee was impaneled. Their first presentments made clear the Unionist strategy. Beginning with Confederate president Jefferson Davis and General Robert E. Lee, Unionists indicted practically every prominent Confederate who had influenced Southern policy in East Tennessee. Those named included Major Generals Simon B. Buckner, James Longstreet, Edmund Kirby Smith, William Hardee, Braxton Bragg, John C. Breckinridge, and John P. McCown and Brigadier Generals John C. Vaughn, William Carroll, Humphrey Marshall, John Hunt Morgan, Danville Leadbetter, Alfred E. Jackson, George Crittenden, and Nathan Bedford Forrest. Loyalists then turned their attention to secessionist leaders in East Tennessee and indicted John Crozier, William Sneed, John Crozier Ramsey, Landon Carter Haynes, William G. Swan, C. W. Charleton, William W. Wallace, Colonel David M. Key, and dozens of others. But loyalist vengeance was not confined to leaders only. Unionists seemed determined to bring a suit against every secessionist of any status at all in East Tennessee, and by January 1867 the court had before it over two thousand presentments for treason or for giving aid and comfort to the enemy.[17]

But again Unionists failed to achieve their full aims. In their zeal to punish as many secessionists as possible, loyalists completely overwhelmed the capacities of the district court. Trying so many cases would take years and monopolize the court's resources, a fact that soon became clear even to many Unionists. For practical reasons, if for no other, Trigg had to find means to settle these cases quickly and clear his docket. More importantly, for a second time secessionists benefited from the shifting political climate. The legal theory on which the treason suits were based was that secession was a conspiracy to overthrow the U.S. government, and anyone who had served as a Confederate official or even voted for separation was a party to that conspiracy. But that theory could not be sustained. President Johnson's reconstruction policies discouraged the mass punishment of secessionists, and his special pardons again protected many Confederates from prosecution. In addition, a number of original Unionist leaders, including Trigg, had concluded that the widespread persecution of secessionists was misguided and instead favored reconciliation.

The result was that most treason suits were quickly settled in favor of the defendants. At the beginning of the winter term of 1864–65 Trigg instituted the practice of dismissing treason cases if the defendant took an oath of allegiance, obtained a special pardon from President Johnson, and paid the thirty-dollar court costs. This practice allowed Trigg to dispose of a large number of cases in a short period of time. By May 1866 794 charges of treason and giving aid and comfort had been dismissed, and almost all the remaining treason cases had been cleared by the end of 1868. Ultimately the U.S. Supreme Court simply threw out the few that remained. In the end, not a single defendant was convicted of treason in the district court at Knoxville.[18]

Radical Unionists were bitterly disappointed at the court's leniency. But secessionists did not escape entirely unscathed. Many spent time in jail, and all experienced at least some financial loss, inconvenience, and embarrassment. Even a routine dismissal required many defendants to travel to Knoxville, remain there several days, pay legal fees, and risk violence from Unionists. Several prominent secessionists suffered more severe penalties. John Crozier Ramsey was arrested several times before his case was dismissed, and he, Landon Carter Haynes, and William H. Sneed were repeatedly harassed. And three of Brownlow's enemies, John Aikin, James Sperry, and Robert P. Fox, were arrested in 1864, denied bail, threatened by Unionist mobs in Knoxville, and mistreated by their prison guards. Sperry settled his case in January 1865, but Fox died in prison, and Aikin was not released until December 1866.[19]

The Unionist legal campaign had other effects as well. In conjunction with the ongoing violence, these prosecutions prevented some Confederates from returning to East Tennessee and forced others who had come home to flee again. David Sullins, indicted for treason for counseling Nelson and Johnson not to speak at Blountville in May 1861, fled to Virginia and did not return for two years. Colonel Henry M. Doak received numerous threats after returning to Jonesborough and eventually moved to Louisiana. William G. McAdoo and Charles McClung both took refuge in Georgia and remained there until 1867. J. G. M. Ramsey fled to North Carolina in 1864 after his estate was burned by Federal soldiers and did not come home until 1871. William Sneed moved to Atlanta, while Landon Carter Haynes chose Memphis. And other secessionists made homes in Virginia, Kentucky, Arkansas, Texas, Kansas, or even Brazil.[20]

The magnitude of the secessionist exodus was astonishing. In July 1865 William Stakely listed thirty-one prominent Confederate families, including the McAdoos, Sneeds, Croziers, Swans, McClungs, Doaks, Charletons, Wallaces, and Ramseys, who had left Knoxville or been expelled by Federal authorities. John Crozier Ramsey reported that "no prominent Southern men [from Knoxville] have returned and those who are there are making arrangements to leave." In December 1865 Frank McClung claimed that he "saw East Tennesseans at almost every town, depot, and station in Georgia." David T. Patterson testified to Congress that by early 1866 there were few Confederates left in East Tennessee. And in April 1867 John Crozier Ramsey reported that while some secessionist refugees in North Carolina were planning to return to their homes, others had chosen to remain there permanently.[21]

Of course not all secessionists became refugees. David M. Key secured a special pardon from Johnson in May 1865, got the treason charges against him dismissed, returned home to resume his law practice, and eventually enjoyed a distinguished political career. But many secessionists who did not become permanent exiles still had great difficulty resuming normal lives. Captain William W. Stringfield was jailed for thirty days, indicted for treason, threatened by Unionist bands, and chased from his home at Strawberry Plains. William Gibbs Allen was repeatedly harassed by Union authorities, threatened with violence, and robbed at least twice. And Brigadier General Alfred E. Jackson was charged with treason, indicted for several offenses in the Washington County and Knox County Courts, and had most of his land seized by the Federal government as abandoned enemy property. Jackson attributed his difficulties to "the radical policy inaugurated in E. Tenn of persecution and impoverishment" and to the feeling that he had "not been sufficiently humbled and impoverished."[22]

Thus, though they were not able to accomplish all they wished, East Tennessee loyalists punished hundreds of secessionists for their support of the South and permanently reduced the Confederate population in the region. Equally important, Unionism, trans-formed into Republicanism, became the dominant political force in the region and remained so even when most of the rest of the South returned to the control of the Democratic Party. But this victory was not without its price. The economic costs of the war were im-mense and in some areas nearly fatal. Confederate and Union troops, along with guerrilla bands, repeatedly stripped the region of supplies, taking food stocks, draft animals, and seed and destroying houses, barns, fences, and implements. Thousands of men left the region to join the Union and Confederate armies, and though women assumed many new responsibilities, labor remained in short supply. The threat of guerrillas forced many rural families to aban-don their farms and flee to the towns for safety. Finally, like the rest of the South, the economy of East Tennessee was damaged by inflation and the Union blockade. The results were devastating. Agricultural and industrial production dropped sharply, many fami-lies suffered from hunger and exposure, and in some areas recovery seemed impossible without outside aid. Fortunately, that aid was forthcoming. In 1864 Unionists, led by Thomas W. Humes and Nathaniel G. Taylor, organized a relief committee and appealed to the North for aid. Boston, New York City, Philadelphia, and other cities responded generously and provided thousands of dollars for immediate relief and rebuilding. This aid prevented much suffering, but the task of rebuilding was nonetheless painfully slow.[23]

The old Unionist Party of 1861 was also a casualty of the conflict. The increasing social and moral costs of the national war and the partisan conflict had very different effects on loyalists and eventually split them into two factions. One group, the conservatives, were ap-palled at the war's destructiveness, and by 1864 many concluded that even the division of the Union was preferable to continued blood-shed. Radicals, conversely, became increasingly bitter and violent as the war progressed and called for ever harsher measures to defeat the South. While conservatives argued that the preservation of con-stitutional restraints and free government took precedence even over the salvation of the Union, radicals viewed policies such as the suspension of the writ of habeas corpus, confiscation, and even emancipation as essential to the achievement of victory. Most of the original Unionist leaders became conservatives, while increasingly the radical ranks were filled with younger men who had served in the Federal army. During Reconstruction radicalism would become transformed into Republicanism.

The division between radicals and conservatives had deep roots. As early as June 1861 the Greeneville Convention had revealed a divergence between Unionists who insisted on remaining within constitutional bounds and those who were ready to resort to violence and revolution. Then, in 1862, Nelson parted company with the Lincoln administration, Military Governor Johnson, and Brownlow over emancipation. But the radical-conservative split was not fully revealed until April 1864, when Johnson asked Nelson to call into session the Unionist Convention. Since 1862 Johnson had labored to restore Federal authority in Tennessee, build a Union Party, and establish a new state government. But secessionists in Middle and West Tennessee resisted his every move and intimidated potential supporters. Johnson established strict franchise restrictions and held some local elections in 1863 and 1864, but despite his precautions Unionists failed to win a number of contests. Johnson, therefore, turned to East Tennessee for a public endorsement of his policies and a base for a loyal state government. But, unknown to Johnson, Nelson hoped to use the convention to voice disapproval of Lincoln's policies and organize support for conservative Unionist candidates who would oppose disfranchisement, emancipation, and the continuation of the war.

From the beginning, therefore, the convention was hopelessly divided. The Committee on Resolutions, which was responsible for developing a platform, was forced to issue two opposing documents. The majority, conservative report called for an immediate end to the war and a negotiated settlement between the North and the South. The minority report supported the continued prosecution of the war and approved Johnson's policies. These differences could not be compromised, and the delegates became mired in an increasingly acrimonious debate. In his usual extravagant manner, Brownlow called for the complete subjugation of the Confederacy and bitterly condemned conservatives for their tenderness toward secessionists. Conservatives in turn criticized Johnson's policies as divisive and unconstitutional, and appealed for reconciliation with Confederates. By April 15 it was clear that further discussion was useless, and the delegates agreed to adjourn. The following day radical Unionists met in their own convention and passed a series of resolutions, written by Johnson himself though presented as Brownlow's, that fully endorsed the governor's policies for the reconstruction of the state government.[24]

From that point the two groups took separate ways. Radicals campaigned vigorously for the Lincoln-Johnson ticket, while con-

servatives attempted to mobilize support for the Democratic presidential candidate, Major General George B. McClellan. The conservative cause was hopeless, however. McClellan found little support in East Tennessee, and in October Brownlow reported to Johnson that "a McClellan man cannot make a speech anywhere in this District without being mobbed." Further, Johnson's franchise restrictions, which required voters to swear to "cordially oppose all armistices or negotiations for peace with rebels in arms," effectively precluded McClellan supporters from voting. Nelson, William B. Campbell, and other conservatives appealed to Lincoln for justice, but Lincoln stated that he had no power to interfere with the conduct of a state election and asserted that Johnson's only intention was to protect loyal voters in Tennessee. Conservatives then withdrew from the election.[25]

In January 1865 Tennessee Unionists met in Nashville to initiate the formation of a loyal state government. Bypassing the established constitutional requirement of first electing delegates to a convention, which would then amend the constitution, loyalists immediately repealed the Tennessee ordinance of secession, wrote an amendment to the state constitution abolishing slavery, and scheduled elections for state and local offices. Brownlow's status as the most celebrated Unionist in Tennessee guaranteed his nomination as governor.[26]

On March 4 loyalist voters elected Brownlow and a legislature dominated by radical Unionists. Brownlow came to office with the stated intention of punishing Confederate supporters and expunging from the state all traces of secession, and his administration was characterized by vindictiveness and increasingly desperate measures to bar Confederates from politics. In June 1865, at Brownlow's urging, the state legislature passed a franchise bill designed to ensure Unionist political dominance. Legislators confined the right to vote to three groups: persons who had been discharged honorably from the Federal army, had voted in the elections of March 1864 and March 1865, or could prove that they had always supported the Union. To guard against fraud, qualified voters had to obtain a court document certifying their right to the franchise. Confederate military and civilian officials, persons who had left Federal or state offices to serve the new government, and persons who had fled Union-occupied territory, were denied the right to vote for the next fifteen years. All other Confederates in Tennessee were disfranchised for five years and could regain the right to vote only by taking an "iron-clad" loyalty oath and securing witnesses who would swear to their loyalty.[27]

This bill prevented most outright secessionists from voting, but it failed to bar conservative Unionists who opposed Brownlow's reconstruction policies. In April and May 1866, therefore, the legislature passed an even more restrictive act. All persons who had voluntarily fought against the U.S. government, held Confederate office, or voluntarily supported a government hostile to the United States were permanently disfranchised. All voters except Union veterans were required to prove their right to the franchise by taking an iron-clad loyalty oath and presenting in court the testimony of two persons who already possessed voting certificates. The legislature also authorized Brownlow to appoint in each county special registrars to judge each voter's qualifications. Finally, to enforce these measures legislators granted Brownlow the power to organize special militia companies to guard polling places against threats from the Klan, protect voting registrars, enforce the franchise restrictions, and prevent interference with an election.[28]

These acts strained executive powers to the limit and gave Brownlow the ability to determine outright the outcome of many elections. Conservatives condemned these acts as unconstitutional and tyrannical and accused Brownlow of usurpation. But radicals argued that these measures, while extreme, were both just and essential. In their view, persons who had supported the Confederacy had committed treason and should not again be trusted to vote, at least not for some time. Radical Unionists also believed that their survival depended on the maintenance of absolute political control. Though Brownlow was following policies very similar to those Johnson had used while military governor, the president now opposed franchise restrictions. For a variety of reasons, including his opposition to attempts to improve the position of African Americans and alter the South's political and economic system and his desire to restore Southern states to the Union as quickly as possible, Johnson attempted to ensure that participation in the establishment of the new state governments would be open to almost all prewar voters, including Confederate supporters. Radical Unionists in Tennessee thus felt abandoned and isolated. Brownlow turned to congressional radicals for support, but his supporters also determined that they would use whatever means necessary to bar their former enemies from power. In May 1866 a loyalist from Harrison predicted that "the people of Middle and West Tennessee numerically are in the ascendancy and will disregard the franchise law and crush us." A group of Unionists from Jonesborough insisted that "we must fight the enemies of our country, and fight them everywhere and in every way. We are satisfied that President Johnson is an enemy to the loyal people of the South, and intends to crush them if he can." Brownlow agreed with this assessment, stating in August 1866 that "we are to have another war. Johnson has gone over to the rebels, and in the next rebellion will take the place of Jeff Davis." The *Knoxville Whig* also portrayed Johnson as the tool of former Confederates and warned that secessionists were plotting to regain control of the state government, reenslave African Americans, and take revenge on Unionists.[29]

A second wedge between conservatives and radicals was the old issue of race. In 1861 no East Tennessee Unionist leader had questioned the institution of slavery. But the war had forced radical Unionists to accept changes in racial relations. In 1863 Brownlow, Johnson, Horace Maynard, and other Unionists had endorsed emancipation as a military measure, though they opposed any radical change in the position of blacks. In 1865 loyalist voters, anxious to secure Tennessee's readmission to the Union, ratified the Thirteenth Amendment to the U.S. Constitution by a large margin. Few Unionists expected racial relations to be altered further, but political conditions dictated otherwise. By 1866 it was clear that white Unionists constituted a vulnerable minority in Tennessee and required allies if they were to maintain their control of the state government. Even with the franchise restrictions, conservatives won a number of elections in Middle and West Tennessee, and secessionists were becoming increasingly restive and ready to resort to violence. The Tennessee legislature rejected a franchise bill in 1866, but the following year, in response to pressure from Brownlow and increasing threats from conservatives, reluctant legislators granted the franchise to African American males. Subsequent bills added the right to hold office and sit on juries. These actions were unpopular in East Tennessee, but Brownlow insisted that without black votes future Unionist administrations would not survive.[30]

A number of other issues contributed to the split in Unionist ranks. Conservatives were appalled at the continuing hatred, violence, and vengeance that characterized postwar East Tennessee, and in May 1865 Nelson, Thomas W. Humes, and almost one hundred other conservative Unionists petitioned Brownlow to use his influence to halt the outbreak of loyalist violence. But Brownlow saw the petition as an attempt to embarrass him politically. Though he issued a proclamation that advised Unionists to seek justice in the courts, the governor then stated that if justice could not be had it was inevitable that Unionists would take revenge on their own. Brownlow also dwelt at length on the wrongs that Unionists had suffered and called upon secessionists to cease their resistance to the reestablishment of Federal authority and make reparations for their persecution of Unionists. Finally, Brownlow's egotism and limitless ambition alienated even some of his most enduring supporters. His constant acts of self-promotion well served an editor, but they were ill suited to a governor attempting to build a new political party. Brownlow's decision to claim a second term as governor in 1867 angered Andrew Jackson Fletcher, who had served as Brownlow's secretary of state and expected to be his successor. And Brownlow's successful bid for a Senate seat in 1869 embittered Fletcher, Maynard, and a number of Middle Tennessee Unionists, all of whom had faithfully supported Brownlow and expected to be rewarded for their loyalty.[31]

Radical Unionists stumbled badly in their attempts to seize control of the state government and reconstruct Tennessee politics and society. Even with the franchise restrictions, Brownlow's administration grew steadily weaker, and Confederates and conservatives became increasingly determined to regain control of the state. Further, black and white Unionists found it impossible to cooperate, and Brownlow's attempts to build a broad base of support failed. Brownlow recognized that his time was short, and in February 1869 he exchanged the governorship for a seat in the U.S. Senate. Brownlow appointed DeWitt Senter, an original Unionist leader from Grainger County, as his successor. Senter had campaigned against secession in February and June 1861, been briefly imprisoned in May 1862, suffered repeated secessionist threats, and finally fled to Kentucky. He had returned to East Tennessee with the Union army in 1863, won a seat in the Tennessee Senate in March 1865, and faithfully supported Brownlow's policies. But by the late 1860s Senter had become disenchanted with radical reconstruction. Like Brownlow, he recognized the failure of radical policies, and he determined to make an alliance with Democrats in Middle and West

Tennessee. Shortly after his appointment Senter disbanded the state militia, the institution that conservatives despised most. Then in August, Senter ran for a second term with the promise to end the franchise restrictions and dismantle completely Brownlow's program. Senter's opponent was William B. Stokes, a former Union officer and a radical who pledged to maintain Brownlow's policies. To Stokes's dismay, Brownlow supported Senter, who won by a large majority.[32]

With Senter's victory radical reconstruction in Tennessee came to an end. As would soon happen in other Southern states, Democrats resumed control of the government, eliminated programs that Republicans had established for economic reform, and eventually forced African Americans back into a second-class status. Brownlow's radical policies had alienated even many East Tennesseans, and for a time East Tennessee Republicans suffered. Their support declined, and the party floundered in its attempts to define new, more acceptable issues. But Republicanism survived in East Tennessee. In the mid-1870s a group of younger leaders led by Leonidas Houk reorganized and revived the party. Houk, a Federal veteran and a supporter of Brownlow, based his appeal on the Unionist experience in the Civil War, but he adopted modern party techniques, created an efficient political machine, and shifted the emphasis from Reconstruction to local economic and political issues. Under Houk's leadership the Republican Party, with its roots in Civil War Unionism, became the dominant political force in East Tennessee, and the region remained divided from much of the rest of the South.[33]

CONCLUSION

Unionists and secessionists in East Tennessee divided over competing ideologies, political attachments, and visions of the future of
their region. Secessionists identified with Southern interests and
grievances and believed that they would prosper under a Confederate government. But Unionists feared the implications of Southern
rule and declined to give up the nation and the government that
they revered. A large number of factors, including party affiliation,
slaveholding, residence, political and personal conflicts in the antebellum period, and business contacts, influenced individual choices
for or against the Confederacy. The political terrain of this region
was as varied as its geography, and no single factor explains the loyalties of East Tennesseans.

The division between Unionists and secessionists in East Tennessee hardened with surprising speed. Within months the two
sides viewed each other as aliens, concluded that they could not
both live in the same region, and began to harass and assault each
other. Their struggle for control of East Tennessee was complex.
Unionists and secessionists employed traditional political methods
to build and maintain support, legal measures to intimidate and
punish their enemies, propaganda to create sympathy for themselves
and influence the policies of the Confederate and Union governments, and partisan violence. They also served as spies, guides, and
soldiers for the Northern and Southern armies.

The war between Unionists and Confederate troops, and that
between secessionists and Federal soldiers, was largely a stalemate.
Conventional troops were superior in discipline, tactics, and resources, but partisans nullified these advantages by their unconventional methods, their knowledge of the area, and their ability to hide
their identities. Neither the Confederacy nor the Union enjoyed
notable success in controlling dissent, and their frustrations led not
only to growing brutality among the troops but also to increasingly
harsh political measures and occupation policies.

The relationship between the East Tennessee guerrillas and the
regular Confederate and Union armies was a story of contradic-
tions. Officially authorities on both sides condemned irregular warfare, even by their supporters, and sought to curb it. Both sides also

refused to recognize bushwhackers as legitimate combatants and defined guerrillas as criminals. Yet Confederate and Union authorities frequently cooperated with partisans and even sponsored irregular units when it suited their purposes.

Though the military operations of the East Tennessee guerrillas were not negligible, their political operations were much more significant. Through their campaign of murder, intimidation, and destruction, Unionists gained control of much of East Tennessee, impeded Confederate policies, and ensured a significant role for Unionists in the formation and implementation of Federal occupation policies. By the time the war ended in 1865 East Tennessee had become a stronghold of radical Unionism in the South. It provided the foundation for Tennessee's reconstruction, and it remained Republican when most of the South reverted to the control of the Democratic Party. But secessionists were not silent, and in southern East Tennessee they devastated Unionist communities and forced many loyalists to flee.

The intensity of the guerrilla war stemmed partly from the personalization of the conflict and partly from the lack of institutions to channel and regulate the violence. Partisan fighting corrupted all institutions in East Tennessee, and partisans employed the political system, the military, and even the churches as weapons. Only one establishment, the courts, proved somewhat resistant to manipulation for partisan purposes. Confederate district court judge West Humphreys refused to cooperate with attempted persecutions of Unionists, and dozens of Unionists found refuge in his court. Similarly, during Reconstruction the Federal district court blocked the attempted prosecution of secessionists for treason, and even many state and county courts eventually undermined attempts at revenge. Thus the East Tennessee war reveals the importance of institutions and laws in controlling the use of force.

Confederate commanders attempted but failed to find a combination of conciliation and coercion that would subdue the loyalist population. Three factors hampered their efforts to end the Unionist resistance. The first was the strategic insignificance of this department. East Tennessee's most valuable assets were its copper deposits and its rail lines, which connected the Gulf states with Virginia and sent thousands of Deep South recruits to the defense of Richmond. These factors were not negligible, but in the scope of the whole conflict East Tennessee was a backwater theater. It held no major cities, ports, rivers, or industrial centers that demanded defense, and politically its influence was small. Other areas took precedence over East Tennessee, and commanders there were constantly short on manpower and supplies.[1]

A second problem was lack of consistency in Confederate policy. This weakness stemmed partly from policy shifts in Richmond and partly from the rapid turnover of department commanders. In the twenty-eight months that the Confederacy held formal control of East Tennessee, eight different men headed the department. The longest tenure, that of General Edmund Kirby Smith, was ten months; the shortest was seventeen days. This revolving door of command prevented both the implementation of consistent policies and the establishment of trust, or at least understanding, between the commander and the rebellious population. Promising initiatives lapsed, and Unionists felt unable to trust any Confederate pronouncements.[2]

A final difficulty was the attitudes of the officers and men stationed in this theater. The people of East Tennessee possessed a reputation as ignorant and primitive, and many Confederate soldiers despised the people they were sent to govern. East Tennessee was also far from the major battlefields of the war, and there was little glory to be won there. Finally, occupation duty was dull and demoralizing, and many soldiers hated service in East Tennessee and were glad to leave. These attitudes made it difficult for Confederate forces to act as a reconciling agent.

Federal authorities made few attempts to conciliate the secessionist population. Instead, they relied on loyalty oaths, mass arrests, and Unionist forces to control dissent. Union officers established very strict standards of loyalty, and they freely jailed or exiled anyone considered a possible threat. But the harshness of Union policy aroused great bitterness, even among loyalists. Furthermore, Federal authorities failed either to protect their own supporters against Confederate bands or curb the depredations of Union troops.

Confederate and Union policies in East Tennessee exhibited a number of similarities. Union commanders rotated in and out of the theater almost as frequently as their Confederate counterparts, and many Federal troops demonstrated the same hostility and resentment toward the population. Northern and Southern commanders also adopted equivalent legal positions concerning disloyalty, and they utilized many of the same measures to control dissent, including imprisonment, loyalty oaths, confiscation, and exile. And commanders on both sides were frustrated in their attempts to persuade their governments to adopt flexible policies in this troubled region.

The differences between the two occupations are equally significant. The primary Confederate aims were to win the loyalties of the population and persuade or force Unionists to submit to conscription and other war measures. Thus their policies for controlling disloyalty were essentially political. Union authorities, conversely, took a police approach. Beyond circulating Lincoln's Proclamation of Amnesty and Reconstruction, they did little to attempt to win over the secessionist population. The thrust of Union policy was to bind all secessionists through the loyalty oath and remove or silence anyone threatening Federal control. In part, these differences were a response to variations in the situation that each side faced, but in part they also reflected fundamental differences in perspective and philosophy. In the Southern view, East Tennesseans were Confederate citizens, subject to common obligations and burdens, but also entitled to common rights and protections. This perception eroded as Confederate frustrations increased, but it did moderate Southern policies. Brigadier General Felix K. Zollicoffer, Major General Edmund Kirby Smith, and Major General Sam Jones all advocated restraint and attempted to deflect demands from Richmond and East Tennessee secessionists for harsher measures against Unionists.

Conversely, Union authorities viewed East Tennessee as enemy territory and felt less obliged to conciliate, persuade, or woo the disaffected. As a consequence, Union policies were less restrained than Confederate. Federal authorities freely arrested and banished a large number of secessionists, and nowhere in Union records does one find the references to restraint and moderation that were so common in Confederate exchanges. Evidence for the relative harshness of Federal policy can also be found by comparing the number of prisoners held by each side. The most complete list of Federal prisoners in the District of East Tennessee shows that between November 1863 and April 1865 925 citizens were detained at Knoxville at one time or another, the great majority for political offenses. A separate record lists 492 political arrests in the period from September 1863 through April 1864. Given the incompleteness of Union records, as well as the many arrests made by local commanders or deputy provost marshals that never appeared in headquarters records, a conservative estimate would place the number of political arrests at over one thousand. Since East Tennessee recorded about fifteen thousand votes for secession in June 1861, this represents a significant portion of the disloyal population. The number of Unionists confined in Confederate prisons was far smaller. Following the November 1861 uprising, Southern officials arrested perhaps one thousand Unionists and sent over two hundred of these to military prisons in the Deep South. Confederate prison records for 1862 list a total of two hundred Unionists detained for political offenses. These records are also incomplete, but since East Tennessee recorded almost 35,000 Unionist votes in the June 1861 referendum, the Federal total is quite high in comparison with the Confederate.[3]

At the same time, the appearance of Confederate restraint is somewhat deceiving. Where Federal officers employed imprisonment, Confederate officials used conscription to control dissent, forcing loyalists into the army, into hiding, or out of Confederate territory. The flight of thousands of Unionists to Kentucky reduced the threat to Confederate control and thus the need for large numbers of arrests. Most importantly, policies of restraint had little effect on local secessionist officials, who confiscated the property of hundreds of Unionists, or on Confederate troops, who relentlessly pursued loyalist refugees and draft evaders and abused Unionist families. And Confederate commanders, despite their policy of leniency, did little to restrain Southern troops.

Unionists won the war in East Tennessee. They exacted vengeance on their enemies, gained some vindication for their stance in 1861, drove dozens of secessionists from the region, and temporarily excluded Southern supporters from the political process. Though many secessionist refugees eventually returned to East Tennessee, many others did not, and Unionists-turned-Republicans dominated East Tennessee long after the war. At the same time, the increasing demands of the war divided loyalists. The same conservatism that led Unionists such as T. A. R. Nelson and Connelly F. Trigg to oppose secession in 1861 also turned them against the radical policies of emancipation and disfranchisement. The result was that the Unionist victory was diminished.

The tragedy of East Tennessee Unionists was that they fit comfortably into no region and no party. Conservative Unionists could not follow the South in 1861, but they also could not accept many Northern policies during the war and Reconstruction. The Civil War left Southern conservatives with no political home, for they could neither embrace Republicanism nor join with their lifelong opponents in the Democratic Party. In the early 1870s conservatives favored the formation of a third party that would unite moderates in both the North and the South, but this scheme quickly collapsed. Yet many radicals were also uncomfortable with their alliance with the North and the transformation of racial relations, and it is significant that the Republican Party revived in East Tennessee only by distancing itself from Reconstruction policies and focusing on local issues. Well after the war, East Tennesseans remained uncertain of their identity and their future.

Interpretations of East Tennessee Unionism

The desire to preserve the Union intact was widespread in the Upper South in late 1860 and early 1861. Tennessee, Virginia, and North Carolina all developed Unionist parties with substantial support, rejected secession in February 1861, and supported compromise efforts. Unionism in the Upper South was a powerful sentiment, but it was also conditional. When the fighting at Fort Sumter ended hopes for a reconciliation, most Unionists abandoned their position and joined the Confederacy.

Unionism in East Tennessee, therefore, was a distinct sentiment, comparable only to the loyalism of West Virginia. It was not premised on a set of conditions, and it was strong enough to withstand the most strenuous Confederate assaults. A few East Tennessee Unionists did convert at the beginning of hostilities, while others fell away in response to Confederate repression or Northern policies such as emancipation. But there remained a large group of hard-core loyalists whose commitment to the United States was unalterable. Unionism in East Tennessee was an ideological commitment that emerged in December 1860 and reflected a wholesale rejection of secession and the Confederacy.

The causes of East Tennessee's loyalism have received more attention than any other topic in the region's past. One of the first historians of the East Tennessee war, Thomas William Humes, attributed Unionism to two factors: the region's tradition of patriotism and service to the United States, evidenced by such events as the battle of King's Mountain, and its lack of involvement in slavery and cotton production. Humes's contemporary, Oliver P. Temple, agreed that these factors contributed to East Tennessee's rejection of secession, but he emphasized two other elements: the influence of the Whig Party in East Tennessee, and the unyielding stance of East Tennessee's Unionist leaders. Drawing a contrast with the capitulation of John Bell and other Middle Tennessee Whigs, Temple argued that only the refusal of loyalist leaders to submit to secession frustrated Southern machinations and enabled East Tennessee's nascent Unionism to survive and triumph.[1]

Historical studies in the twentieth century have tended to repeat the interpretations developed by Humes and Temple. Thomas Perkins Abernathy attributed East Tennessee's rejection of secession to the influence of party divisions, the effective guidance provided by Unionist leaders, a hatred of the slaveholding elite, and the desire of East Tennesseans to escape the political dominance of Middle Tennessee. Thomas B. Alexander conceded that economic and geographic factors contributed to East Tennessee's rejection of secession, but he agreed with Temple's assertion that without decisive leadership the region's Unionist impulse would never have survived. Stanley J. Folmsbee, Robert E. Corlew, and Enoch L. Mitchell attributed East Tennessee's Unionism to its sense of isolation from the slaveholding South and its sense of uniqueness.[2]

More recent studies have confirmed the importance of party, slavery, and geography in determining voting for or against secession in Tennessee. Ralph Wooster demonstrated that counties choosing secessionist delegates tended to have a higher percentage of slaves in the population, a greater per-capita wealth, and a history of supporting Democratic candidates. He concluded, however, that the most obvious dividing factor in Tennessee was geography. In the February referendum, East Tennessee, the river counties of West Tennessee, and the Highland Rim counties of Middle Tennessee all opposed holding a convention. In June the most obvious split over secession was between East Tennessee and the rest of the state. Similarly, Daniel Crofts concluded that the primary influences in Tennessee were slaveholding and party affiliation. Yet Crofts also pointed out that citizens were more greatly influenced by their community's slaveholding status than by their own as individuals, for nonslaveholders in regions with high slave concentrations tended to support secession. And Crofts agreed with Wooster that in the June referendum the most obvious dividing factor in Tennessee may have been geography.[3]

Other historians have attributed the Unionist-secessionist split to social and political divisions in antebellum East Tennessee. James Patton argued that urban dwellers and more wealthy residents tended to support the Confederacy, while inhabitants of poorer nonslaveholding regions generally clung to the Union. Eric Lacy, while conceding that geography, slavery, and leadership partially explained East Tennessee's loyalism, argued that sectional and political splits within East Tennessee were more influential. Lacy asserted that disagreements among upper, middle, and lower East Tennessee in the antebellum period over funding for internal improvements had divided the region and created resentments that lasted into the Civil War. Pointing out that five of the six East Tennessee counties supporting secession were located in the southern part of the region,

Lacy argued that since the Unionist movement was identified with upper East Tennessee leaders such as T. A. R. Nelson, voters in the lower counties tended to support secession.[4]

The most comprehensive interpretation of East Tennessee Unionism is found in Charles F. Bryan's unpublished dissertation, "The Civil War in East Tennessee: A Social, Political, and Economic Study." Bryan concluded that loyalism resulted primarily from the region's isolation and sense of uniqueness. East Tennessee's physical separation from the rest of the South, its lack of transportation links, and its economic and cultural differences all cut the region off from political currents in the rest of the South and created an alternate set of loyalties. Bryan agreed that resentment concerning the loss of political power to Middle Tennessee and the dominance of the Whig Party played a role, but he denied that there existed any clear correlation between voting on secession and either slavery or wealth.[5]

Finally, W. Todd Groce provided a highly original interpretation of the Confederate side in an unpublished dissertation, "Mountain Rebels: East Tennessee Confederates and the Civil War, 1860–1870." Groce argued that the completion of the East Tennessee rail system in the 1850s altered the political landscape. The railroads created a boom in wheat production, which in turn led to the emergence of a new group of merchants and lawyers who marketed wheat to Southern states such as Georgia. This group tended to be relatively young and relatively wealthy, to live in the towns along the railroads, to have extensive business and personal contacts in other Southern states, and to vote Democratic. Groce portrayed this group as a "rising commercial professional middle class" who had previously been shut out of politics and who were in conflict with an older, more conservative merchant class, which in some cases included their fathers. Groce also argued that farmers who voted for secession tended to inhabit areas that were developing rapidly, while Unionists generally came from areas that were economically stagnant. Groce thus drew a contrast between Southern supporters who had an optimistic view of a future under Southern rule and Unionists who were fearful about their prospects.[6]

To attempt to identify more precisely the causes of East Tennessee's Unionism, this study statistically compared a number of economic and social factors with the votes against secession in the June 1861 referendum. Initially twelve elements from the 1860 census—percent of slaveholders, planters, and slaves in the population, aggregate wealth per free inhabitant, land value (dollars per acre), total farm value, percent of improved acres, farm size, capital invested in manufacturing per free inhabitant, and production of cotton (in bales), tobacco (in pounds), and wheat (in bushels) per farm—were selected. Means for these data were calculated for each of Tennessee's eighty-four counties. Two additional factors, region (East, Middle, West) and the percent of votes for John Bell in the 1860 presidential election, were then added.

The next step was to determine the coefficients of correlation among these twelve characteristics. As Table A-1 shows, a number of these factors are closely related. For example, the percent of slaveholders in the population is highly correlated with the percent of planters, the percent of slaves, and wealth, while land values are also linked with wealth. This study identified all correlations greater than .750 and removed one of the factors. The result was that nine characteristics were retained.

Finally, the regressions between the vote against secession in the June 1861 referendum and these nine characteristics were calculated, first for each single factor and then for combinations of factors. As Tables A-2 and A-3 demonstrate, the most significant factor influencing voting against secession in Tennessee was region, which by itself explained about 55 percent of the vote. The second most significant factor was slaveholding, at 42 percent, while the third was the vote for Bell, at 22 percent. Taken together these three factors explain about 75 percent of the vote against secession, though since slaveholding and region are slightly correlated this figure should be used with caution. (See Table A-4.) These results compare very closely with those obtained by Daniel Crofts in *Reluctant Confederates*. Crofts demonstrated a somewhat stronger link between voting in the 1860 presidential election and voting on secession, but this variation may have resulted from the use of slightly different voting figures and statistical methods. Importantly, no economic factor, either in isolation or in combination with other characteristics, explains a significant percentage of the voting in Tennessee.

These statistical results support two common interpretations of East Tennessee's Unionism, the relative absence of slavery and the influence of the Whig Party. They also suggest that other character-istics that appeared to set East Tennessee apart, including the lack of staple crop production and the substitution of wheat as a money crop, had little effect on the region's attitude toward secession. Fi-nally, these results reveal the impact of sectional divisions on the voting concerning secession. East Tennessee's geographic isolation, its separate sense of identity, and its history created a different set of loyalties and divided much of East Tennessee from the rest of the state and the South. These conclusions concerning voting on seces-sion are rather general, and there is little doubt that local political, social, economic, and cultural influences were equally important in determining individual votes. Yet the fact that most counties voted heavily either for or against secession suggests that large-scale influ-ences were indeed significant.

The validity of other explanations that have been advanced is less certain. The evidence concerning the influence of class, for ex-ample, is quite inconclusive. Some contemporary observers con-cluded that East Tennesseans did divide along the line of wealth. Humes claimed that East Tennessee secessionists came from the ranks of "the rich and persons of the best social position." Confed-erate colonel Samuel Doak asserted that the majority of the lower class took the Union side, and in February 1864 a Methodist minis-ter in Chattanooga reported that "the rich are rebels the poor are ig-norant but beginning to be loyal." But most statements concerning class divisions were made by Confederates who wished to portray the Unionist party as a movement of ignorant, inconsequential men. And certainly Unionist leaders matched or exceeded their secession-ist rivals in terms of wealth and status.[7]

The evidence concerning leadership is also mixed. Unionist lead-ers were undoubtedly courageous and politically shrewd, and An-drew Johnson clearly influenced numbers of Democratic voters in upper East Tennessee. But the leadership interpretation contains at least two flaws. First, it emphasizes the few successes of South-ern Unionist leaders, while ignoring their many failures. Second, it overlooks the mutual influence between leaders and followers. Unionist spokesmen helped mobilize Unionist sentiment, but they could not have campaigned at all if public opinion had been as hos-tile in East Tennessee as it was in the rest of the state.

TABLE A-1. *Coefficients of Correlation*

	SLVH	PLNT	WLTH	LAND	IMPR	FARM	LFRM	MANF	CTTN	TBCO
PLNT	.883									
WLTH	.907	.888								
LAND	.647	.442	.756							
IMPR	.636	.443	.630	.789						
FARM	.643	.562	.832	.878	.632					
LFRM	.675	.812	.788	.388	.445	.630				
MANF	.020	.038	.020	.043	−.061	.154	.081			
CTTN	.337	.437	.371	.045	.053	.146	.414	.004		
TBCO	.288	.155	.154	.159	.122	.070	−.073	.100	.105	
SLVS	.918	.845	.857	.581	.527	.622	.649	.012	.327	.271

Key:

SLVH = percentage of slaveholders in the population.
PLNT = percentage of planters in the population.
WLTH = aggregate wealth per free inhabitant.
LAND = value of land per acre.
IMPR = percentage of improved acres.
FARM = total farm value.
LFRM = percentage of farms 500 acres or greater.
MANF = capital invested in manufacturing per free inhabitant.
CTTN = bales of cotton produced per farm.
TBCO = pounds of tobacco produced per farm.
SLVS = percentage of slaves in population.

TABLE A-2. *Single Regressions, Vote against Secession*

	R-SQ (percent)
SLVH	41.8
LAND	15.0
LFRM	7.9
MANF	0.0
CTTN	6.1
TBCO	2.4
WHEAT	6.5
REGION	54.9
VOTE FOR JOHN BELL	22.3

TABLE A-3. *Multiple Regressions, Vote against Secession*

	R-SQ (percent)
CTTN, TBCO, WHEAT	14.1
SLVH, LAND, LFRM	44.0
SLVH, LAND, LFRM, CTTN, TBCO	43.9
SLVH, CTTN, TBCO, WHEAT	44.3
SLVH, REGION	62.3
SLVH, VOTE FOR JOHN BELL	66.3
REGION, VOTE FOR JOHN BELL	63.0
SLVH, REGION, VOTE FOR JOHN BELL	74.3

TABLE A-4. *Single Regressions, Region*

	R-SQ (percent)
SLVH	36.5
LAND	5.9
LFRM	7.1
MANF	0.0
CTTN	13.1
WHEAT	32.1
VOTE FOR JOHN BELL	7.9

Unionist Informants and the Death of John Hunt Morgan

On September 3, 1864, Brigadier General John Hunt Morgan, then in command of the Confederate District of East Tennessee and West Virginia, was killed by Federal cavalry at Greeneville, Tennessee. Three Federal regiments surprised Morgan's troopers at night and shot Morgan in a garden outside the house where he had been sleeping. Morgan was a dramatic and heroic figure, and his death was a sensational event that quickly became surrounded by legends. Many Confederates asserted that Morgan had been betrayed, while many Unionists claimed credit for leading Union cavalry to Morgan's location.

One of these was loyalist James Leahy, a twelve-year-old farm boy. Leahy asserted that he had met some of Morgan's men on the road near Greeneville and that they had stolen a bag of meal that he was carrying home. Angry at his loss, Leahy claimed that he had sought out Major General Alvin C. Gillem and informed him that Confederate cavalry were at Greeneville. Gillem then mounted the expedition that led to Morgan's death. James A. Ramage, one of Morgan's biographers, accepted Leahy's story as valid and noted that after the war Gillem took Leahy to Nashville and paid for his education.[1]

But Leahy's story did not go uncontested. Sarah Thompson, a loyalist woman from Greeneville, asserted that it was she who provided the critical intelligence to Union officers. Thompson's story was quite dramatic. She claimed that after the Federal invasion her husband had served as a Union courier and had been captured and executed as a spy by some of Morgan's men in 1864. A few months after this event Morgan and some his cavalry rode into Greeneville, came to Thompson's house, stole a quantity of food, and insulted her. In retaliation she rode to Bull's Gap and persuaded Union cavalry to ride to Greeneville, setting off the engagement that took Morgan's life. After the war Colonel John Brownlow (First Tennessee Cavalry), Lieutenant Edward J. Brooks (Tenth Michigan Cavalry), Lieutenant John Johnson (Thirteenth Tennessee Cavalry), Provost Marshal General Samuel P. Carter, and President Andrew

Johnson all gave depositions that corroborated Thompson's claims. But Thompson told this story in an attempt to secure pension benefits, and her veracity is questionable. Further, in the early 1890s Brownlow gave a much different account, stating that it was in fact Leahy who led Union forces to Morgan.[2]

Finally, there is a third version of this story, which states that a different Greeneville woman, Lucy Williams, betrayed Morgan to Federal troops. Williams was the daughter-in-law of Catherine Williams, the owner of the house where Morgan was staying when he was killed. Catherine Williams was a Confederate sympathizer, but Lucy Williams supported the Union, and her husband was a Federal soldier. She was therefore an obvious suspect. But a second Morgan biographer, Cecil Fletcher Holland, concluded that pieces of the evidence concerning Lucy Williams's whereabouts the night Morgan was killed are so conflicting as to make this story implausible. Holland in fact rejected all loyalist claims and concluded that chance alone brought Federal cavalry to Greeneville that night.[3]

Vote on Secession in Tennessee, June 1861

TABLE C-1 *Vote on Secession, by Region and County*

County	Yes	%	No	%	Total
EAST TENNESSEE					
Anderson	97	7.1	1,278	92.9	1,375
Bledsoe	197	28.3	500	71.7	697
Blount	418	19.1	1,766	80.9	2,184
Bradley	507	26.8	1,382	73.2	1,889
Campbell	59	5.6	1,000	94.4	1,059
Carter	86	6.0	1,343	94.0	1,429
Claiborne	250	16.7	1,243	83.3	1,493
Cocke	518	30.4	1,185	69.6	1,703
Cumberland	not available		not available		
Grainger	586	28.2	1,492	71.8	2,078
Greene	744	21.7	2,691	78.3	3,435
Hamilton	854	40.4	1,260	59.6	2,114
Hancock	279	30.7	630	69.3	909
Hawkins	908	38.3	1,460	61.7	2,368
Jefferson	603	23.3	1,987	76.7	2,590
Johnson	111	12.4	787	87.6	898
Knox	1,214	27.6	3,196	72.4	4,415
McMinn	904	44.1	1,144	55.9	2,048
Marion	414	40.8	600	59.2	1,014
Meigs	481	64.3	267	35.7	748
Monroe	1,096	58.6	774	41.4	1,870
Morgan	50	7.4	630	92.6	680
Polk	738	70.0	317	30.0	1,055
Rhea	360	64.1	202	35.9	562
Roane	454	22.5	1,568	77.5	2,022
Scott	19	3.5	521	96.5	540
Sequatchie	153	60.5	100	39.5	253
Sevier	60	3.8	1,528	96.2	1,588
Sullivan	1,586	71.7	627	28.3	2,213
Union	not available		not available		
Washington	1,022	41.4	1,445	58.6	2,467
MIDDLE TENNESSEE					
Bedford	1,595	68.7	727	31.3	2,322
Cannon	1,149	90.0	127	10.0	1,276
Cheatham	702	92.7	55	7.3	757

County	Yes	%	No	%	Total
Coffee	1,276	98.0	26	2.0	1,302
Davidson	5,635	93.3	402	6.7	6,037
Dekalb	883	57.9	642	42.1	1,525
Dickson	1,141	94.1	72	5.9	1,213
Fentress	128	16.4	651	83.6	779
Franklin	1,652	100.0	0	0.0	1,652
Giles	2,458	99.6	11	0.4	2,469
Grundy	528	98.3	9	1.7	537
Hardin	498	32.1	1,051	67.9	1,549
Hickman	1,400	99.8	3	0.2	1,403
Humphreys	1,042	100.0	0	0.0	1,042
Jackson	1,483	67.5	714	32.5	2,197
Lawrence	1,124	93.7	75	6.3	1,199
Lewis	223	94.1	14	5.9	237
Lincoln	2,912	100.0	0	0.0	2,912
Macon	447	39.1	697	60.1	1,144
Marshall	1,642	94.2	101	5.8	1,743
Maury	2,731	97.9	58	2.1	2,789
Montgomery	2,631	98.8	33	1.2	2,664
Overton	1,471	80.2	364	19.8	1,835
Putnam	not available		not available		
Robertson	3,839	99.6	17	0.4	3,856
Rutherford	2,392	97.0	73	3.0	2,465
Smith	1,249	64.9	676	35.1	1,925
Stewart	1,839	94.9	99	5.1	1,938
Sumner	6,465	98.9	69	1.1	6,534
Van Buren	308	96.0	13	4.0	321
Warren	1,419	99.2	12	0.8	1,431
Wayne	409	31.1	905	68.9	1,314
White	1,370	91.9	121	8.1	1,491
Williamson	1,949	98.6	28	1.4	1,977
Wilson	2,329	86.8	353	13.2	2,682

WEST TENNESSEE

County	Yes	%	No	%	Total
Benton	798	77.8	228	22.2	1,026
Carroll	967	41.8	1,349	58.2	2,316
Decatur	310	36.0	550	64.0	860
Dyer	811	87.5	116	12.5	927
Fayette	1,364	98.3	23	1.7	1,387
Gibson	1,999	88.2	268	11.8	2,267
Hardeman	1,526	98.1	29	1.9	1,555
Haywood	930	87.0	139	13.0	1,069
Henderson	801	44.2	1,013	55.8	1,814
Henry	1,746	84.6	317	15.4	2,063
Lauderdale	763	99.1	7	0.9	770
McNairy	1,318	69.2	586	30.8	1,904

County	Yes	%	No	%	Total
Madison	2,754	99.3	20	0.7	2,774
Obion	2,996	97.9	64	2.1	3,060
Perry	780	82.3	168	17.7	948
Shelby	7,132	99.9	5	0.1	7,137
Tipton	943	98.3	16	1.7	959
Weakley	1,189	49.7	1,201	50.3	2,390

NOTES

ABBREVIATIONS

DU   William R. Perkins Library, Manuscript Department, Duke
        University, Durham, N.C.
LC   Library of Congress, Manuscript Division, Washington, D.C.
MC   McClung Collection, Lawson McGhee Library, Knoxville, Tenn.
MHI   Military History Institute, Carlisle Barracks, Carlisle, Pa.
OR   *The War of the Rebellion. A Compilation of the Official Records of the
        Union and Confederate Armies.* 128 vols. Washington, D.C.:
        Government Printing Office, 1880–1900. Cited by volume and page
        number, with part number, where relevant, in parentheses. All
        references are to Series 1 unless otherwise indicated.
NA   National Archives, Washington, D.C.
NASR   National Archives, Southeast Region, Atlanta, Ga.
NSCA   North Carolina State Archives, Raleigh
SHC   Southern Historical Collection, University of North Carolina
        Library, Chapel Hill
TSLA   Tennessee State Library and Archives, Nashville
UTSC   University of Tennessee Library, Special Collections, Knoxville

INTRODUCTION

1. Fellman, *Inside War*; Ash, *When the Yankees Came*; Grimsley, *Hard Hand of War*; Ash, *Middle Tennessee Society Transformed*; Escott, *Many Excellent People*; Barrett, *Civil War in North Carolina*; Brownlee, *Gray Ghosts*.

2. Rhea, *Battle of the Wilderness*; Cozzens, *This Terrible Sound*; Linderman, *Embattled Courage*.

3. Readers interested in the effects of the Civil War on East Tennessee's society, economy, and racial system should consult Charles F. Bryan's excellent "The Civil War in East Tennessee: A Social, Political, and Economic Study," (Ph.D. diss., University of Tennessee, 1978).

CHAPTER ONE

1. Bryan, "East Tennessee," stresses East Tennessee's geographic and political isolation from the rest of the South as a cause of that region's peculiar loyalties. For studies of other Southern Appalachian regions, see Noe, *Southwest Virginia's Railroad*; Inscoe, *Mountain Masters*; Dunn, *Cades Cove*; Paludan, *Victims*.

2. Folmsbee, Corlew, and Mitchell, *Short History*, 50–59, 64–70.

3. Ibid., 56–57.

4. Ibid., 59–78; Temple, *East Tennessee*, 4–38; Humes, *Loyal Mountaineers*, 37–56.

5. Lacy, "Franklin"; Folmsbee, Corlew, and Mitchell, *Short History*, 79–94; Samuel Cole Williams, *Lost State of Franklin*; Abernathy, *Frontier*, 67–90, 310; Humes, *Loyal Mountaineers*, 57–76.

6. Folmsbee, Corlew, and Mitchell, *Short History*, 98–113.

7. Bergeron, *Politics*, 1–8; Folmsbee, Corlew, and Mitchell, *Short History*, 126–36, 164–66.

8. Bergeron, *Politics*; Walton, "Second Party System"; Folmsbee, Corlew, and Mitchell, *Short History*, 178–210.

9. Bergeron, *Politics*, 32–34, 148–56; Lowrey, "Tennessee Voters."

10. Lacy, *Vanquished Volunteers*; Alexander, *Political Reconstruction*, 12–13.

11. Humphrey, *Brownlow*, 1–17; Coulter, *Brownlow*, 1–34, 53–83; Brownlow, *Secession*, 16–21.

12. Bellamy, "Landon Carter Haynes"; Humphrey, *Brownlow*, 18–23, 60–64; Coulter, *Brownlow*, 36–40; Patton, *Unionism*, 78–79.

13. Humphrey, *Brownlow*, 17–18, 99–102; Coulter, *Brownlow*, 46–48; Patton, *Unionism*, 79–80.

14. Coulter, *Brownlow*, 48–49; Brownlow, *Secession*, 214–17; *Knoxville Whig*, Aug. 31, 1860.

15. Humphrey, *Brownlow*, 143–46; Turner, "William Montgomery Churchwell."

16. Haskins, "Internecine Strife"; Alexander, "Strange Bedfellows."

17. Abernathy, *Frontier*, 1–32, 181–93; Mary Emily Robertson Campbell, *Attitude*, 35; Carroll, "Tennessee Sectionalism," 120–23, 190, 355.

18. Bergeron, *Politics*, 41–42, 66, 112–18; Folmsbee, Corlew, and Mitchell, *Short History*, 108–9, 136–37, 141; Alexander, *Nelson*, 41–46; Folmsbee, *Sectionalism*, 147, 184–85, 196–97, 212–21.

19. Trefousse, *Johnson*, 48; Bergeron, *Politics*, 41–42; Lacy, *Volunteers*, 121; Bryan, "East Tennessee," 48; Lacy, "Franklin," 321–32; Carroll, "Sectionalism," 418–28; D. C. Trewhitt to L. C. Houk, May 23, 1866, Leonidas Campbell and John C. Houk Papers, MC; W. B. Reese to Oliver P. Temple, Apr. 21, 1866, Oliver P. Temple Papers, UTSC.

20. Dunn, *Cades Cove*, 123–29; Degler, *Other South*, 79–81; Dillon, "Anti-Slavery Editors"; Folmsbee, Corlew, and Mitchell, *Short History*, 172–76, 223–25; Mooney, "Question of Slavery"; Coulter, *Brownlow*, 89–91; Temple, *East Tennessee*, 85–95, 111.

21. Hsiung, "Isolation and Integration," 1–80; Folmsbee, Corlew, and Mitchell, *Short History*, 5–11; Law, *Geography of Tennessee*; Clarke, *Yeomen*, 13, 22–26; John C. Campbell, *Highlander*.

22. Groce, "Mountain Rebels," 1–29; Dunn, *Cades Cove*, 63–89; U.S. Census Bureau, *Statistics*, 132–39, 215.

23. Hsiung, "Isolation and Integration," 81–124; Coulter, *Brownlow*, 85–86; U.S. Census Bureau, *Statistics*, 238–39, 348.

24. Folmsbee, Corlew, and Mitchell, *History of Tennessee*, 1:371–400; Coul-

ter, *Brownlow*, 86–89; Abernathy, *Frontier*, 153–58; Abernathy, "Whig Party"; John C. Campbell, *Highlander*, 46–48.

25. Hsiung, "Isolation and Integration," 154–96; Folmsbee, "Railroad Movement"; James W. Holland, "East Tennessee & Virginia"; James W. Holland, "East Tennessee & Georgia."

26. Groce, "Mountain Rebels," 1–52. For a description of similar developments in another Southern Appalachian region, see Noe, *Southwest Virginia*.

27. Clark, *Yeomen*, 8–9, 26–68; Owsley, "Rural Tennessee"; U.S. Census Bureau, *Statistics*, 132–39, 215.

28. Mary Emily Robertson Campbell, *Attitude*, 26; U.S. Census Bureau, *Statistics*, 132–39, 215.

29. Mary Emily Robertson Campbell, *Attitude*, 17–19; England, "Free Negro"; Clark, *Yeomen*, 9–20; U.S. Census Bureau, *Statistics*, 238–39, 348.

30. U.S. Census Bureau, *Statistics*, 238–39, 348.

31. Haskins, "Internecine Strife," portrays antebellum East Tennessee as a region of conflicting economic and political tendencies.

CHAPTER TWO

1. Bergeron, *Politics*, 103–47; Mary Emily Robertson Campbell, *Attitude*, 34–123; Joseph H. Parks, *John Bell*, 289–330; Joseph H. Parks, "Tennessee Whigs"; Webb, "Slavery Question."

2. Crofts, *Reluctant*, 81–89; Bergeron, *Politics*, 162–66; Mary Emily Robertson Campbell, *Attitude*, 104–35; Folmsbee, Corlew, and Mitchell, *Tennessee*, 3:23–28.

3. Crofts, *Reluctant*, 90–102; Mary Emily Robertson Campbell, *Attitude*, 134–44, 154–55; Folmsbee, Corlew, and Mitchell, *Tennessee*, 3:28–30; William G. McAdoo Diary, Nov. 9, 1860, Nov. 12, 1860, Jan. 1, 1861, Floyd-McAdoo Papers, LC.

4. Trefousse, *Johnson*, 128–29; Lacy, *Volunteers*, 170; Temple, *East Tennessee*, 147–49, 166–79; Humes, *Loyal Mountaineers*, 80–81; Brownlow, *Secession*, 191–207; *Knoxville Whig*, Aug. 11, 1860, Nov. 17, 1860, Jan. 19, 1861; Andrew Jackson Fletcher to T. A. R. Nelson, Dec. 18, 1860, Andrew Jackson Fletcher Correspondence, TSLA.

5. Crofts, *Reluctant*, 144–53; Mary Emily Robertson Campbell, *Attitude*, 158–63; Folmsbee, Corlew, and Mitchell, *Tennessee*, 3:31–32.

6. Crofts, *Reluctant*, 146–47, 149–52; Mary Emily Robertson Campbell, *Attitude*, 175–79, 288–90.

7. Temple, *East Tennessee*, 147–49; William G. McAdoo Diary, Nov. 30, Dec. 12, Dec. 20, 1860, Floyd-McAdoo Papers, LC.

8. Crofts, *Reluctant*, 90–91, 102–4, 144–53; Mary Emily Robertson Campbell, *Attitude*, 171–75; Humes, *Loyal Mountaineers*, 90–92; Brownlow, *Secession*, 28–30; Joseph C. C. McDannel to Andrew Johnson, Dec. 29, 1860, Mortier F. Johnson to Johnson, Dec. 31, 1860, Richard M. Edwards to Johnson, Jan. 2, 1862, Graf, Haskins, and Bergeron, *Johnson Papers*, 4:102, 107–8, 119–20; *Knoxville Whig*, Jan. 12, 1861.

9. Crofts, *Reluctant*, 130–36, 153–54, 164–95; Henry, "Revolution"; Patton, *Unionism*, 7.

10. Crofts, *Reluctant*, 262–73, 277–83, 296–97, 327; Henry, "Revolution"; Blackstone McDannel to Johnson, Mar. 18, 1861, John C. McGaughy to Johnson, Mar. 28, 1861, Robert M. Barton to Johnson, Apr. 4, 1861, Charles A. Rice to Johnson, Apr. 5, 1861, Richard M. Edward to Johnson, Apr. 8, 1861, Graf, Haskins, and Bergeron, *Johnson Papers*, 4:404–5, 437–38, 459–61, 466–68, 469–70.

11. Crofts, *Reluctant*, 323–30; Mary Emily Robertson Campbell, *Attitude*, 190–96; Folmsbee, Corlew, and Mitchell, *Tennessee*, 3:32–38; Patton, *Unionism*, 7, 16–17.

12. Mary Emily Robertson Campbell, *Attitude*, 194–99; Folmsbee, Corlew, and Mitchell, *Tennessee*, 3:32–33, 37–38, 41; Patton, *Unionism*, 18–19.

13. Temple, *East Tennessee*, 121–25, 132–46, 158–76, 191–207, 231–32, 333–34; Humes, *Loyal Mountaineers*, 94–97; Hurlbut, *Bradley County*, 38–39, 46–49; Brownlow, *Secession*, 49, 92–95, 115–18; John Lellyet to Johnson, Jan. 23, 1861, Graf, Haskins, and Bergeron, *Johnson Papers*, 4:184–85; Oliver P. Temple to T. A. R. Nelson, Apr. 18, 1861, N. M. Heche to Nelson, Apr. 24, 1861, T. A. R. Nelson Papers, MC.

14. Alexander, *Nelson*, 76–83; Temple, *East Tennessee*, 179–204; Humes, *Loyal Mountaineers*, 100–102.

15. Stryker, *Johnson*, 86–87; Winston, *Johnson*, 194–95, 204; *Knoxville Whig*, Dec. 22, 1860, Jan. 12, 1861, Jan. 26, 1861. For a more complete account of the Unionist interpretation of secession, see Fisher, "Definitions of Loyalty."

16. Horace Maynard, "How, By Whom, and for What the War Was Begun," Mar. 20, 1862, and "To the Slaveholders of Tennessee," July 4, 1863, Horace Maynard Papers, UTSC; Temple, *East Tennessee*, 309, 558; William Randolph Carter, *First Tennessee*, 14–15, 19. For a discussion of the relationship between republicanism, race, and the concept of independence, see Stephanie McCurry, "The Two Faces of Republicanism: Gender and Proslavery Politics in Antebellum South Carolina," *Journal of American History* 78 (1991–92): 1245–64.

17. D. Young to Governor William B. Campbell, June 3, 1861, Campbell Family Papers, DU; C. M. Melville to T. A. R. Nelson, May 9, 1861, T. A. R. Nelson Papers, MC; David M. Key to Lizzie, Loudon, May 6, 1861, David McKendree Key Papers, SHC.

18. Trefousse, *Johnson*, 53–54, 61; Graf, "Andrew Johnson"; Winston, *Johnson*, 50, 164–65; Clifton R. Hall, *Johnson*, 20–31, 91–92; *Knoxville Whig*, Feb. 20, 1864; J. J. Jones to Johnson, June 15, 1861, Graf, Haskins, and Bergeron, *Johnson Papers*, 4:486–87, C. M. Melville to Johnson, Nov. 29, 1861, Graf, Haskins, and Bergeron, *Johnson Papers*, 5:38. For slaveholding by Unionists, see Trefousse, *Johnson*, 45; Alexander, *Nelson*, 47–48; Coulter, *Brownlow*, 79–80; Temple, *Notable Men* , 9; Brownlow, *Secession*, 7, 37, 105–13.

19. Clifton R. Hall, *Johnson*, 28; Temple, *East Tennessee*, 121–25, 132–46, 158–76, 191–207, 231–32, 333–34, 558; Hurlbut, *Bradley County*, 38–39, 46–49; Brownlow, *Secession*, 49, 92–95, 115–18; *Knoxville Whig*, Jan. 12, 1861;

John Lellyet to Johnson, Jan. 23, 1861, Graf, Haskins, and Bergeron, *Johnson Papers*, 4:184–85; Oliver P. Temple to T. A. R. Nelson, Apr. 18, 1861, N. M. Heche to Nelson, Apr. 24, 1861, T. A. R. Nelson Papers, MC.

20. *Knoxville Whig*, Jan. 26, 1861; Alexander, *Nelson*, 76–83; Temple, *East Tennessee*, 557–58; A. W. Howe to T. A. R. Nelson, Apr. 14, 1861, T. A. R. Nelson Papers, MC.

21. Alexander, *Nelson*, 76–83; Sullins, *Recollections*, 192–95; W. M. Stakely to Carrie Stakely, Apr. 27, 1861, Mary Caldwell to "Callie," May 14, 1861, Hall-Stakely Family Papers, MC; W. H. Churchwell to Colonel Landon Carter Haynes, May 6, 1861, A. E. Jackson to Haynes, May 17, 1861, John C. Gaut to T. A. R. Nelson, May 26, 1861, Nelson Papers, MC; L. F. Johnson to Johnson, May 6, 1861, Elkenah D. Rader to Johnson, Mar. 20, 1861, Graf, Haskins, and Bergeron, *Johnson Papers*, 4:418–19, 476; William A. Sorrell to Judge James S. Havron, May 8, 1861, Havron Collection, TSLA.

22. Winston, *Johnson*, 195–96; Temple, *East Tennessee*, 154–56; Humes, *Loyal Mountaineers*, 100, 347; Brownlow, *Secession*, 55–58.

23. Temple, *East Tennessee*, 192–95; Humes, *Loyal Mountaineers*, 120–21; Brownlow, *Secession*, 277–79.

24. Groce, "Mountain Rebels," 53–89; Crouch, "Merchant and Senator"; Stryker, *Johnson*, 79; Temple, *East Tennessee*, 233–36; Humes, *Loyal Mountaineers*, 81–85, 102; Brownlow, *Secession*, 208–9; R. M. Fisher et al. to Nelson, May 17, 1861, T. A. R. Nelson Papers, MC; [C. W. Charleton] to Amos A. Lawrence, May 15, May 23, June 6, 1861, Graf, Haskins, and Bergeron, *Johnson Papers*, 4:476–77; Colonel William W. Churchwell to Secretary of War L. P. Walker, May 25, 1861, copies of letters sent to the Confederate secretary of war and President Davis, RG 109, NA.

25. Bryan, "Tories"; Temple, *East Tennessee*, 340–43; Humes, *Loyal Mountaineers*, 103–15, 347–55; Mary Emily Robertson Campbell, *Attitude*, 201–4.

26. Groce, "Mountain Rebels," 53–89; Crofts, *Reluctant*, 342–44; Alexander, *Nelson*, 83–85; Mary Emily Robertson Campbell, *Attitude*, 205–7, 291–94; Folmsbee, Corlew, and Mitchell, *Tennessee*, 3:34–35; Temple, *East Tennessee*, 205–23; Humes, *Loyal Mountaineers*, 103–5; Brownlow, *Secession*, 222–23; W. R. Henly to Nelson, May 8, 1861, T. A. R. Nelson Papers, MC; Robert Johnson to Johnson, Apr. 29, 1861, Graf, Haskins, and Bergeron, *Johnson Papers*, 4:474–76.

27. Burns and Blankenship, *Fiddles*, 40–42, 49–50; Order No. 33, June 5, 1861, Orders, East Tennessee Brigade, 1861, RG 109, NA; David M. Key to Lizzie Key, June 10, 1861, David McKendree Key Papers, SHC; W. G McKinly to Newton Lillard, June 10, 1861, Lillard Family Papers, TSLA; George Ryan to Johnson and Emerson Etheridge, Aug. 24, 1861, H. C. Thompson to Andrew Johnson, Apr. 28, 1862, Graf, Haskins, and Bergeron, *Johnson Papers*, 4:693–94, 5:346–47.

28. Graf, Haskins, and Bergeron, *Johnson Papers*, 4:487, note 2; Crofts, *Reluctant*, 164–94.

29. Bryan, "Tories"; Alexander, *Nelson*, 84–87; Mary Emily Robertson Campbell, *Attitude*, 207–9; Ridenour, *Campbell County*, 57–58; Temple,

East Tennessee, 343–65, 565–73; Humes, *Loyal Mountaineers*, 115–19, 347–55; Temple, *Notable Men*, 104.

30. For defenses of the conservative course, see Temple, *East Tennessee*, 354–60; B. Frazier to Nelson, June 15, 1861, T. A. R. Nelson Papers, MC. For criticisms, see J. J. Jones to Nelson, June 8, 1861, John Murphy to Nelson, July 14, 1861, T. A. R. Nelson Papers, MC.

31. Dickson, *Violence*, 178–93; Franklin, *Militant South*, 131–33.

CHAPTER THREE

1. Folmsbee, Corlew, and Mitchell, *Short History*, 298.

2. Temple, *Notable Men*, 104; Ridenour, *Campbell County*, 57–58; William G. McAdoo Diary, Aug. 18, 1861, Floyd-McAdoo Papers, LC.

3. Livingood, *Hamilton County*, 157–61; Temple, *Notable Men*, 95–96; Hurlbut, *Bradley County*, 61–62, 68–77; William G. Swan to President Jefferson Davis, July 11, 1861, *OR*, Series 2, 1:828; General James E. Rains to his wife, Aug. 15, 1861, James E. Rains Letters, TSLA; Thomas Doak Edington Memoir, TSLA; David M. Key to Lizzie, July 30, 1861, David McKendree Key Papers, SHC; Milton P. Jarnagin, "Reminiscences of the War," TSLA; Robert A. Crawford to Nelson, July 18, 1861, T. A. R. Nelson Papers, MC; Samuel S. Bush to Johnson, July 15, 1861, Graf, Haskins, and Bergeron, *Johnson Papers*, 4:580–81.

4. General Orders No. 5, Aug. 26, 1861, General Orders No. 7, Sept. 7, 1861, General Orders No. 10, Sept. 10, 1861, General Orders No. 11, Aug. 26, 1861, General Orders No. 12, Sept. 1, 1861, General Orders No. 13, Sept. 12, 1861, General Orders No. 14, Sept. 14, 1861, General Orders No. 15, Sept. 19, 1861, Circulars, Letters, Orders Issued by Various Commands, Brigadier General Felix K. Zollicoffer, East Tennessee Brigade, 1861, RG 109, NA; Brigadier General Felix K. Zollicoffer to Colonel William F. Baldwin, Aug. 26, 1861, Sept. 1, 1861, Lieutenant Colonel George R. McClelland to Colonel William B. Wood, Nov. 9, 1861, Letter Book of Colonel W. B. Wood, Commanding Post at Knoxville, Tennessee, Oct. 14–Nov. 25, 1861, RG 109, NA; John Lillard to his father, July 12, 1861, John Lillard to his wife, Aug. 13, 1861, Lillard Family Papers, TSLA; G. M. White to Carrie Stakely, Aug. 13, 1861, Hall-Stakely Family Papers, MC.

5. Humes, *Loyal Mountaineers*, 131–32; William G. McAdoo Diary, Aug. 23, 1861, Floyd-McAdoo Papers, LC; George W. Keith to Johnson, July 12, 1861, Graf, Haskins, and Bergeron, *Johnson Papers*, 4:560–61.

6. Temple, *Notable Men*, 70–71, 123–27; Andrew Jackson Fletcher to Oliver P. Temple, July 26, 1861, Oct. 15, 1861, June 18, 1864, Oliver P. Temple Papers, UTSC.

7. David Campbell Scales to "William," Aug. 10, 1861, Scales and Campbell Family Papers, TSLA; John F. Milhollin to "Eve," Aug. 1, 1861, John F. Milhollin Letters, MHI; William G. McAdoo Diary, Aug. 20, 1861, Floyd-McAdoo Papers, LC; H. Watterson to William Watterson, June 7, 1861, MC.

8. H. R. Cox to Governor Isham G. Harris, June 10, 1861, S. B. Cockerill to

Governor Isham G. Harris, Aug. 8, 1861, Papers of the Governors, Isham G. Harris, TSLA; James W. Rogan to "His Excellency Jefferson Davis," July 1, 1861, Jefferson Davis Papers, DU; Harris to Davis, July 13, 1861, Isham G. Harris Papers, TSLA.

9. McKee, "Zollicoffer"; Stamper, "Zollicoffer"; Patton, *Unionism*, 15–16; Felix K. Zollicoffer to William B. Campbell, May 11, 1861, Campbell Family Papers, DU.

10. Adjutant and Inspector General Samuel Cooper to Zollicoffer, July 31, 1861, *OR* 4:377.

11. "To the People of East Tennessee," Aug. 7, 1861, Orders, East Tennessee Brigade, 1861, RG 109, NA.

12. Humes, *Loyal Mountaineers*, 120–23; *Knoxville Whig*, July 6, June 29, July 6, July 13, Oct. 12, Oct. 19, 1861; General Orders No. 5, Aug. 23, 1861, Orders and Letters Sent, Brigadier General Felix K. Zollicoffer, Aug. 1861–Jan. 1862, RG 109, NA; William G. McAdoo Diary, Aug. 18, 1861, Floyd-McAdoo Papers, LC.

13. Order 16, May 22, 1861, Special Order, Oct. 1861, East Tennessee Brigade, Orders, 1861, RG 109, NA; General Orders No. 48, Jan. 1, 1862, Orders and Letters Sent, Aug. 1861–Jan. 1862, Brigadier General Felix K. Zollicoffer, RG 109, NA.

14. Major General Leonidas Polk to Colonel Robertson Topp, Judge R. Caruthers, Dr. Jeptha Fowlkes, D. M. Leatherman, July 29, 1861, Robertson Topp Papers, TSLA; A. M. Lea to A. J. Bledsoe, Aug. 26, 1861, *OR* 4:393–94; Topp to Robert Josselyn, Oct. 20, 1861, copies of letters sent to the Confederate secretary of war and President Davis, RG 109, NA; Alex M. Clayton to Davis, July 31, 1861, Robertson Topp Papers, TSLA; Johnson and William B. Carter to Abraham Lincoln, Aug. 6, 1861, Graf, Haskins, and Bergeron, *Johnson Papers*, 4:669–70.

15. Landon Carter Haynes to Harris, June 15, 1861, Landon Carter Haynes Letters, TSLA; Sam Tate to Robert Toombs, June 28, 1861, P. G. T. Beauregard to Davis, June 27, 1861, J. L. Calhoun to Secretary of War L. P. Walker, June 30, 1861, *OR* 52(2):115–17, Polk to Davis, July 9, 1861, 4:365–66; Samuel P. Carter to Johnson, Aug. 7, 1861, Graf, Haskins, and Bergeron, *Johnson Papers*, 4:671–72.

16. Mary Emily Robertson Campbell, *Attitude*, 185–89, 210–12; Brownlow, *Secession*, 224–44; William G. Brownlow to Campbell, May 6, 1861, Campbell Family Papers, DU; George Bridges to Nelson, July 10, 1861, T. A. R. Nelson Papers, MC; R. M. McEwen to Temple, July 12, 1861, Oliver P. Temple Papers, UTSC.

17. McKee, "Zollicoffer," 45–46; Governor Harris to Walker, Aug. 3, 1861, Aug. 16, 1861, *OR*, Series 2, 1:830–31; Zollicoffer to Cooper, Aug. 6, 1861, Orders and Letters Sent, Brigadier General Felix K. Zollicoffer, Aug. 1861–Jan. 1862, RG 109, NA; Hannibal Paine to "Miss Jenny," Aug. 18, 1861, Paine Family Papers, TSLA.

18. Alexander, *Nelson*, 87–93; Temple, *East Tennessee*, 367–69; Zollicoffer to Cooper, Aug. 6, 1861, Orders and Letters Sent, Brigadier General Felix K. Zollicoffer, Aug. 1861–Jan. 1862, RG 109, NA; William H. Humphreys to Zolli-

coffer, Aug. 13, 1861, Nelson to Davis, "Statement" by Nelson, Aug. 12, 1861, T. A. R. Nelson Papers, MC.

19. Humes, *Loyal Mountaineers*, 141–46; Brownlow, *Secession*, 134–40; Robertson Topp to Robert Josselyn, Oct. 20, 1861, copies of letters sent to the Confederate secretary of war and President Davis, RG 109, NA; William G. McAdoo Diary, Oct. 12, 1861, Floyd-McAdoo Papers, LC; Andrew Jackson Fletcher to Temple, Oct. 15, 1861, Oliver P. Temple Papers, UTSC.

20. Groce, "Mountain Rebels," 152–80; Bryan, "East Tennessee," 75–76; *OR* 4:588–92; *OR*, Series 2, 1:1368–70.

21. Bryan, "East Tennessee," 79–82; Brownlow to Topp, Oct. 1, 1861, Robertson Topp Papers, TSLA.

22. Charles Wallace to Harris, Oct. 29, 1861, Reuben Davis to Davis, Nov. 4, 1861, *OR* 4:510–11; Zollicoffer to Cooper, Oct. 26, 1861, Colonel William B. Wood to Zollicoffer, Oct. 28, 1861, Wood to Secretary of War Judah P. Benjamin, Nov. 4, 1861, Letter Book of Colonel W. B. Wood, Commanding Post at Knoxville, Tennessee, Oct. 14–Nov. 25, 1861, RG 109, NA.

23. Zollicoffer to Lieutenant Colonel George C. McClelland, Oct. 25, 1861, McClelland to Wood, Oct. 29, 1861, McClelland to Zollicoffer, Nov. 4, 1861, McClelland to Zollicoffer, Nov. 5, 1861, Zollicoffer to Wood, Oct. 30, Nov. 5, Nov. 7, 1861, Letter Book of Colonel W. B. Wood, Commanding Post at Knoxville, Tennessee, Oct. 14–Nov. 25, 1861, RG 109, NA.

24. Zollicoffer to Wood, Oct. 30, 1861, Wood to Benjamin, Nov. 4, 1861, Zollicoffer to Wood, Nov. 5, 1861, Letter Book of Colonel W. B. Wood, Commanding Post at Knoxville, Tennessee, Oct. 14–Nov. 25, 1861, RG 109, NA; Zollicoffer to McClelland, Oct. 28, 1861, Orders and Letters Sent, Brigadier General Felix K. Zollicoffer, Aug. 1861–Jan. 1862, RG 109, NA.

25. Francis McKinney, *Education in Violence*, 109–19; Samuel P. Carter Memoirs, UTSC; William Nelson to Johnson, July 11, July 16, July 17, July 25, 1861, Montgomery Blair to Johnson, Aug. 8, 1861, Amos A. Lawrence to Johnson, June 25, 1861, July 3, 1861, Graf, Haskins, and Bergeron, *Johnson Papers*, 4:514, 539, 557–58, 586–88, 673–74; Crouch, "Merchant and Senator."

26. Madden, "Unionist Resistance"; Burt, "East Tennessee"; Temple, *Notable Men*, 88–93; Temple, *East Tennessee*, 370–77; "President Lincoln's Plan of Campaign—1861—undated," *OR* 52(1):191–92; J. G. Burrfield, "Statement Relating to the Union Men Who Was Enlisted to Burn the Railroad Bridges at Union Sullivan County Tennessee. Under Special Orders from General George H. Thomas Nov 1861," Samuel Mays Arnell Papers, UTSC.

27. Madden, "Resistance," 28–29; Burt, "East Tennessee," 12; William B. Carter to Brigadier General George Thomas, Oct. 22, 1861, Oct. 27, 1861, *OR* 4:317, 320.

28. Burt, "East Tennessee," 12; Francis McKinney, *Education in Violence*, 117–19; Lewis, *Sherman*, 195–98; Johnson to William T. Sherman, Oct. 30, 1861, Graf, Haskins, and Bergeron, *Johnson Papers*, 5:29–30.

29. Madden, "Resistance," 30–34; Burt, "East Tennessee," 18; Temple, *East Tennessee*, 380–85; J. G. Burrfield, "Statement," UTSC; Abraham Jobe Diary, TSLA; Zollicoffer to Cooper, Nov. 9, Nov. 11, 1861, Wood to Cooper, Nov. 11, 1861, "Statement Furnished Colonel Wood by Messrs. Wiseman and Fain,"

Letter Book of Colonel W. B. Wood, Commanding Post at Knoxville, Tennessee, Oct. 14–Nov. 25, 1861, RG 109, NA.

30. Scott and Angel, *Thirteenth Regiment*, 81; Ellis, *Adventures*, 28–30; Abraham Jobe Diary, TSLA; Wood to Cooper, Nov. 11, 1861, John L. Hopkins to "W. H. Sneed, John H. Crozier, Mag. C. William, Genl. Zollicoffer, or Col. Wood," Nov. 11, 1861, Zollicoffer to Lieutenant Colonel William Mackall, Nov. 20, 1861, Maj. L. J. Cannon to Wood, Nov. 10, 1861, Zollicoffer to Brigadier General William H. Carroll, Aug. 12, 1861, Letter Book of Colonel W. B. Wood, Commanding Post at Knoxville, Tennessee, Oct. 14–Nov. 25, 1861, RG 109, NA; Carroll to General Albert Sidney Johnston, Dec. 5, 1861, Henry Clark to Benjamin, Nov. 16, Nov. 18, 1861, Benjamin to Clark, Nov. 21, 1861, Governor Joseph E. Brown to Benjamin, Nov. 17, 1861, Carroll to Johnston, Dec. 17, 1861, *OR* 52(2):209–10, 214, 228–29, 232; Zollicoffer to Cooper, Nov. 14, 1861, *OR* 4:243; Carroll to Benjamin, Dec. 7, 1861, *OR*, Series 2, 1:852.

31. Temple, *East Tennessee*, 387; Ellis, *Adventures*, 28–30; Abraham Jobe Diary, TSLA; Colonel Danville Leadbetter to Cooper, Nov. 28, 1861, *OR* 7:712–13; Zollicoffer to Lieutenant Colonel William Mackall, Nov. 20, 1861, Letter Book of Colonel W. B. Wood, Commanding Post at Knoxville, Tennessee, Oct. 14–Nov. 25, 1861, RG 109, NA.

32. Temple, *East Tennessee*, 400–401; H. C. Young to D. M. Currin, Dec. 19, 1861, *OR* 7:777–79.

33. Scott and Angel, *Thirteenth Regiment*, 92–93; Humes, *Loyal Mountaineers*, 135–37, 152–53, 308; Ellis, *Adventures*, 29–30; Hancock, *Diary*, 77; Zollicoffer to Wood, Nov. 9, Nov. 10, 1861, Wood to Cooper, Knoxville, Nov. 11, 1861, Wood to Zollicoffer, Nov. 10, 1861, Commissioner Robert B. Reynolds to Wood, Nov. 14, 1861, Letter Book of Colonel W. B. Wood, Commanding Post at Knoxville, Tennessee, Oct. 14–Nov. 25, 1861, RG 109, NA; Zollicoffer to Colonel W. L. Stratham, Nov. 14, 1861, Zollicoffer to Cooper, Nov. 14, 1861, Zollicoffer to Mackall, Nov. 17, 1861, Orders and Letters Sent, General Felix K. Zollicoffer, Aug. 1861–Jan. 1862, RG 109, NA; Carroll to Harris, Nov. 14, 1861, Papers of the Governors, Isham G. Harris, TSLA; Carroll to Benjamin, Nov. 12, 1861, *OR* 45(2):206; Leadbetter to Johnston, Nov. 13, 1861, *OR* 52(2):207; Leadbetter to Cooper, Nov. 28, 1861, Carroll to Benjamin, Nov. 26, 1861, "Proclamation," Dec. 11, 1861, *OR* 7:704–5, 712–13, 760; Post Commandant, Knoxville, General Orders No. 5, Nov. 13, 1861, Samuel Powell III Papers, DU.

34. Zollicoffer to Wood, Nov. 12, 1861, Letter Book of Colonel W. B. Wood, Commanding Post at Knoxville, Tennessee, Oct. 14–Nov. 25, 1861, RG 109, NA; Zollicoffer to Mackall, Nov. 20, 1861, Zollicoffer to Cooper, Nov. 22, 1861, Orders and Letters Sent, Brigadier General Felix K. Zollicoffer, Aug. 1861–Jan. 1862, RG 109, NA.

35. Wood to Benjamin, Nov. 20, 1861, Benjamin to Wood, Leadbetter, and Carroll, Nov. 25, 1861, Letter Book of Colonel W. B. Wood, Commanding Post at Knoxville, Tennessee, Oct. 14–Nov. 25, 1861, RG 109, NA. Judge David T. Patterson was Andrew Johnson's son-in-law and was thought to be a leader in the resistance movement in Greene County. He was arrested, detained

for a few days, and released. Levi Pickens was an outspoken Unionist whose son was suspected of involvement in the bridge burnings. He died in Confederate captivity.

36. Temple, *East Tennessee*, 393–409; Humes, *Loyal Mountaineers*, 146; Brownlow, *Sketches*, 308–28, 369–70; John Crozier Ramsey to Benjamin, Nov. 28, 1861, Benjamin to Ramsey, Nov. 28, 1861, Leadbetter to Benjamin, Nov. 30, Dec. 8, 1861, Carroll to Benjamin, Nov. 29, 1861, Benjamin to Carroll, Dec. 10, 1861, Carroll to Benjamin, Dec. 11, 1861, *OR* 7:700–701, 720, 726, 747–48, 754, 759–60; Benjamin to Brigadier General John M. Withers, Dec. 26, 1861, Leadbetter to Cooper, Jan. 7, 1861, *OR*, Series 2, 1:859, 869; Record of Political Prisoners, Knoxville, 1862, Department of East Tennessee, Record of Political Prisoners, 1862, RG 109, NA; "J. Pickens vs. John Crozier, D. B. Reynolds, W. H. Sneed," Feb. 1865, T. A. R. Nelson Papers, MC.

37. Brownlow, *Secession*, 280–305, 337–81; John Crozier Ramsey to Benjamin, Dec. 6, 1861, *OR* 7:740.

38. Special Orders No. 216, Adjutant and Inspector General's Office, Nov. 11, 1861, Benjamin to Crittenden, Dec. 13, 1861, *OR* 7:685, 764.

39. J. G. M. Ramsey to Benjamin, Nov. 29, 1861, *OR* 7:721–22; Leadbetter to Cooper, Dec. 24, 1861, *OR*, Series 2, 1:859.

40. Temple, *East Tennessee*, 406–20; John Baxter to Benjamin, Nov. 30, 1861, Governor Isham G. Harris to General Albert Sidney Johnston, Dec. 31, 1861, *OR* 7:725–26, 811–12; John C. Burch to Davis, Jan. 20, 1862, "Citizens Petition for Release of James S. Bradford and Levi Trewhitt, Bradley County" and "Statement by Colonel James W. Gillespie, 43rd Tennessee Volunteers," Jan. 20, 1862, Benjamin to Landon Carter Haynes, Feb. 4, 1862, "Statement by Judah P. Benjamin to the Tennessee Delegation, Confederate Congress," Feb. 24, 1862, *OR*, Series 2, 1:870–71, 871–73, 879–80.

41. Burt, "East Tennessee," 23; Dykeman, *French Broad*, 89; Black, *Railroads*, 69; Temple, *East Tennessee*, 400–401; Leadbetter to Johnston, Nov. 13, 1861, *OR* 52(2):207; James T. Shelby to Johnson, Dec. 28, 1861, Graf, Haskins, and Bergeron, *Johnson Papers*, 5:84–85.

CHAPTER FOUR

1. Temple, *Notable Men*, 79–80, 94–100; Sensing, *Ferguson*, 2–11; Michael L. Patterson to Johnson, Jan. 31, 1862, Robert Johnson to Johnson, Feb. 13, 1862, Graf, Haskins, and Bergeron, *Johnson Papers*, 5:113–14, 143–44. Though Fentress and White Counties were officially part of Middle Tennessee, Unionists in these counties were linked to the loyalist network in East Tennessee, and Confederate guerrillas from Fentress and White fought with Unionist partisans in bordering East Tennessee counties. Further, the Union forces that invaded East Tennessee in 1863 were responsible for occupying these counties. For these reasons, White and Fentress are included in this study. For a discussion of the structure of guerrilla bands in other parts of the South, see Ash, *Yankees*, 44–50.

2. Guerrillas were identified primarily from the following prison records: Department of East Tennessee, Record of Political Prisoners, 1862, RG 109, NA; District of East Tennessee, Records of the Provost Marshal General, Roll of Prisoners in Custody; District of East Tennessee, Records of the Provost Marshal General, Record of Political Prisoners Confined in Citizens Prison, Apr. 6, 1864; District of East Tennessee, Records of the Provost Marshal General, Register of Names of Political Prisoners Confined in U.S. Military Prison at Knoxville, Tennessee, RG 393, NA. Information on occupation and wealth was derived from *Eighth Census, Manuscript Returns of Free Inhabitants, Tennessee*, NA.

3. Temple, *East Tennessee*, 427–28; Humes, *Loyal Mountaineers*, 364–66.

4. Temple, *Notable Men*, 196; Temple, *East Tennessee*, 426–27; Ellis, *Adventures*; Hurlbut, *Bradley County*, 213–18.

5. Paludan, *Victims*, 66–67; Temple, *East Tennessee*, 426–28; Daniel H. Kelly to Johnson, June 17, 1863, Graf, Haskins, and Bergeron, *Johnson Papers*, 6:257–58; Twenty-third Army Corps, Special Orders No. 111, Nov. 13, 1863, Twenty-third Army Corps, Special Orders and Circulars, June 1863–May 1864, RG 393, NA; "Statement," Brigadier General Samuel P. Carter, Dec. 31, 1864, Provost Marshal General, District of East Tennessee, Press Copies of Letters Sent, 1864, RG 393, NA; Lieutenant Colonel Edward Maynard to Dr. Pick, July 6, 1862, Horace Maynard Papers, UTSC; Major General Edmund Kirby Smith to Adjutant and Inspector General Samuel Cooper, Apr. 2, 1862, Kirby Smith to Brigadier General Samuel P. Carter, Knoxville, Apr. 12, 1862, Letters and Telegrams Sent, Department of East Tennessee, Mar.–Sept. 1862, RG 109, NA.

6. Barrett, *North Carolina*, 237–39; Humes, *Loyal Mountaineers*, 159–63, 198–99, 357–63; Ellis, *Adventures*, passim; Reminiscences of Chris D. Livesay, Chris D. Livesay Papers, TSLA; William Williams Stringfield, "History of the Sixty-Ninth Regiment of North Carolina Volunteers," NCSA.

7. Temple, *East Tennessee*, 424–25, 470; Humes, *Loyal Mountaineers*, 159–63, 165–66, 357–63; Captain John M. Carmek to Colonel John E. Toole, Jan. 27, 1862, *OR*, Series 2, 1:878–79; Brigadier General George W. Morgan to Captain Oliver D. Greene, Apr. 19, 1862, *OR* 10(2):114; Kirby Smith to Lieutenant Julius M. Rhett, Apr. 23, 1862, Department of East Tennessee, Letters and Telegrams Sent, Mar.–Sept. 1862, RG 109, NA; Brigadier General Felix K. Zollicoffer to Colonel William B. Wood, Nov. 12, 1861, Zollicoffer to Cooper, Nov. 14, 1861, Letter Book of Colonel W. B. Wood, Commanding Post at Knoxville, Tennessee, Oct. 14–Nov. 25, 1861, RG 109, NA; Christopher L. Johnsen to Johnson, Aug. 8, 1862, Graf, Haskins, and Bergeron, *Johnson Papers*, 5:599–600.

8. Thomas Doak Edington Diary, Mar. 2–7, 1862, UTSC.

9. Ragan, *Escape*, 12–36.

10. Current, *Loyalists*, 29–60, 213–15; Dyer, *Compendium*, 1:11–12; Anderson, *Southern Federals*, 11; William Randolph Carter, *First Tennessee*, 19; Edward Maynard to Horace Maynard, Sept. 1, 1861, Horace Maynard Papers, UTSC; Wood to Secretary of War Judah P. Benjamin, Nov. 4, 1861, *OR*, Series

2, 1:837; Carter to Captain J. B. Fry, Mar. 9, 1862, Kirby Smith to Major T. A. Washington, Apr. 26, 1862, *OR* 10(2):23, 453–54; David C. Bradley to his mother, Aug. 10, 1863, David C. Bradley Letters, MHI.

11. G. M. Hall to Callie, Mar. 23, 1862, Hall-Stakely Family Papers, MC; Kirby Smith to Brigadier General Danville Leadbetter, Mar. 27, 1862, Kirby Smith to Cooper, Knoxville, Apr. 19, 1862, Department of East Tennessee, Letters and Telegrams Sent, Mar.–Sept. 1862, RG 109, NA.

12. Kirby Smith to Washington, Apr. 3, 1862, Department of East Tennessee, Letters and Telegrams Sent, Mar.–Sept. 1862, RG 109, NA; Fuller Manly to his parents, Aug. 26, 1862, Basil Manly (Sr.) Papers, SHC.

13. Colonel Henry M. Doak Memoirs, TSLA; Colonel Baxter Smith, "History of the Regiment," MHI; Major John Morgan Brown to Colonel Samuel A. Gilbert, Jan. 3, 1863, *OR* 20(1):159–61.

14. Thomas B. Hill to his father, Aug. 18, 1862, TSLA; Abraham Jobe Memoirs, TSLA; Stephen F. Whitaker to his father, Aug. 2, 1863, Stephen F. Whitaker Papers, NCSA.

15. William Williams Stringfield, "History of the Sixty-Ninth North Carolina," William Williams Stringfield Papers, NCSA; Stephen F. Whitaker to his wife, Aug. 13, 1862, Stephen F. Whitaker Papers, NCSA; Colonel Alex M. Wallace to his wife, Tazewell, Aug. 15, 1862, Alex M. Wallace Letters, MHI.

16. Kirby Smith to Lieutenant Colonel W. L. Eakin, Captain William H. Thomas, and Captain W. C. Kain, July 1, 1862, Department of East Tennessee, Letters and Telegrams Sent, Mar.–Sept. 1862, RG 109, NA; Major General Simon B. Buckner to Brigadier General A. Greeley, May 20, 1863, Department of East Tennessee, Telegrams Sent, Apr. 1863–Sept. 1864, RG 109, NA; Major General Dabney H. Maurey to Major General Joseph E. Johnston, May 11, 1863, Department of East Tennessee, Letters, Orders, Circulars, Apr. 1863–Oct. 1864, RG 109, NA; Campbell Wallace and John R. Braemen to President Jefferson Davis, July 17, 1863, Jefferson Davis Papers, DU; Davis to Major General Braxton Bragg, Sept. 10, 1863, *OR* 52(2):524.

17. Kirby Smith to Colonel William Mackell, Mar. 14, 1862, Department of East Tennessee, Letters and Telegrams Sent, Mar.–Sept. 1862, RG 109, NA; Alexander D. Coffee to his wife, Nov. 3, 1861, Alexander Donelson Coffee Papers, SHC; Franklin Gaillard to Maria Gaillard, Nov. 10, 1863, Franklin Gaillard Letters, SHC; Major John M. Brown to Colonel Samuel A. Gilbert, Jan. 3, 1863, *OR* 20(1):159–61.

18. William Randolph Carter, *First Tennessee*, 16; Humes, *Loyal Mountaineers*, 184–85; "Morgan's Defeat by Sarah Thompson, Herself," Sarah Thompson Papers, DU; Hannibal Paine to Oliver Paine, July 18, 1864, Paine Family Papers, TSLA; Zollicoffer to Lieutenant Colonel G. R. McClelland, Oct. 28, 1861, Letter Book of Colonel W. B. Wood, Commanding Post at Knoxville, Tennessee, Oct. 14–Nov. 25, 1861, RG 109, NA.

19. Kephart, *Highlanders*, 124, 130.

20. Livingood, *Hamilton County*, 157–61; Temple, *Notable Men*, 99; Hurlbut, *Bradley County*, 68–77; Brigadier General George W. Morgan to Secretary of War Edwin M. Stanton, May 24, 1862, *OR* 10(2):213; Morgan to Johnson, May 24, 1862, Graf, Haskins, and Bergeron, *Johnson Papers*, 5:415–16; Kirby Smith

to Brigadier General Henry Heth, Aug. 10, 1862, Kirby Smith to Colonel S. J. Smith, Aug. 23, 1862, Department of East Tennessee, Letters and Telegrams Sent, Mar.–Sept. 1862, RG 109, NA; Colonel James R. Howard to Kirby Smith, Oct. 17, 1862, *OR* 16(1):1143; Colonel William Clift to "Adjutant General, United States Army," Oct. 28, 1862, *OR* 16(1):858–59.

21. Buckner to Brigadier General A. E. Jackson, July 28, 1863, Telegrams Sent, Department of East Tennessee, Apr. 1863–Sept. 1864, RG 109, NA; William Gibbs Allen Memoir, TSLA; Chris D. Livesay Reminiscences, Chris D. Livesay Papers, TSLA.

22. Temple, *Notable Men*, 78–79; Lyman Potter Spencer Diary, June 19, 1864, LC; Sam Houston Hyrd to Ann Hyrd, May 27, 1862, *Records of East Tennessee*; William Franklin Draper to his wife, Oct. 7, 1863, William Franklin Draper Letters, LC. For accounts of women acting as spies and other types of auxiliaries, see Victoria Bynum, *Unruly Women: The Politics of Social and Sexual Control in the Old South, 1840–1865* (Chapel Hill: University of North Carolina Press, 1992), 130–50; Lyde Cullen Sizer, "Acting Her Part: Narratives of Union Women Spies," in *Divided Houses: Gender and the Civil War*, ed. Catherine Clinton and Nina Silber (New York: Oxford University Press, 1992), 114–33; Bell Irvin Wiley, *Confederate Women* (Westport, Conn.: Greenwood Press, 1975).

23. Major General Sam Jones to Colonel L. M. Allen, Sept. 30, 1862, Jones to Lieutenant Colonel George N. Fowlkes, Sept. 26, Oct. 13, 1862, Jones to Colonel D. R. Hundley, Oct. 20, 1862, Department of East Tennessee, Letters and Telegrams Sent, Sept.–Nov. 1862, RG 109, NA.

24. William Sloan Diary, Feb. 21, 1862–Apr. 9, 1863, TSLA.

25. Leadbetter to Cooper, Nov. 28, Dec. 8, 1861, *OR* 7:712–13, 747–48.

26. William Sloan Diary, Mar. 9, 1862, Feb. 10, 1863, TSLA.

27. J. W. Gash to Mr. Eli Patton, Oct. 30, 1862, J. W. Gash Papers, NCSA; James Bennett McCrey Diary, Oct. 12, 1862, DU.

28. Joel Haley to Enoch Farr, Dec. 11, 1861, Joel Haley Letters, TSLA; William Gibbs Allen Memoirs, TSLA; William Sloan Diary, Mar. 9, 1862, TSLA.

29. Joel Haley to Enoch Farr, Dec. 11, 1861, Joel Haley Letters, TSLA; William Sloan Diary, Jan. 11, 1863, TSLA. For a discussion of similar attitudes held by Union soldiers in Missouri, see Fellman, *Inside War*, 81–131, 148–66.

30. William Sloan Diary, Sept. 28, 1862, Oct. 22, 1862, Feb. 6, 1863, TSLA; J. C. Gruar to his wife, [Jan. or Feb. 1864], John Calvin Gruar Papers, TSLA; Captain W. F. Parker to [illegible], Oct. 17, 1864, Samuel Wheeler Worthington Collection, NCSA.

31. Paludan, *Victims*, 56–99.

32. Assistant Adjutant General Henry L. Clay to Brigadier General C. S. Stevenson, June 26, 1862, Clay to Colonel A. W. Reynolds, July 8, 1862, Department of East Tennessee, Letters and Telegrams Sent, Mar.–Sept. 1862, RG 109, NA; Jones to Allen, Sept. 30, 1862, Jones to Hundley, Oct. 20, 1862, Jones to Fowlkes, Oct. 13, 1862, Department of East Tennessee, Letters and Telegrams Sent, Sept.–Nov. 1862, RG 109, NA.

33. Humes, *Loyal Mountaineers*, 229; Major General Ambrose Burnside to

Colonel Foster, Sept. 4, 1863, Army of the Ohio, Letters Sent, Aug. 1863–Jan. 1865, RG 393, NA; Captain John Shrady to his wife, Nov. 1, 1863, John Shrady Letters, UTSC; Hugh T. Carlisle Reminiscences, MHI; David S. Stanley, West-Stanley-Wright Family Memoirs, MHI.

34. Temple, *East Tennessee*, 498–510; Humes, *Loyal Mountaineers*, 262–64; Poe, *Personal Recollections*, 47; Dykeman, *French Broad*, 104–7; Creekmore, *Knoxville*, 101–2, 108–9; Burnside to Colonel James Biddle, Nov. 21, 1863, Twenty-third Army Corps, Letters Sent, June 1863–May 1864, RG 393, NA.

35. Wilson, *Column South*, 205–6; Trowbridge, *Tenth Michigan*, 18–19; Major General O. O. Howard to Major General William T. Sherman, Dec. 9, 1863, *OR* 31(3):364–65; Colonel Edward McCook to Brigadier General Edward E. Potter, Feb. 13, 1864, *OR* 32(2):386–87; David F. Beatty to Matty Patton, June 9, 1864, Boren Family Papers, MC; Colonel C. G. Howley to Captain W. P. Ammen, Jan. 8, 1865, *OR* 45(2):551–52; Thomas Smith Hutton Diary, Feb. 21, 1865, TSLA.

36. Colonel Robert K. Byrd to Major General George Thomas, Feb. 27, 1864, *OR* 32(1):485; Lieutenant George W. Ross to Brigadier General Davis Tillson, Jan. 29, 1865, Captain Thomas A. Stevenson to Captain Dean, Jan. 31, 1865, Stevenson to Tillson, Feb. 3, 1865, District of East Tennessee, Telegrams Received, 1864–65, RG 393, NA; [unidentified author] to Johnson, Jan. 30, 1865, Graf, Haskins, and Bergeron, *Johnson Papers*, 7:447–48.

37. Albert A. Pope Diary, MHI; Captain John M. Shrady to his wife, Nov. 1, 1863, July 20, 1864, Sept. 4, 1864, John M. Shrady Letters, UTSC; Lieutenant Colonel M. S. Patterson to Brigadier General Jacob Ammen, June 19, 1864, District of East Tennessee, Telegrams Received, 1864–65, RG 393, NA; Major General D. S. Stanley to Major General George Thomas, Apr. 20, 1865, *OR* 49(2):414; George P. Hawkes Diary, Dec. 26, 1863, MHI.

38. Escott, *Many Excellent People*, 76–81; Paludan, *Victims*, 70–75, 84–85; Lonn, *Desertion*, 25, 62–63, 79; Moore, *Conscription*, 152, 219–21; William Cole to Cornelia Cole, June 24, 1863, William Cole Letters, MHI; Brigadier General John H. Morgan to Cooper, July 1, 1864, Department of East Tennessee, Letters, Orders, Circulars, Apr. 1863–Oct. 1864, RG 109, NA; Lieutenant Colonel J. I. Daniel to Colonel H. G. Gibson, [1865], Lieutenant G. A. Deal to Gibson, Apr. 3, 1865, Second Brigade, Fourth Division, Department of the Cumberland, Letters and Telegrams Received, 1865, RG 393, NA.

39. Daniel, "Special Warfare," 146–54; Burns and Blankenship, *Fiddles*, 59–61, 269; Sensing, *Ferguson*, passim; Leroy S. Clements to Johnson, Apr. 9, 1862, Andrew J. Hall to Johnson, June 15, 1862, Graf, Haskins, and Bergeron, *Johnson Papers*, 5:286–87, 478; Colonel Henry C. Gibson to Johnson, Nov. 7, 1863, Graf, Haskins, and Bergeron, *Johnson Papers*, 6:459–60; Colonel John M. Hughes to Captain Walter Weir, Sept. 8, 1863, *OR* 30(2):646–47; Hughes to Weir, Feb. 14, 1864, *OR* 32(1):55–57.

40. Rowell, *Yankee Cavalrymen*, 60–61; William Randolph Carter, *First Tennessee*, 109–11; Lieutenant Colonel James P. Brownlow to Colonel A. P. Campbell, Nov. 25, Dec. 1, 1863, *OR* 31(1):573, 591.

41. Colonel Robert K. Byrd to Thomas, Feb. 27, 1864, *OR* 32(1):485; Johnson to Major General William S. Rosecrans, Nashville, Oct. 12, 1863, *OR*

30(4):308; Thomas to Johnson, Chattanooga, Jan. 10, 1864, *OR* 32(3):64–65; Department of the Cumberland, Special Field Orders No. 24, Jan. 24, 1864, Special Field Orders No. 141, May 22, 1864, *OR* 52(1):513, 555; Colonel William B. Stokes to Captain B. H. Polk, Feb. 24, Mar. 28, 1864, *OR* 32(1):416–17, 494–95; Major Thomas H. Reeve to Lieutenant P. S. Abbot, July 9, July 20, 1864, *OR* 39(1):351–54.

42. Colonel Robert K. Byrd to Brigadier General Samuel P. Carter, May 2, 1864, District of East Tennessee, Letters Received, 1863–64, RG 393, NA; Johnson to Thomas, Nashville, Aug. 16, 1864, William G. Brownlow to Johnson, Feb. 7, 1865, Graf, Haskins, and Bergeron, *Johnson Papers*, 7:98, 460–61; Ellis, *Adventures*, 289–305; Carter to Thomas Sanderson, Oct. 29, 1864, Provost Marshal General, District of East Tennessee, Press Copies of Letters Sent, Sept. 1863–64, RG 393, NA; Brigadier General Speed S. Fry to Captain J. S. Butler, Dec. 2, 1864, *OR* 45(2):28; twenty citizens and sixteen officers and men of the Seventh Tennessee Mounted Infantry to Tillson, Mar. 18, 1865, District of East Tennessee, Letters Received, 1863–64, RG 393, NA; William Heard to Brownlow, May 4, 1865, Papers of the Governors, William G. Brownlow, TSLA.

43. Lillard, *Bradley County*, 63–64; A. J. Williams, *Polk County*, 28; Hurlbut, *Bradley County*, 130–33, Appendix, 6–13; Captain J. W. Branson to Carter, Aug. 8, 1864, Provost Marshal General, District of East Tennessee, Press Copies of Letters Sent, Sept. 1863–64, RG 393, NA; Lieutenant Colonel Joseph Destiny to Assistant Adjutant General W. P. Ammen, Dec. 14, 1864, Telegrams Received, District of East Tennessee, 1864–65, RG 393, NA; Peter Smith to William B. Reynolds, Dec. 8, 1864, Jan. 17, 1865, William B. Reynolds Papers, DU.

44. Carter to "Comdg. Officer S Plains," Oct. 17, 1864, Provost Marshal General, District of East Tennessee, Press Copies of Telegrams Sent, RG 393, NA; Major General George C. Stoneman to Colonel H. G. Gibson, May 15, 1865, District of East Tennessee, Letters Sent, Apr. 1864–Mar. 1866, RG 393, NA.

45. Mary Jane Reynolds to S. B. Reynolds, Jan. 26, 1864, Mary Jane Reynolds Letters, TSLA; Franklin Gaillard to Maria, Mar. 27, 1864, Franklin Gaillard Papers, SHC; Skipper and Gove, "Stray Thoughts."

46. Ellis, *Adventures*, 261–65.

47. Dunn, *Cades Cove*, 131–41. For a similar incident, or perhaps an alternative account of the same incident, see Dugger, *War Trails*, 112–17.

48. M. B. C. Ramsey to Robert, July 10, 1861, Ramsey Family Papers, UTSC; Carrie Stakely to Margaret, Aug. 12, 1861, Hall-Stakely Family Papers, MC; R. P. Wells to Nelson, Apr. 11, 1862, T. A. R. Nelson Papers, MC; John B. Logan to Johnson, Mar. 19, 1862, Graf, Haskins, and Bergeron, *Johnson Papers*, 5:204–5.

49. Bryan, "East Tennessee," 274–78, 289–90.

50. Ibid., 273–74, 284–89.

51. Wilson, *Column South*, 140; Ellis, *Adventures*, 281–88; Paul Turner Vaughn to his father, Jan. 20, 1864, Paul Turner Vaughn Letters, SHC; J. C. Gruar to his wife, Mar. 20, 1864, John Calvin Gruar Papers, SHC.

52. Major General John M. Schofield to Major George W. Kirk, Feb. 13, 1864, Schofield to Kirk, June 12, 1864, Army of the Ohio, Letters Sent, Aug. 1863–Jan. 1865, RG 393, NA; Assistant Adjutant General Robert Morrow to Schofield, July 15, 1864, Schofield to Kirk, July 24, 1864, Army of the Ohio, Letters Sent, May 1864–Jan. 1865, RG 393, NA; Tillson to Lieutenant Colonel G. W. Bascom, Jan. 17, 1865, *OR* 45(2):608–9; S. A. Key to "Kendree," Jan. 11, 1864, David McKendree Key Papers, SHC; L. Cowles to Mary, July 24, 1864, Calvin J. Cowles Papers, NCSA.

53. Camp, *Sequatchie County*, 61–62; Alexander, "Neither Peace nor War"; James B. Campbell, "East Tennessee"; Humes, *Loyal Mountaineers*, 209; Brigadier General John Pegram to Colonel J. J. Morrison, July 1, 1863, Department of East Tennessee, Letters, Orders, Circulars, Apr. 1863–Oct. 1864, RG 109, NA; Captain H. H. Thomas to Captain William Reynolds, Dec. 6, 1863, Provost Marshal General, District of East Tennessee, Press Copies of Letters Sent, Sept. 1863–64, RG 393, NA; Lieutenant Colonel Frank S. Curtis to Captain W. P. Ammen, Jan. 4, 1865, Lieutenant Colonel William C. Bartlett to Tillson, Feb. 22, 1865, District of East Tennessee, Telegrams Received, 1864–65, RG 393, NA; Mrs. John C. Williams to Rufus Williams, Sept. 22, 1864, John and Rhoda Campbell Williams Papers, MC.

54. Mary Jane Reynolds to S. B. Reynolds, [Feb. 1864], Feb. 26, 1864, Mary Jane Reynolds Letters, TSLA; Carter to Colonel Dunlop, Jan. 15, 1864, Provost Marshal General, District of East Tennessee, Press Copies of Letters Sent, Sept. 1863–64, RG 393, NA; William Sloan Diary, Mar. 15, Mar. 16, Aug. 11, 1864, TSLA.

55. Wyatt Lipscomb to Mr. Lenoir, Feb. 4, 1865, Lenoir Family Papers, SHC; M. S. Temple to Temple, Aug. 31, 1864, Oliver P. Temple Papers, UTSC; Carter to Colonel Crawford, Oct. 28, 1863, Provost Marshal General, District of East Tennessee, Press Copies of Letters Sent, Sept. 1863–64, RG 393, NA; Colonel W. Y. Dillard to W. P. Ammen, Oct. 7, 1864, District of East Tennessee, Telegrams Received, 1864–65, RG 393, NA; District of East Tennessee, General Orders No. 56, June 10, 1865, General Orders No. 57, Aug. 2, 1865, District of East Tennessee and Fourth Division, Twenty-third Army Corps, General Orders, RG 393, NA.

56. Trowbridge, *Tenth Michigan*, 18–19; Morgan to Secretary of War Edwin M. Stanton, July 13, 1862, *OR* 16(2):142.

57. Lieutenant Colonel Robert Klein to Assistant Adjutant General, Department of the Ohio, Jan. 14, 1864, Colonel Thomas J. Harrison to Brigadier General William D. Whipple, Jan. 14, 1864, *OR* 32(1):65–66, 70; Lieutenant Colonel George A. Gowin to Major General James B. Steedman, Feb. 2, 1865, *OR* 49(1):33.

58. Ammen to Dillard, Oct. 14, 1864, Bartlett to Ammen, Dec. 1, Dec. 29, 1864, District of East Tennessee, Letters Received, 1863–64, RG 393, NA; Bartlett to Tillson, Jan. 28, Feb. 7, 1865, District of East Tennessee, Telegrams Received, 1864–65, RG 393, NA.

59. Carter to Lieutenant William Estrada, June 7, 1864, Provost Marshal General, District of East Tennessee, Press Copies of Letters and Telegrams Sent, 1864–65, RG 393, NA.

60. Burns and Blankenship, *Fiddles*, 232; Chauncey B. Welton to his parents, May 1, 1864, Chauncey B. Welton Letters, SHC; Hugh T. Carlisle Reminiscences, MHI.

61. Grimsley, *Hard Hand*, 145–51; Garner, "General Orders 100"; Freidel, "General Orders 100."

62. Carter to Captain S. C. Honeycutt, June 22, 1864, Provost Marshal General, District of East Tennessee, Press Copies of Letters and Telegrams Sent, 1864–65, RG 393, NA; Bartlett to Ammen, Dec. 10, 1864, Ammen to Bartlett, Dec. 21, 1864, Jan. 6, 1865, District of East Tennessee, Letters Sent, Apr. 1864–Mar. 1866, RG 393, NA; Harvey Washington Wiley Diary, June 16, 1864, Harvey Washington Wiley Papers, LC; John Emerson Anderson Memoir, LC.

63. Captain William A. Cochran to Tillson, Mar. 2, 1865, Tillson to Cochran, Mar. 2, 1865, District of East Tennessee, Letters Sent, Apr. 1864–Mar. 1866, RG 393, NA; Major General George Stoneman to Colonel James Parsons, Apr. 21, 1865, District of East Tennessee, Letters Sent, Apr. 1864–Mar. 1866, RG 393, NA.

64. Michael Fellman noted a similar development among Union troops in Missouri. See Fellman, *Inside War*, 166–92.

CHAPTER FIVE

1. Joseph H. Parks, *Kirby Smith*, 12–110.

2. Ibid., 110–21.

3. Ibid., 121–54.

4. Major General Edmund Kirby Smith to Cassie, Mar. 3, Mar. 13, Mar. 26, 1862, Edmund Kirby Smith Papers, SHC; Kirby Smith to Colonel William W. Mackall, Mar. 14, 1862, Department of East Tennessee, Letters and Telegrams Sent, Mar.–Sept. 1862, RG 109, NA.

5. Colonel Danville Leadbetter to Adjutant and Inspector General Samuel Cooper, Dec. 24, 1861, *OR* 7:791; Kirby Smith to President Jefferson Davis, Mar. 10, 1862, Kirby Smith to Cooper, Mar. 13, Mar. 23, 1862, Kirby Smith to Major General Albert Sidney Johnston, Mar. 9, 1862, Kirby Smith to Cooper, Apr. 2, 1862, Department of East Tennessee, Letters and Telegrams Sent, Mar.–Sept. 1862, RG 109, NA; Kirby Smith to Cassie, Mar. 15, 1862, Kirby Smith to Governor Isham G. Harris, May 29, 1862, SHC.

6. Archer Jones, *Command and Strategy*, 157–59; Cooling, *Henry and Donelson*; McDonough, *Shiloh*.

7. Kirby Smith to Colonel James E. Raines, Mar. 29, 1862, Kirby Smith to Brigadier General S. B. Moxey, Mar. 29, 1862, Kirby Smith to Colonel John C. Vaughn, Apr. 14, 1862, Kirby Smith to Colonel Thomas Taylor, June 28, 1862, Kirby Smith to "Lieutenant Colonel Davidson, Colonel J. B. Cooke, Comd Officer Thirty-First Alabama & Forty-Second Georgia," June 11, 1862, Kirby Smith to Colonel R. G. Faine, Aug. 27, 1862, General Orders No. 2, Sept. 27, 1862, Department of East Tennessee, Letters and Telegrams Sent, Mar.–Sept. 1862, RG 109, NA.

8. Kirby Smith to Major T. A. Washington, Apr. 3, 1862, Kirby Smith to Cooper, Apr. 2, 1862, Department of East Tennessee, Letters and Telegrams Sent, Mar.–Sept. 1862, RG 109, NA.

9. Bryan, "East Tennessee," 190–98; Kirby Smith to "Colonel Danville Leadbetter, Colonel James E. Rains, Captain W. L. Brown, Captain A. W. Hoge, Captain Chambers, Major W. L. Eakin, and Captain Ashby," Apr. 2, 1862, Kirby Smith Papers, SHC.

10. Temple, *Notable Men*, 203–5; Assistant Adjutant General Henry L. Clay to Major W. L. Eakin, Apr. 14, 1862, Department of East Tennessee, Letters and Telegrams Sent, Mar.–Sept. 1862, RG 109, NA; Samuel P. Johnson Diary, Apr. 22–June 15, 1862, Samuel P. Johnson Papers, UTCS.

In March Kirby Smith also arrested John Baxter and attempted, unsuccessfully, to have him tried for treason. See Kirby Smith to Johnston, Mar. 25, 1862, Kirby Smith to Bragg, Apr. 4, 1862, Clay to Captain W. L. Brown, Apr. 8, 1862, Department of East Tennessee, Letters and Telegrams Sent, Mar.–Sept. 1862, RG 109, NA.

11. Groce, "Mountain Rebels," 152–70; Bryan, "East Tennessee," 190–98; Kirby Smith to Cooper, Mar. 23, Apr. 2, 1862, Kirby Smith to Major F. A. Washington, Apr. 3, 1862, Department of East Tennessee, Letters and Telegrams Sent, Mar.–Sept. 1862, RG 109, NA.

12. Radley, *Rebel Watchdog*, 178–79, 194–95; War Department, Adjutant and Inspector General's Office, General Orders No. 21, Apr. 8, 1862, *OR* 10(2):402; Clay to Hon. F. W. Turby, Knoxville, Apr. 14, 1862, Clay to R. Lovel, Apr. 24, 1862, Department of East Tennessee, Letters and Telegrams Sent, Mar.–Sept. 1862, RG 109; T. H. Watts to Secretary of War George W. Randolph, Apr. 19, 1862, Confederate States Papers, Opinions of the Attorney General 1861–65, SHC.

13. Brownlow, *Secession*, 451–55; "Application to Amend Sequestration Petition," Jan. 18, 1862, "Writ of Attachment," Jan. 18, 1862, Horace Maynard to Johnson, Apr. 30, 1862, William G. Brownlow to Johnson, May 3, 1862, "Confederacy vs. Estate of Andrew Johnson," Dec. 10, 1862, Graf, Haskins, and Bergeron, *Johnson Papers*, 5:105–8, 352–53, 357–58; 6:95–96.

14. Robert Johnson to Johnson, Apr. 8, 1862, Graf, Haskins, and Bergeron, *Johnson Papers*, 5:280–82; Clay to Vaughn, Apr. 18, 1862, Clay to First Lieutenant Julius M. Rhett, Apr. 23, 1862, Department of East Tennessee, Letters and Telegrams Sent, Mar.–Sept. 1862, RG 109, NA.

15. Kirby Smith, "Proclamation," Apr. 18, 1862, Kirby Smith, "To the East Tennesseans in the United States Army," Aug. 13, 1862, Department of East Tennessee, Letters and Telegrams Sent, Mar.–Sept. 1862, RG 109, NA; Colonel William M. Churchwell, "To the Disaffected People of East Tennessee," Apr. 23, 1862, *OR* 10(2):641.

16. Kirby Smith to Cooper, Mar. 13, 1862, Kirby Smith to Colonel R. Morgan, May 11, 1862, Kirby Smith to Davis, May 9, 1862, Kirby Smith to Cooper, May 13, 1862, Department of East Tennessee, Letters and Telegrams Sent, Mar.–Sept. 1862, RG 109, NA; Major General Robert E. Lee to Kirby Smith, Apr. 7, 1862, Davis to Kirby Smith, May 13, 1862, *OR* 10(2):397–98, 521.

17. Archer Jones, *Command and Strategy*, 65–69; Joseph H. Parks, *Kirby Smith*, 159–92; Kirby Smith to Washington, Apr. 25, May 3, 1862, Kirby Smith to Cooper, June 15, 1862, Department of East Tennessee, Letters and Telegrams Sent, Mar.–Sept. 1862, RG 109, NA; Kirby Smith to Cassie, Mar. 23, June 12, July 15, 1862, Edmund Kirby Smith Papers, SHC.

18. McDonough, *War in Kentucky*; Joseph H. Parks, *Kirby Smith*, 198–245.

19. Kirby Smith to Davis, Aug. 11, 1862, Major General John P. McCown to Randolph, Sept. 1, Sept. 3, Sept. 17, 1862, endorsement, Randolph, Sept. 17, 1862, Department of East Tennessee, Letters and Telegrams Sent, Mar.–Sept. 1862, RG 109, NA. For Jones's background, see Ezra J. Warner, *Generals in Gray* (Baton Rouge: Louisiana State University Press, 1959), 265–66.

20. Major General Sam Jones to Randolph, Oct. 14, 1862, Department of East Tennessee, Letters and Telegrams Sent, Sept.–Nov. 1862, RG 109, NA.

21. Randolph to Jones, Sept. 19, 1862, *OR* 16(2):851.

22. McCown to Randolph, Sept. 3, 1862, Department of East Tennessee, Letters and Telegrams Sent, Mar.–Sept. 1862, RG 109, NA; William Sloan Diary, Jan. 11, 1863, TSLA.

23. Jones to Nelson, Sept. 25, 1862, T. A. R. Nelson Papers, MC; Jones to Randolph, Oct. 4, Oct. 14, 1862, Department of East Tennessee, Letters and Telegrams Sent, Sept.–Nov. 1862, RG 109, NA; William G. McAdoo Diary, Oct. 3, 1862, Floyd-McAdoo Papers, LC.

24. Jones to Randolph, Oct. 4, Oct. 14, 1862, Seth J. W. Lucky to Jones, Oct. 11, 1862, Rev. F. E. Pitts to Hon. Nat Taylor, Sept. 24, 1862, Taylor to Pitts, Oct. 2, 1862, Jones to Editor, *Athens Post*, Oct. 4, 1862, Assistant Adjutant General Charles Stringfellow to "Neale and Cowwan," Oct. 6, 1862, Department of East Tennessee, Letters and Telegrams Sent, Sept.–Nov. 1862, RG 109, NA.

25. "Address of Hon. T. A. R. Nelson to the People of East Tennessee," *Knoxville Register*, Oct. 3, 1862.

26. James P. McDoult et al. to Nelson, Oct. 6, 1862, William McCampbell to Nelson, Oct. 8, 1862, James Sevier et al. to Nelson, Oct. 8, 1862, T. P. Fickle et al. to Nelson, Oct. 6, 1862, T. A. R. Nelson Papers, MC.

27. Alexander, *Nelson*, 97–98; Jones to Nelson, Oct. 17, 1862, Kirby Smith to Nelson, Nov. 17, 1862, T. A. R. Nelson Papers, MC; Thomas Doak Edington Memoirs, TSLA.

28. Jones to Randolph, Oct. 4, Oct. 14, Oct. 17, 1862, Jones to Editor, *Athens Post*, Knoxville, Oct. 4, 1862, Department of East Tennessee, Letters and Telegrams Sent, Sept.–Nov. 1862, RG 109, NA; Kirby Smith to Cassie, July 22, Oct. 27, 1862, Edmund Kirby Smith Papers, SHC.

29. Jones to Randolph, Sept. 23, Sept. 24, Oct. 17, Oct. 18, 1862, Department of East Tennessee, Letters and Telegrams Sent, Sept.–Nov. 1862, RG 109, NA.

30. Endorsements, Randolph and Davis, Oct. 24, 1862, to Jones's letter of Oct. 17, Department of East Tennessee, Letters and Telegrams Sent, Sept.–Nov. 1862, RG 109, NA.

31. Jones to Randolph, Sept. 25, 1862, Jones to Cooper, Oct. 5, Oct. 10,

1862, Cooper to Jones, Oct. 10, 1862, Jones to Cooper, Oct. 18, 1862, Department of East Tennessee, Letters and Telegrams Sent, Sept.–Nov. 1862, RG 109, NA.

32. Fuller Manly to his parents, Aug. 26, 1862, Basil Manly (Sr.) Papers, SHC; G. W. Hunt to Brigadier General John Hunt Morgan, Nov. 26, 1864, Duke-Morgan Papers, SHC; Paul Turner Vaughn to his father, Jan. 20, 1864, Paul Turner Vaughn Letters, SHC.

33. Burns and Blankenship, *Fiddles*, 188; Alexander D. Coffee to Ann Coffee, Wartburg, Nov. 20, 1861, Alexander Donelson Coffee Papers, SHC; Oliver Paine to Hannibal Paine, Nov. 20, 1862, Paine Family Papers, TSLA; William G. McAdoo Diary, Oct. 1, 1862, Floyd-McAdoo Papers, LC; Captain Charles Stringfield, "History of the Sixty-Ninth North Carolina Infantry," NCSA; Jones to McCown, Oct. 16, 1862, Department of East Tennessee, Letters and Telegrams Sent, Sept.–Nov. 1862, RG 109, NA.

34. A. J. Williams, *Polk County*, 27–28; Leadbetter to Cooper, Dec. 8, 1861, *OR* 7:712–13, 747–48; William Sloan Diary, Mar. 18, 1863, TSLA; Reverend Henry M. Sneed to Brigadier General Samuel P. Carter, Jan. 5, 1864, *OR* 32(2):29; L. B. K. Cowles to William Holden, July 26, 1864, Calvin J. Cowles Papers, NCSA; Jones to Captain Fitzgerald, Oct. 18, 1862, Department of East Tennessee, Letters and Telegrams Sent, Sept.–Nov. 1862, RG 109, NA.

35. Major General Daniel S. Donelson to Colonel Ewell, Feb. 10, 1863, Secretary of War James A. Seddon to Donelson, Feb. 27, 1862, *OR* 23(2): 631, 651–52; Buckner to Cooper, July 28, 1863, Buckner to Mr. Abe Tipton, July 25, 1863, Colonel V. Shelikan to Buckner, May 30, 1863, Department of East Tennessee, Letters, Orders, Circulars, Apr. 1863–Oct. 1864, RG 109, NA.

36. Kirby Smith to Cassie, July 22, 1862, Edmund Kirby Smith Papers, SHC; "J. Pickens vs. John Crozier, D. B. Reynolds, W. H. Sneed, Others," T. A. R. Nelson Papers, Feb. 1865, MC.

37. Brigadier General William H. Carroll to Benjamin, Nov. 29, 1861, *OR* 7:720–21; Benjamin to Colonel William B. Wood, Leadbetter, Carroll, Nov. 25, 1861, Letter Book of Colonel W. B. Wood, Commanding Post at Knoxville, Tennessee, Oct. 14–Nov. 25, 1861, RG 109, NA; Kirby Smith to Brigadier General George W. Morgan, Aug. 1, 1862, Clay to Brigadier General C. S. Stevenson, June 26, 1862, Clay to Colonel A. W. Reynolds, July 8, 1862, Department of East Tennessee, Letters and Telegrams Sent, Mar.–Sept. 1862, RG 109, NA; Assistant Adjutant General Charles S. Stringfellow to Lieutenant W. O. Cain, Sept. 21, 1862, Stringfellow to Colonel Hudly, Oct. 20, 1862, Acting Assistant Adjutant General Giles B. Cocke to Colonel Alex D. Smith, Oct. 3, 1862, Department of East Tennessee, Letters and Telegrams Sent, Sept.–Nov. 1862, RG 109, NA.

38. Colonel Orlando M. Poe to Eleanor, Aug. 26, 1863, Orlando M. Poe Papers, LC; William Franklin Draper to his wife, Sept. 25, 1863, William Franklin Draper Papers, LC; R. E. Jameson to his mother, Knoxville, Oct. 3, 1863, Robert Edwin Jameson Papers, LC; Marshall M. Miller to his wife, Knoxville, Jan. 22, 1864, Marshall Mortimer Miller Letters, LC.

CHAPTER SIX

1. Hattaway and Jones, *How the North Won*, 56–63; T. Harry Williams, *Generals*, 47–59, 182–85, 205–36.

2. Andrew Johnson and Horace Maynard to Major General Don Carlos Buell, Dec. 7, 1861, Maynard to Johnson, Apr. 29, 1862, Johnson to Brigadier General George W. Morgan, May 14, 1862, Johnson to Major General Henry W. Halleck, June 5, 1862, Halleck to Johnson, June 22, 1862, Johnson to Morgan, July 25, 1862, Graf, Haskins, and Bergeron, *Johnson Papers*, 5:43–44, 348–49, 396–97, 442–43, 494, 570; Mrs. Horace Maynard to Washburne Maynard, Mar. 27, 1863, Horace Maynard Papers, UTSC.

3. Clifton R. Hall, *Johnson*, 56; Johnson to Lewis Wallace, June 30, 1862, Johnson to Major General George H. Thomas, Aug. 16, 1862, Johnson to President Abraham Lincoln, Sept. 1, 1862, Johnson to Lincoln, May 29, 1863, Graf, Haskins, and Bergeron, *Johnson Papers*, 5:532–34, 617, 6:4–6, 233.

4. Coulter, *Brownlow*, 205–42; Brownlow, *Secession*, 337–444.

5. Brownlow, *Secession*, 216–17.

6. Army of the Ohio, General Field Orders No. 2, Aug. 14, 1863, General Field Orders No. 13, Sept. 17, 1863, Department and Army of the Ohio, Printed Copies of General Orders, Aug. 1862–Dec. 1864, RG 393, NA; Major General Ambrose E. Burnside to Lincoln, Sept. 10, 1863, *OR* 30(3):323.

7. Temple, *East Tennessee*, 480; Humes, *Loyal Mountaineers*, 211–12; Colonel Orlando M. Poe to Eleanor Poe, Sept. 4, 1863, Orlando M. Poe Papers, LC; August Valentine Kautz Diary, Oct. 17, Oct. 23, 1863, August Valentine Kautz Papers, MHI; Major General Ambrose E. Burnside to Rev. Thomas W. Humes, Dec. 11, 1863, Army and Department of the Ohio, Letters Sent, Aug. 1863– Jan. 1865, RG 393, NA.

8. Cozzens, *Chickamauga*.

9. Archer Jones, *Command and Strategy*, 174–75; Marvel, *Burnside*, 270–94; Poe, *Recollections*, 4–8; Daniel Larned to Henry, Sept. 28, 1863, Daniel Larned Papers, LC.

10. Marvel, *Burnside*, 270–94.

11. Marvel, *Burnside*, 295–324; Longstreet, *Manassas*, 480–96; Poe, *Recollections*, 9–19; August Valentine Kautz Diary, Oct. 28–31, 1863, August Valentine Kautz Papers, MHI; Albert A. Pope Diary, Nov. 15–29, 1863, MHI.

12. Marvel, *Burnside*, 331–33; Poe, *Recollections*, 42–44; Major General John G. Foster to Brigadier General W. L. Elliot, Dec. 14, 1863, Army and Department of the Ohio, Letters Sent, Aug. 1863–Jan. 1865, RG 393, NA.

13. Marvel, *Burnside*, 324–34; Burt, "East Tennessee," 59, 66–71; Longstreet, *Manassas*, 497–508; Poe, *Recollections*, 42–45; Temple, *East Tennessee*, 511–15; Foster to Elliot, Dec. 14, 1863, Army and Department of the Ohio, Letters Sent, Aug. 1863–Jan. 1865, RG 393, NA; Major General Ulysses S. Grant to Halleck, Feb. 12, 1864, *OR* 32(2):374–75.

14. Longstreet, *Manassas*, 509–50; William Randolph Carter, *First Tennessee*, 114–35; "From East Tennessee Unionists to Johnson," Graf, Haskins, and Bergeron, *Johnson Papers*, 7:52–53; Colonel W. Y. Dillard to Brigadier General Jacob Ammen, Aug. 1, 1864, *OR* 39(2):216.

15. Starr, *Union Cavalry*, 3:559–63; Davis, *Breckinridge*, 463–67; Van Noppen, *Stoneman*, 1–11; Clifton R. Hall, *Johnson*, 157–58, 186–88; Trowbridge, *Tenth Michigan*, 20–39; Alvin C. Gillem to Johnson, May 14, 1862, Graf, Haskins, and Bergeron, *Johnson Papers*, 5:390–92, Johnson to Halleck and Secretary of War Edwin M. Stanton, June 21, 1862, *OR* 16(1):47; Stanton, "Authorization to Raise Troops," Washington, Mar. 25, 1863, Johnson, "Order Re Governor's Guard," Nashville, Aug. 1, 1864, Graf, Haskins, and Bergeron, *Johnson Papers*, 6:198–99; Major General John M. Schofield to Johnson, Oct. 18, 1864, William G. Brownlow to Johnson, Nov. 14, 1864, Johnson to Ammen, Nov. 17, 1864, Graf, Haskins, and Bergeron, *Johnson Papers*, 7:241, 285, 299–300; Johnson to Joseph S. Fowler, Sept. 22, 1863, Joseph S. Fowler Papers, SHC; Brigadier General Alvin C. Gillem to Fowler, Nov. 27, 1864, Joseph S. Fowler Papers, SHC; G. W. Hunt to Brigadier General John Hunt Morgan, Nov. 26, 1864, Duke-Morgan Papers, SHC.

16. Marvel, *Burnside*, 221–38.

17. Ash, *Yankees*, 56–67; Grimsley, *Hard Hand*, 48–51, 85–91, 111–19; Fellman, *Inside War*, 126–28; Brownlee, *Ghosts*, 157–79; Maslowski, *Treason*, 74–96; Clifton R. Hall, *Johnson*, 39–44; Wayne W. Smith, "Experiment in Counterinsurgency"; Freidel, "General Orders 100."

18. Army of the Ohio, General Field Orders No. 9, Sept. 4, 1863, Department and Army of the Ohio, Printed Copies of General Orders, Aug. 1862–Dec. 1864, RG 393, NA; Samuel P. Carter Memoirs, UTSC.

19. Fourth Division, Twenty-third Army Corps, General Orders No. 3, Jan. 20, 1865, District of East Tennessee and Fourth Division, Twenty-third Army Corps, General Orders Issued, RG 393, NA. For Carter's background, see Ezra J. Warner, *Generals in Blue* (Baton Rouge; Louisiana State University Press, 1964), 74; Campbell H. Brown, "East Tennessee Raid"; Samuel P. Carter Memoirs, UTSC.

20. Samuel P. Carter Memoirs, UTSC; [first entry, no date], Ninth Army Corps, Entry of Prisons and Prisoners, RG 393, NA; Carter to Brigadier General Edward E. Potter, Dec. 15, 1863, Provost Marshal General, District of East Tennessee, Press Copies of Letters Sent, Sept. 1863–64, RG 393, NA; Carter to Brigadier General Davis Tillson, June 13, 1864, Provost Marshal General, District of East Tennessee, Press Copies of Letters and Telegrams Sent, 1864–65, RG 393, NA; Office of the Provost Marshal General of East Tennessee, Special Orders No. 2, June 14, 1864, No. 18, July 20, 1864, No. 27, Aug. 13, 1864, No. 29, Aug. 16, 1864, No. 30, Aug. 17, 1864, No. 31, Aug. 20, 1864, No. 52, Oct. 19, 1864, No. 76, Dec. 4, 1864, District of East Tennessee, Special Orders Issued by the Provost Marshal General, RG 393, NA; Fourth Division, Twenty-third Army Corps, Special Orders No. 46, Aug. 3, 1864, No. 51, Aug. 18, 1864, District of East Tennessee and Fourth Division, Twenty-third Army Corps, Special Orders Issued, Apr. 1864–Mar. 1866, RG 393, NA.

21. Army of the Ohio, General Field Orders No. 6, Aug. 19, 1863, Department and Army of the Ohio, Printed Copies of General Orders, Aug. 1862–Dec. 1864, RG 393, NA; Army of the Ohio, Special Field Orders No. 75, Nov. 10, 1863, *OR* 31(3):111–12; Assistant Adjutant General Lewis Richmond to Lieutenant Colonel H. C. Ransom, n.d., Army and Department of the Ohio,

Letters Sent, Aug. 1863–Jan. 1865, RG 393, NA; Carter to the Officer of the Prisoner Guard, Oct. 29, 1863, Carter to Captain W. A. Harris, Dec. 2, 1863, Provost Marshal General, District of East Tennessee, Press Copies of Letters Sent, Sept. 1863–64, RG 393, NA; Brigadier General Samuel D. Sturgis to Foster, Dec. 22, 1863, Department of the Ohio, Letters Sent, 1861–65, RG 393, NA.

22. Army of the Ohio, General Field Orders No. 10, Sept. 15, 1863, Army and Department of the Ohio, Printed Copies of General Orders, Aug. 1862–Dec. 1864, RG 393, NA.

23. Army of the Ohio, General Field Orders No. 10, Sept. 15, 1863, General Field Orders No. 25, Nov. 4, 1863, Army and Department of the Ohio, Printed Copies of General Orders, Aug. 1862–Dec. 1864, RG 393, NA; Samuel P. Carter Memoirs, UTSC; Carter to Captain Branson, June 3, 1864, District of East Tennessee, Press Copies of Telegrams Sent by the Provost Marshal General, RG 393, NA.

24. Richmond to Colonel W. C. Lerner, Sept. 17, 1863, Department and Army of the Ohio, Letters Sent, Aug. 1863–Jan. 1865, RG 393, NA; Assistant Adjutant General R. H. Goddard to Lieutenant Colonel Drake, Oct. 4, 1863, Twenty-third Army Corps, Telegrams Received, 1864–65, RG 393, NA; Schofield to Lieutenant Colonel G. W. Bascom, July 27, 1864, Department of North Carolina and Army of the Ohio, Telegrams Sent, Apr. 1864–Jan. 1865, RG 393, NA; Ammen to Lieutenant Edward G. Fechet, Nov. 8, Dec. 17, Dec. 24, 1864, Major General George Stoneman to Fechet, Mar. 11, Mar. 15, Apr. 1, Apr. 4, Apr. 13, Apr. 19, 1865, District of East Tennessee, Letters Sent, Apr. 1864–Mar. 1866, RG 393, NA; Lieutenant Colonel W. C. Bartlett to Ammen, Dec. 30, 1864, District of East Tennessee, Telegrams Received, 1864–65, RG 393, NA.

25. Wilson, *Column South*, 134; William Randolph Carter, *First Tennessee*, 134–36; Foster to Grant, Knoxville, Jan. 16, 1864, Department and Army of the Ohio, Telegrams Sent, Dec. 1863–Dec. 1864, RG 393, NA; Bartlett to Tillson, Jan. 28, 1865, District of East Tennessee, Telegrams Received, 1864–65, RG 393, NA; Tillson to Gibson, Feb. 10, 1865, District of East Tennessee, Letters Sent, Apr. 1864–Mar. 1866, RG 393, NA; Carter to Tillson, June 4, 1864, Provost Marshal General, District of East Tennessee, Press Copies of Letters and Telegrams Sent, 1864–65, RG 393, NA; "Resolutions," Zion Hill Church, Anderson County, Oct. 6, 1864, District of East Tennessee, Letters Received, 1863–64, RG 393, NA; "Declaration of the Home Guard, Carter County, Tennessee, 1865," TSLA.

26. Folmsbee, Corlew, and Mitchell, *Tennessee*, 3:74–75; James B. Campbell, "East Tennessee," 66–67, 75–76; Humes, *Loyal Mountaineers*, 265–66; Coulter, *Brownlow*, 250–57.

27. Carter to Colonel John M. Foster, Sept. 12, 1863, Provost Marshal General, District of East Tennessee, Press Copies of Letters Sent, Sept. 1863–64, RG 393, NA; Office of the Provost Marshal General of East Tennessee, Circular No. 9, Dec. 22, 1863, Ninth Army Corps, Entry of Prisons and Prisoners, RG 393, NA.

28. Livingood, *Hamilton County*, 206; Lillard, *Bradley County*, 62–63;

Temple, *East Tennessee*, 410; Edward Maynard to Dr. Pick, Nov. 17, 1863, Horace Maynard Papers, UTSC; Carter to Knoxville post commander, Dec. 28, 1864, Carter to Lieutenant S. F. Shaw, Dec. 29, 1864, Jan. 10, 1865, Provost Marshal General, District of East Tennessee, Press Copies of Letters Sent, Sept. 1863–64, RG 393, NA; William G. Swan to J. G. M. Ramsey, Feb. 13, 1865, Ramsey Family Papers, UTSC; Ellen McClung to her brother, Oct. 13, 1864, Campbell Family Papers, DU.

29. Schofield to Bascom, July 24, 1864, Department of North Carolina and Army of the Ohio, Letters Sent, Apr. 1864–Jan. 1865, RG 393, NA; Mary Jane Reynolds to S. B. Reynolds, Loudon, Feb. 17, June 5, June 20, 1864, Mary Jane Reynolds Letters, UTSC; Carter, "Statements," June 28, 1864, Carter to Captain J. W. Branson, June 28, 1864, Provost Marshal General, District of East Tennessee, Press Copies of Letters and Telegrams Sent, 1864–65, RG 393, NA; Bascom to Carter, Aug. 15, 1864, Department and Army of the Ohio, Letters Sent, Aug. 1863–Jan. 1865, RG 393, NA; Colonel James B. Brownlow to Oliver P. Temple, Sept. 9, 1864, Oliver P. Temple Papers, UTSC.

30. Headquarters United States Forces, Kingston, General Orders No. 4, June 25, 1864, John Wilson Hines Papers, SHC; Carter to Branson, Aug. 6, 1864, Provost Marshal General, District of East Tennessee, Press Copies of Letters and Telegrams Sent, 1864–65, RG 393, NA.

31. Carter to Lieutenant Colonel Brownlow, Jan. 10, 1864, Provost Marshal General, District of East Tennessee, Press Copies of Letters Sent, Sept. 1863–64, RG 393, NA; Mary Jane Reynolds to S. B. Reynolds, Mar. 13, Apr. 18, 1864, Mary Jane Reynolds Letters, UTSC; Schofield to Brigadier General William D. Whipple, Apr. 26, 1864, District of East Tennessee, Press Copies of Letters and Telegrams Sent, 1863–64, RG 393, NA; Carter to Major John McGaughy, Aug. 5, 1864, Provost Marshal General, District of East Tennessee, Press Copies of Letters and Telegrams Sent, 1864–65, RG 393, NA; Carter to Brigadier General Thomas Meegher, Dec. 28, 1864, Provost Marshal General, District of East Tennessee, Press Copies of Letters Sent, Sept. 1863–64, RG 393, NA.

For accounts of resistance by white women to Federal occupation, see Ash, *Yankees*, 41–44; Catherine Clinton and Nina Silber, eds., *Divided Houses: Gender and the Civil War* (New York: Oxford University Press, 1992); George C. Rable, *Civil Wars* (Urbana: University of Illinois Press, 1989); Bell Irvin Wiley, *Confederate Women* (Westport, Conn.: Greenwood Press, 1975).

32. Fourth Division, Twenty-third Army Corps, General Orders No. 24, Oct. 19, 1864, General Orders No. 10, Jan. 31, 1865, District of East Tennessee and Fourth Division, Twenty-third Army Corps, General Orders Issued, RG 393, NA; Major General George Stoneman to Mr. M. L. Hall, May 17, 1865, District of East Tennessee, Letters Sent, Apr. 1864–Mar. 1866, RG 393, NA.

33. Oath of Allegiance, n.d., Ninth Army Corps, Entry of Prisons and Prisoners, RG 393, NA; Oath of Allegiance, First Brigade, Fourth Division, Twenty-third Army Corps, n.d., District of East Tennessee and Fourth Division, Twenty-third Army Corps, RG 393, NA.

34. Schofield to Carter, June 14, 1864, Schofield to Carter, July 3, 1864, Department of North Carolina and Army of the Ohio, Telegrams Sent, Apr. 1864–Jan. 1865, RG 393, NA; Carter to George W. Ross, June 14, 1864, Carter to Major J. A. Campbell, June 14, 1864, Carter to McGaughy, June 18, 1864, Carter to Major General J. A. Webster, June 27, 1864, Provost Marshal General, District of East Tennessee, Press Copies of Letters and Telegrams Sent, 1864–65, RG 393, NA.

35. Major General William T. Sherman to Brigadier General Stephen G. Burbridge, June 21, 1864, Military Division of the Mississippi, Letters Sent in the Field, RG 393, NA.

36. Army of the Ohio, General Orders No. 150, Sept. 15, 1863, Department and Army of the Ohio, Printed Copies of General Orders, Aug. 1862–Dec. 1864, RG 393, NA; Fourth Division, Twenty-third Army Corps, General Orders No. 10, July 12, 1864, No. 19, Aug. 30, 1864, No. 22, Oct. 1, 1864, No. 4, Jan. 23, 1865, District of East Tennessee and Fourth Division, Twenty-third Army Corps, General Orders Issued, RG 393, NA; Army of the Ohio, General Orders No. 87, Oct. 13, 1864, No. 93, Oct. 27, 1864, No. 7, Dec. 31, 1864, Department and Army of the Ohio, Printed Copies of General Orders, Aug. 1862–Dec. 1864, RG 393, NA. For an excellent discussion of the establishment of Union military commissions in general and the problems associated, see Neely, *Liberty*, 161–69.

37. District of East Tennessee, Records of the Provost Marshal General, Roll of Prisoners in Custody, RG 393, NA; District of East Tennessee, Records of the Provost Marshal General, Record of Political Prisoners Confined in Citizens Prison, Knoxville, Apr. 6, 1864, RG 393, NA; District of East Tennessee, Records of the Provost Marshal General, Register of Names of Political Prisoners Confined in U.S. Military Prison at Knoxville, Tennessee, RG 393, NA; Ninth Army Corps, Entry of Prisons and Prisoners, RG 393, NA.

38. Carter to Ammen, Knoxville, Jan. 4, 1865, District of East Tennessee, Office of the Provost Marshal General, Press Copies of Letters Sent, Nov. 1864–65, RG 393, NA; W. M. Clarkson to Nelson, June 2, 1864, John Murell to Nelson, Oct. 30, 1864, T. A. R. Nelson Papers, MC; W. C. Kaine and J. R. McCann to William B. Campbell, Jan. 15, 1866, Campbell Family Papers, DU.

39. Assistant Adjutant General Lewis Richmond to Colonel William Elliot, Dec. 4, 1863, Department and Army of the Ohio, Letters Sent, Aug. 1863–Jan. 1865, RG 393, NA; John C. Gaut and David T. Patterson to Johnson, Feb. 14, 1864, Graf, Haskins, and Bergeron, *Johnson Papers*, 6:605–6; Memoirs of Thomas H. McCallie, published in *Chattanooga Free Press*, Sept. 21, 1938, Wells Family Papers, TSLA.

40. Carter to Bascom, June 21, 1864, Carter to David S. Patterson, Oct. 3, 1864, Provost Marshal General, District of East Tennessee, Press Copies of Letters and Telegrams Sent, 1864–65, RG 393, NA.

41. Scott and Angel, *Thirteenth Tennessee*, 336; Carter, "Announcement," Office of the Provost Marshal General of East Tennessee, Sept. 28, 1863, T. A. R. Nelson Papers, MC.

42. Folmsbee, Corlew, and Mitchell, *Tennessee*, 3:74–75; Alexander, "Nei-

ther Peace nor War"; James B. Campbell, "East Tennessee," 66–67; Patton, *Unionism*, 69–70; Coulter, *Brownlow*, 273; Horace Maynard to Johnson, Sept. 28, 1863, Graf, Haskins, and Bergeron, *Johnson Papers*, 6:387–88.

43. Carter to Captain J. W. Reilly, Oct. 22, 1863, Carter to Lieutenant Underdown, June 3, 1864, Provost Marshal General, District of East Tennessee, Press Copies of Letters Sent, Sept. 1863–64, RG 393, NA; Assistant Adjutant General H. H. Thomas to Wade Newman, June 20, 1864, Provost Marshal General, District of East Tennessee, Press Copies of Letters and Telegrams Sent, 1864–65, RG 393, NA; Bascom to Captain S. F. Bryan, May 4, 1865, District of East Tennessee, Letters Sent, Apr. 1864–Mar. 1866, RG 393, NA.

44. Army of the Ohio, General Field Orders No. 10, Sept. 15, 1863, Army and Department of the Ohio, Printed Copies of General Orders, Aug. 1862–Dec. 1864, RG 393, NA.

45. Army of the Ohio, General Field Orders No. 2, Aug. 14, 1863, General Field Orders No. 11, Aug. 31, 1863, General Field Orders No. 13 and 14, Sept. 17, 1863, Department and Army of the Ohio, Printed Copies of General Orders, Aug. 1862–Dec. 1864, RG 393, NA; Twenty-third Army Corps, General Orders No. 29, Sept. 8, 1863, Twenty-third Army Corps, General Orders and Circulars, May 1863–May 1864, RG 393, NA; First Division, Ninth Army Corps, Circular, Sept. 23, 1863, Ninth Army Corps, Circulars, Dec. 1862–Mar. 1864, RG 393, NA; Army of the Ohio, Circular, Nov. 22, 1863, General Field Orders No. 40, Dec. 12, 1863, Department and Army of the Ohio, General Orders, Dec. 1863–May 1864, Jan. 1865, RG 393, NA. See also Grimsley, *Hard Hand*, 23–35, 54–66.

46. Carter to Lieutenant Colonel Selfridge, Dec. 10, 1863, Carter to Potter, Dec. 19, 1863, Carter to Potter, Dec. 26, 1863, Nelson to Carter, Dec. 26, 1863, *OR* 31(3):372, 447–48, 506–8; Cavalry Corps, Army of the Ohio, Circular, Dec. 28, 1863, Circular, Jan. 4, 1864, Sturgis to Potter, Jan. 24, 1864, *OR* 32(1):114–15; Foster to Major General John G. Parke, Jan. 27, 1864, Army and Department of the Ohio, Letters Sent, Aug. 1863–Jan. 1865, RG 393, NA; Twenty-third Army Corps, General Orders No. 8, Jan. 28, 1864, Twenty-third Army Corps, General Orders and Circulars, May 1863–May 1864, RG 393, NA.

47. Humes, *Loyal Mountaineers*, 216; William F. Draper to his wife, Sept. 23, 1863, William F. Draper Papers, LC; William H. Bradbury to his wife, Aug. 23, 1863, William H. Bradbury Papers, LC.

48. William H. Bradbury to his wife, Aug. 27, 1863, William H. Bradbury Papers, LC; Army of the Ohio, General Orders No 14, Jan. 28, 1864, Department and Army of the Ohio, Printed Copies of General Orders, Aug. 1862–Dec. 1864, RG 393, NA; Brigadier General John Beatty to Thomas, Oct. 14, 1863, *OR* 30(4):366–70; Chauncey B. Welton to his brother, Sept. 29, 1863, Chauncey B. Welton Letters, SHC; Albert A. Pope Diary, Jan. 3, 1864, MHI; Hugh Carlisle Reminiscences, MHI; Foster to Halleck, Dec. 14, 1863, Jan. 11, 1864, Army and Department of the Ohio, Letters Sent, Aug. 1863–Jan. 1865, RG 393, NA; Potter to Major General Gordon Granger, Jan. 26, 1864, *OR* 32(2):218; Cavalry Corps, Army of the Ohio, Circular, Feb. 26, 1864, Department of the Ohio, Letters Sent, 1861–65, RG 393, NA.

49. Clifton R. Hall, *Johnson*, 73; William B. Carter to Johnson, Feb. 19, 1862, William S. Speer to Johnson, Feb. 19, 1862, Johnson to Lincoln, June 5, 1862, Johnson to Major General Lorenzo Thomas, Aug. 18, 1862, Thomas to Johnson, Aug. 18, 1862, Graf, Haskins, and Bergeron, *Johnson Papers*, 5:149, 150, 445–46, 623; Major General Edmund Kirby Smith to Brigadier General George C. Morgan, Aug. 1, 1862, Department of East Tennessee, Letters and Telegrams Sent, Mar.–Sept. 1862, RG 109, NA. Hostage taking was not an uncommon practice in the Civil War. See Neely, *Liberty*, 151–58.

50. Judge T. Nixon van Dyke to President Jefferson Davis, Jan. 28, 1864, *OR*, Series 2, 1:890–91; Mrs. E. T. Helms to Nelson, Dec. 13, 1864, T. A. R. Nelson Papers, MC; Carter to Shaw, Aug. 5, 1864, Carter to Gillem, Oct. 28, 1864, Provost Marshal General, District of East Tennessee, Press Copies of Letters and Telegrams Sent, 1864–65, RG 393, NA; Tilson to Deputy Provost Marshal M. McTeer, Feb. 21, 1865, District of East Tennessee, Letters Sent, Apr. 1864–Mar. 1866, RG 393, NA; Captain W. A. Cochran to Tillson, Mar. 2, 1865, District of East Tennessee, Telegrams Received, 1864–65, RG 393, NA; Branson to Schofield, Aug. 8, 1864, *OR* 39(1):460–61; Carter to Deputy Provost Marshal Thomas Sanderson, Nov. 6, 1864, Provost Marshal General, District of East Tennessee, Press Copies of Letters Sent, Sept. 1863–64, RG 393, NA; Tillson to Stoneman, Feb. 15, 1865, District of East Tennessee, Letters Received, 1863–65, RG 393, NA.

51. Brigadier General John Hunt Morgan to Inspector and Adjutant General Samuel Cooper, July 22, 1864, Department of East Tennessee, Telegrams Sent, Apr. 1863–Sept. 1864, RG 109, NA; Brigadier General John C. Vaughn to Colonel David M. Key, Sept. 28, 1864, David McKendree Key Papers, SHC.

52. For informal exchanges, see Schofield to Lieutenant General James Longstreet, Feb. 10, Mar. 23, 1864, Department and Army of the Ohio, Letters Sent, Aug. 1863–Jan. 1865, RG 393, NA; Carter to Colonel F. Foote, June 8, 1864, Carter to Colonel William Hoffman, June 15, 1864, Carter to Vaughn, Knoxville, June 17, 1864, Provost Marshal General, District of East Tennessee, Press Copies of Letters and Telegrams Sent, 1864–65, RG 393, NA.

For Morgan's proposal and the Union response, see Morgan to Carter, Aug. 7, 1864, Department of East Tennessee, Letters, Orders, Circulars, Apr. 1863–Oct. 1864, RG 109, NA; Bascom to Gillem, Aug. 23, Sept. 27, 1864, Army and Department of the Ohio, Telegrams Sent, Dec. 1863–Dec. 1864, RG 393, NA; Carter to Morgan, Aug. 15, 1864, *OR*, Series 2, 7:597; Schofield to Gillem, Sept. 2, 1864, Department and Army of the Ohio, Letters Sent, Aug. 1863–Jan. 1865, RG 393, NA; Carter to Gillem, Sept. 22, 1864, Provost Marshal General, District of East Tennessee, Press Copies of Letters and Telegrams Sent, 1864–65, RG 393, NA; Gillem to Dillard, Sept. 22, 1864, District of East Tennessee, Letters Received, 1863–64, RG 393, NA; Vaughn to Major General John C. Breckinridge, Oct. 26, 1864, *OR*, Series 2, 7:1046.

53. Adjutant and Inspector General's Office, Special Orders No. 267, Nov. 9, 1864, Colonel Robert Ould to Secretary of War James A. Seddon, Nov. 17, 1864, *OR*, Series 2, 7:1114–15, 1125. For J. B. Heiskell, see Office of the Provost Marshal General of East Tennessee, Special Orders No. 43, Sept. 27, 1864, District of East Tennessee, Special Orders Issued by the Provost Marshal

General, RG 393, NA; Johnson to Sherman, Aug. 8, 1864, Graf, Haskins, and Bergeron, *Johnson Papers*, 7:125.

54. Carter to Schofield, Nov. 20, 1864, *OR*, Series 2, 7:1145; Schofield to Carter, Nov. 20, 1864, Department of North Carolina and Army of the Ohio, Telegrams Sent, Apr. 1864–Jan. 1865, RG 393, NA; Carter and Vaughn, "Articles of Agreement for Exchange," Dec. 1, 1864, *OR*, Series 2, 7:1175; Carter to Captain Robert Morrow, Dec. 3, 1864, Trowbridge to Morrow, Mar. 5, 1865, Provost Marshal General, District of East Tennessee, Press Copies of Letters and Telegrams Sent, 1864–65, RG 393, NA; Vaughn to Secretary of War James A. Seddon, Dec. 5, 1864, *OR*, Series 2, 7:1192–93.

55. Carter to Stoneman, Dec. 10, 1864, Provost Marshal General, District of East Tennessee, Press Copies of Letters and Telegrams Sent, 1864–65, RG 393, NA; Carter to Vaughn, Dec. 10, 1864, Provost Marshal General, District of East Tennessee, Press Copies of Letters Sent, Sept. 1863–64, RG 393, NA; Carter to Major General Ethan Allan Hitchcock, Dec. 10, 1864, Hitchcock to Carter, Dec. 23, 1864, *OR*, Series 2, 7:1208, 1263–64; Office of the Provost Marshal General of East Tennessee, Special Orders No. 80, Dec. 12, 1864, Carter to Vaughn, Knoxville, Dec. 21, 1864, District of East Tennessee, Special Orders Issued by the Provost Marshal General, RG 393, NA.

56. Seddon to Vaughn, Dec. 15, 1864, *OR*, Series 2, 7:1299; Trowbridge to Morrow, Mar. 5, 1865, Provost Marshal General, District of East Tennessee, Press Copies of Letters and Telegrams Sent, 1864–65, RG 393, NA; Carter to Hitchcock, Jan. 8, 1865, *OR*, Series 2, 8:25–26.

57. Trowbridge to Vaughn, Feb. 8, Feb. 14, 1865, Trowbridge to Morrow, Mar. 5, Mar. 10, 1865, Provost Marshal General, District of East Tennessee, Press Copies of Letters Sent, Sept. 1863–64, RG 393, NA; Vaughn to Breckinridge, Feb. 19, 1865, Vaughn to Trowbridge, Feb. 20, 1865, *OR*, Series 2, 8:267, 272–74.

58. Samuel W. Melton to Vaughn, Mar. 2, 1865, Secretary of War John C. Breckinridge to Colonel Robert Ould, Mar. 8, 1865, and Ould, Indorsement, *OR*, Series 2, 8:335, 368.

CHAPTER SEVEN

1. Major General D. S. Stanley to Major General George Thomas, Apr. 13, 1865, Brigadier General Davis Tillson to Major George Bascom, May 5, 1865, *OR* 49(2):343, 625; Colonel James Parsons to Bascom, May 16, 1865, District of East Tennessee, Telegrams Received, 1864–65, RG 393, NA; B. W. Howard "to Gen. Gibson or the Commander of the Post at Knoxville," Apr. 17, 1865, Major H. L. Barnes to Captain Dean, Apr. 23, 1865, Lieutenant Thomas B. McKenzie to Colonel Thomas J. Harrison, Apr. 27, 1865, District of East Tennessee and Fourth Division, Department of the Cumberland, Letters and Telegrams Received, 1865, RG 393, NA; Captain James W. Harrington to Major General George Stoneman, Rutledge, Apr. 30, 1865, *OR* 49(2):528–29.

2. Burns and Blankenship, *Fiddles*, 278; Thomas to Tillson, Apr. 17, 1865,

Stoneman to Parsons, Apr. 21, 1865, Stoneman to Harrington, Apr. 25, May 1, 1865, District of East Tennessee, Letters Sent, Apr. 1864–Mar. 1866, RG 393, NA; Harrington to Stoneman, Apr. 30, 1865, Brigadier General William D. Whipple to Major General L. H. Rousseau, May 25, 1865, Whipple to Stoneman, May 25, 1865, Whipple to Thomas, May 30, 1865, Whipple to Stoneman, May 30, 1865, Whipple to Brigadier General R. W. Johnson, June 1, 1865, *OR* 49(2):528–29, 904–5, 931, 933, 946; Parsons to Major George Bascom, May 16, 1865, District of East Tennessee, Telegrams Received, 1864–65, RG 393, NA; Captain Robert Morrow to Brigadier General Alvin C. Gillem, June 5, 1865, District of East Tennessee, Telegrams Sent, July–Nov. 1865, RG 393, NA; Colonel Croft to Morrow, June 10, 1865, District of East Tennessee, Telegrams Sent, May–Sept. 1865, RG 393, NA.

3. Stoneman to Thomas, Apr. 25, 1865, Thomas to Major General James Steedman, Stoneman, Major General Cadwallader Washburne, Rousseau, Colonel Smith, Colonel Gilfillan, May 1, 1865, *OR* 49(2):465, 552–53; Post Commandant, Jonesborough, General Orders No. 2, Apr. 24, 1865, John Wilson Hines Papers, SHC.

4. Alexander, *Reconstruction*, 72; Sensing, *Ferguson*; Emmet Ramsey to Carrie Stakely, May 5, 1865, Sue Coffee to Margaret Stakely, Mar. 19, 1866, Hall-Stakely Papers, MC; Major General Alvin Gillem to Johnson, Nov. 11, 1865, Graf, Haskins, and Bergeron, *Johnson Papers*, 7:372–73.

5. Fourth Division, Department of the Cumberland, Special Orders No. 29, May 10, 1865, District of East Tennessee and Fourth Division, Department of the Cumberland, Special Orders Issued, Mar.–Sept. 1865, RG 393, NA; Major Lawson to Major Wright, June 10, 1865, District of East Tennessee and Fourth Division, Department of the Cumberland, Letters and Telegrams Received, 1865, RG 393, NA; Gillem to Lieutenant Colonel M. L. Courtrey, Sept. 15, 1865, District of East Tennessee, Telegrams Sent, July–Nov., 1865, RG 393, NA; District of East Tennessee, General Orders No. 27, Apr. 29, 1865, General Orders No. 31, May 6, 1865, District of East Tennessee and Fourth Division, Twenty-third Army Corps, General Orders Issued, RG 393, NA.

6. Groce, "Mountain Rebels," 189–93; Bailey, *Confederate Generation*, 106–11, 117; Lyman Potter Spencer Diary, May 1, 1865, LC; Elizabeth Caswell to William Caswell, June 19, 1865, William Richard Caswell Papers, MC; David Anderson Deaderick Journal, May 1865, MC; William Gibbs Allen Memoirs, TSLA; Major J. B. Atkins to Lieutenant Bradford, May 25, 1865, Second Brigade, Fourth Division, Department of the Cumberland, Letters and Telegrams Received, RG 393, NA; Marion S. Wofford to Johnson, Sept. 11, 1865, Andrew Johnson Correspondence, TSLA.

7. Sullins, *Recollections*, 307; Mary Stakely to Callie, May 28, 1865, Hall-Stakely Papers, MC; A. L. Mims to Nelson, Nov. 8, 1865, May 17, 1866, T. A. R. Nelson Papers, MC; William Henry Maxwell to Johnson, Nov. 2, 1865, Graf, Haskins, and Bergeron, *Johnson Papers*, 9:336–38; David M. Key to Lizzie, Feb. 14, 1866, David McKendree Key Papers, SHC.

8. Elizabeth Caswell to William Caswell, June 19, 1865, William Richard Caswell Papers, MC; David Anderson Deaderick Journal, May 1865, MC;

W. W. Wallace to Nelson, Aug. 26, 1865, John G. King to Nelson and John Netherland, Oct. 23, 1865, Wallace to Nelson, Aug. 23, Nov. 20, 1865, Jan. 8, 1866, "James M. Trewhitt, adm of Levi Trewhitt, decd., vs. William H. Tibbs, etc.," T. A. R. Nelson Papers, MC; Hugh Bogle to Temple, Jan. 6, 1866, Brigadier General Alfred E. Jackson to Temple, June 28, 1866, Oliver P. Temple Papers, UTSC.

9. Ragan, *Escape*, 47; W. L. Eakin to Key, Sept. 20, 1865, David McKendree Key Papers, SHC; Key to Rufus T. Lenoir, Jan. 15, 1866, Lenoir Family Papers, SHC; Bird G. Manard to Nelson, June 28, 1865, Mrs. Joseph B. Heiskell to Nelson, July 26, 1865, T. A. R. Nelson Papers, MC; Father Abraham Ryan to Miss Canny, Sept. 12, 1865, Father Abraham Ryan Correspondence, TSLA; Samuel Milligan to Johnson, Sept. 1, 1865, Thomas to Johnson, Nashville, Sept. 7, 1865, Graf, Haskins, and Bergeron, *Johnson Papers*, 9:10–11, 41.

10. Groce, "Mountain Rebels," 215; Alexander, *Reconstruction*, 183; Alexander, "Ku Kluxism"; James B. Campbell, "Reconstruction," 96–97, 103–4; Trelease, *White Terror*, 3–46, 177; Brownlow to General Joseph A. Cooper, July 25, 1867, Papers of the Governors, William G. Brownlow, TSLA; F. A. Brabson to C. W. Slagle, Feb. 21, 1868, Jacob Siler Papers, SHC.

11. Patton, *Unionism*, 106; Robert Johnson to Johnson, May 31, 1865, Graf, Haskins, and Bergeron, *Johnson Papers*, 8:155–56; George L., John C., and David C. Boren to their father, July 28, 1865, Boren Family Papers, MC; Mrs. Horace Maynard to Washburne Maynard, Sept. 26, 1865, Horace Maynard Papers, UTSC.

12. Memorial from Washington County Citizens, Apr. 20, 1866, Graf, Haskins, and Bergeron, *Johnson Papers*, 10:435–37; David Anderson Deaderick Journal, May 1865, MC; Mrs. Joseph B. Heiskell to T. A. R. Nelson, July 26, 1865, O. R. Broyles to Nelson, July 24, 1865, T. A. R. Nelson Papers, MC; Father Abraham Ryan to Miss Canny, Sept. 12, Sept. 16, 1865, Father Abraham Ryan Correspondence, TSLA.

13. James A. Rhea to Nelson, Oct. 11, 1865, Wright McKissick to Nelson, Mar. 31, 1866, W. R. Wilson to Nelson, Apr. 22, 1866, "William Brecht vs. John Carmichael," May 31, 1865, Levi W. Lynes to Nelson, Jan. 16, 1867, T. A. R. Nelson Papers, MC; James M. Hickman to Temple, Apr. 24, 1865, Oliver P. Temple Papers, UTSC; William Williams Stringfield, "History of the Sixty-Ninth North Carolina," NCSA; William Gibbs Allen Memoirs, TSLA.

14. Coulter, *Brownlow*, 274–75; "James Pickens vs. W. H. Sneed, John Crozier, W. B. Reynolds," Feb. 1865, "James M. Trewhitt vs. William H. Tibbs, Thomas J. Campbell, James W. Gillespie, Elizah F. Johnson, William L. Brown, Robert L. McClung, C. L. Hardwicke, J. M. Horton, Joseph Tucker, Robert S. Holt, John M. Dunn, James Donahue, John B. Coxie," Sept. 8, 1865, T. A. R. Nelson Papers, MC.

15. Key to Rufus T. Lenoir, Jan. 15, 1866, Lenoir Family Papers, SHC; Samuel T. Logan to Nelson, Nov. 25, 1867, T. A. R Nelson Papers, MC; David Anderson Deaderick Journal, 1868, MC; Tom Brabson to C. W. Slagle, June 13, 1865, Jacob Siler Papers, SHC.

16. Alexander, *Nelson*, 147–52; Humes, *Loyal Mountaineers*, 346–47; Brownlow to Temple, Jan. 25, 1866, George W. Bridges to Temple, May 11, 1866, Oliver P. Temple Papers, UTSC; Brownlow to Nelson, May 9, 1867, "William G. Brownlow vs. Robert B. Reynolds, Thomas J. Campbell, John H. Crozier, William H. Sneed, John C. Ramsey," Nov. 23, 1867, T. A. R. Nelson Papers, MC; U.S. District Court, Eastern District, Tennessee, Knoxville, Minute Book A, 1864–65, Jan. 27, Feb. 1, 1866, Minute Book B, 1865–70, Jan. 3, 1866, Jan. 7, 1868, RG 21, NASR.

17. Clifton R. Hall, *Johnson*, 131; U.S. District Court, Eastern District, Tennessee, Knoxville, Minute Book A, 1864–65, Minute Book B, 1865–70, RG 21, NASR; "State vs. William H. Sneed," Oct. 10, 1864, T. A. R. Nelson Papers, MC.

18. Temple, *Notable Men*, 212; U.S. District Court, Eastern District, Tennessee, Knoxville, Minute Book A, 1864–65, Minute Book B, 1865–70, RG 21, NASR.

19. U.S. District Court, Eastern District, Tennessee, Knoxville, Minute Book A, 1864–65, June 14, Dec. 29, 1864, Jan. 5, Jan. 11, June 9, 1865, Minute Book B, 1865–70, Dec. 1, Jan. 11, Jan. 12, 1866, RG 21, NASR.

20. Groce, "Mountain Rebels," 210–20; Bryan, "East Tennessee," 182–86; Bellamy, "Haynes," 74–75; Sullins, *Recollections*, 260–61, 295; Colonel Henry M. Doak Memoirs, TSLA; William G. McAdoo Diary, July 8, Dec. 5, 1867, Floyd-McAdoo Papers, LC; Charles McClung to Sue Ramsey, June 8, 1866, Ramsey Family Papers, UTSC; David Anderson Deaderick Journal, 1867, MC; J. G. M. Ramsey to Lizzie, Oct. 12, 1864, Diary of Mrs. Margaret Ramsey, J. G. M. Ramsey, Autobiography, vol. 1, J. G. M Ramsey to John Crozier Ramsey, Oct. 21, 1866, J. G. M. Ramsey Papers, SHC.

For accounts of migrations by other groups during Reconstruction, see Daniel E. Sutherland, *The Confederate Carpetbaggers* (Baton Rouge: Louisiana State University Press, 1988); Leon F. Litwack, *Been in the Storm So Long: The Aftermath of Slavery* (New York: Knopf, 1979); Nell Irvin Painter, *Exodusters: Black Migration to Kansas after Reconstruction* (New York: Knopf, 1976).

21. Alexander, *Reconstruction*, 66; William M. Stakely to Martha, July 18, 1865, Hall-Stakely Papers, MC; John Crozier Ramsey to his sister, Aug. 4, 1865, J. G. M. Ramsey Papers, SHC; Frank McClung to Mrs. McClung, Dec. 20, 1865, Campbell Family Papers, Manuscript Department, DU; John Crozier Ramsey to J. G. M. Ramsey, Knoxville, Apr. 9, 1867, Ramsey Family Papers, UTSC.

22. Lizzie Key to Sarah Lenoir, Jan. 14, 1866, David M. Key to Rufus T. Lenoir, Jan. 15, 1866, Lenoir Family Papers, SHC; Special Pardon from President Andrew Johnson, May 29, 1865, David McKendree Key Papers, SHC; David M. Key to William B. Stokes, Mar. 10, 1870, William B. Stokes Correspondence, TSLA; Ledger, United Confederate Veterans, May 7, 1908, entry for Captain William Williams Stringfield, Hyatt Collections, NCSA; William Williams Stringfield, "History of the Sixty-Ninth North Carolina," NCSA; William Gibbs Allen Memoir, TSLA; Brigadier General Alfred E. Jackson to Temple, June 28, 1866, Oliver P. Temple Papers, UTSC.

23. Humes, *Loyal Mountaineers*, 301–33; Humes, *Relief Association*.

24. Clifton R. Hall, *Johnson*, 12–126; Patton, *Unionism*, 44–45; Temple, *Notable Men*, 44–47, 92, 307; Mary Jane Reynolds to S. B Reynolds, Apr. 17, May 1, 1864, Mary Jane Reynolds Letters, UTSC.

25. Alexander, *Nelson*, 113–17; Clifton R. Hall, *Johnson*, 139–56; Brownlow to Johnson, Nov. 12, 1864, Graf, Haskins, and Bergeron, *Johnson Papers*, 7:235–36; "Protest," signed by William B. Campbell, Nelson, James P. Carter, John Williams, A. Blizzard, Henry Cooper, Bailie Peyton, John Lellyett, Emerson Etheridge, John B. Berryman, 1864, T. A. R. Nelson Papers, MC.

26. Alexander, *Nelson*, 118–20; Alexander, *Reconstruction*, 18–32; Clifton R. Hall, *Johnson*, 157–58; Patton, *Unionism*, 348–50.

27. Alexander, *Reconstruction*, 73–77; Coulter, *Brownlow*, 302–3; Patton, *Unionism*, 70–71, 83–102.

28. Alexander, *Reconstruction*, 99–110, 122–40; Patton, *Unionism*, 114–29, 135, 175–77, 189–95.

29. Alexander, *Nelson*, 122–27; D. C. Trewhitt to L. C. Houk, May 23, 1866, Nat B. Owens to Houk, Sept. 22, 1866, Leonidas Campbell and John C. Houk Papers, MC; Brownlow to [unknown], Aug. 9, 1866, Papers of the Governors, William G. Brownlow, TSLA; *Knoxville Whig*, Mar. 26, 1866. For discussions of Johnson's Reconstruction policies, see David W. Bowen, *Johnson*; McKitrick, *Johnson*.

30. Alexander, *Reconstruction*, 124–30, 141–62; Horace Maynard, "To the Slaveholders of Tennessee," July 4, 1863, Horace Maynard Papers, UTSC; Johnson, "Speech to Union State Convention," Jan. 12, 1865, Graf, Haskins, and Bergeron, *Johnson Papers*, 7:392–400.

31. Humphreys, *Brownlow*, 343–66; Alexander, *Reconstruction*, 59–61, 207, 342–43; Patton, *Unionism*, 227–34; Thomas W. Humes to Brownlow, May 18, 1865, Papers of the Governors, William G. Brownlow, TSLA.

32. Alexander, *Nelson*, 145–46; Alexander, *Reconstruction*, 20–21, 198–225; Patton, *Unionism*, 226; Temple, *Notable Men*, 182–83; Barbour Lewis to John Eaton, Dec. 20, 1868, John Eaton Papers, UTSC; "Agreement Between W. B. Stokes and Gov. Senter," June 18, 1869, Lieutenant A. A. Carter to William B. Stokes, Aug. 11, 1869, William B. Stokes Correspondence, TSLA.

33. Gordon B. McKinney, *Mountain Republicans*, 33–41, 77–86.

CONCLUSION

1. Black, *Railroads*.

2. Brigadier General Felix K. Zollicoffer, July–Dec. 1861; Brigadier General George B. Crittenden, Dec. 1861–Feb. 1862; Major General Edmund Kirby Smith, Feb.–Dec. 1862; Major General John P. McCown, Aug.–Sept. 1862; Major General Sam Jones, Sept.–Oct. 1862; Brigadier General Harry Heth, Dec. 1862–Jan. 1863; Major General Daniel S. Donelson, Jan.–Apr. 1863; Brigadier General Dabney H. Maury, Apr.–May 1863; Major General Simon B. Buckner, May–Sept. 1863.

3. District of East Tennessee, Records of the Provost Marshal General, Roll of Prisoners in Custody, RG 393, NA; District of East Tennessee, Records of the Provost Marshal General, Record of Political Prisoners Confined in Citizens Prison, Apr. 6, 1864, RG 393, NA; District of East Tennessee, Records of the Provost Marshal General, Register of Names of Political Prisoners Confined in U.S. Military Prison at Knoxville, Tennessee, RG 393, NA; Department of East Tennessee, Record of Political Prisoners, 1862, RG 109, NA.

APPENDIX A

1. Temple, *East Tennessee*; Humes, *Loyal Mountaineers*.
2. Folmsbee, Corlew, and Mitchell, *Tennessee*; Alexander, *Nelson*; Abernathy, *Frontier to Plantation*.
3. Crofts, *Reluctant Confederates*; Wooster, *Secession Conventions*.
4. Lacy, *Volunteers*; Patton, *Unionism*.
5. Bryan, "East Tennessee"; Bryan, "Tories."
6. Groce, "Mountain Rebels."
7. Humes, *Loyal Mountaineers*, 91; "Sketch by Colonel Henry M. Doak," Henry M. Doak Papers, TSLA; A. Holman to Bishop Matthew Simpson, Chattanooga, Feb. 1, 1864, Matthew Simpson Correspondence, LC.

For studies of class conflicts in other areas during the Civil War, see Victoria E. Bynum, *Unruly Women: The Politics of Social and Sexual Control in the Old South* (Chapel Hill: University of North Carolina Press, 1992); Bailey, *Confederate Generation*; Escott, *Many Excellent People*; Paludan, *Victims*; Ambrose, "Yeomen Discontent."

APPENDIX B

1. Ramage, *Rebel Raider*; David S. Stanley, West-Stanley-Wright Memoirs, MHI.
2. Sarah Thompson, "Morgan's Defeat by Sarah Thompson, Herself," Statements by Second Lieutenant John G. Johnson, Jan. 10, 1875, Lieutenant Edward J. Brooks, Apr. 13, 1876, Military Governor Andrew Johnson, Nov. 7, 1864, Brigadier General Samuel P. Carter, Jan. 15, 1878, Edward J. Brooks and Sarah E. Thompson, Office of the Commissioner of Claims, Apr. 13, 1876, John B. Brownlow to Hon. W. W. Dudley, Commander of Pensions, July 7, 1882, Sarah Thompson to Secretary of the Treasury John Sherman, Apr. 19, 1879, Sarah Thompson Papers, DU; "Memorandum of Conversation of Colonel John Bell Brownlow about the Death of General John H. Morgan at Greeneville in Sept. 1864, Prepared for Mrs. Ed Ash," UTSC.
3. Cecil Fletcher Holland, *Morgan*.

BIBLIOGRAPHY

ARCHIVAL SOURCES

Library of Congress, Manuscript Division, Washington, D.C.
  John Emerson Anderson Memoir
  William H. Bradbury Papers
  William G. Brownlow Papers
  Horace Capron Papers
  David Anderson Deaderick Papers
  William Franklin Draper Letters
  Robert Edwin Jameson Letters
  August Valentine Kautz Papers
  Daniel Larned Papers
  William G. McAdoo Diary, Floyd-McAdoo Papers
  Marshall Mortimer Miller Papers
  Orlando M. Poe Papers
  Richard Henry Pratt Papers
  Francis Bowes Sayre Papers
  Matthew Simpson Correspondence
  William Farrar Smith Papers
  Spaulding Family Papers
  Lyman Potter Spencer Diary
  Arthur Van Horn Papers
  Harvey Washington Wiley Papers
  James Harrison Wilson Papers
McClung Collection, Lawson McGhee Library, Knoxville, Tenn.
  Boren Family Papers
  Cannon Family Papers
  William Richard Caswell Papers
  Crozier Letters, Edith Scott Manuscripts Collection
  D. A. and Inslee Deaderick Papers
  David Anderson Deaderick Journal
  Hall-Stakely Family Papers
  Leonidas Campbell and John C. Houk Papers
  W. S. McEwen Correspondence, Robert S. Johnson Collection
  T. A. R. Nelson Papers
  William Burton Reynolds Papers
  William Rule Papers
  William and Michael Rule Letters, Mrs. F. Graham Bartlett Collection
  Watterson Family Papers
  John and Rhoda Campbell Williams Papers

Military History Institute, Carlisle Barracks, Carlisle, Pa.
 Quintus Adams Family Papers
 John W. Barringer Papers
 David Benfer Papers
 Henry J. Curtis Jr. Papers
 Liberty Foskett Letters
 August Valentine Kautz Papers
 Levi Neville Diary
 Alex M. Wallace Letters
 David S. Staley Memoirs, West-Staley-Wright Family Papers
 Civil War Miscellaneous Collection
  David C. Bradley Letters
  Hugh T. Carlisle Reminiscences
  William D. Cole Letters
  L. W. Earle Reminiscences
  Robert Moffet Diary
  Curtis C. Pollack Letters
  Baxter Smith History
  Jefferson Gray Thomas Diary
  Asa Zeller Diary
 Civil War Times Illustrated Collection
  John F. Milhollin Letters
  Frederick Pettit Correspondence
  Albert A. Pope Diary
 Harrisburg Civil War Round Table
  Robert A. Rodgers Diary
  George Shuman Letters
 Harrisburg Civil War Round Table, Gregory A. Coco Collection
  George P. Hawkes Diary
  Frederick W. Swift Diary
  Charles D. Todd Diary
National Archives, Washington, D.C.
 Record Group 105, Records of the Bureau of Refugees, Freedmen, and
  Abandoned Lands
 Record Group 109, Confederate Military Records, Department of East
  Tennessee
 Record Group 393, Records of U.S. Army Continental Commands,
  1821–1920, District of East Tennessee
National Archives, Southeast Region, Atlanta, Ga.
 Record Group 21, U.S. District Court, Eastern District, Tennessee,
  Knoxville
North Carolina State Archives, Raleigh
 Calvin J. Cowles Papers
 Mary Gash Family Papers
 Paul E. Hubbell Papers
 Evelyn McIntosh Hyatt Collection

Patterson Family Papers
William Williams Stringfield Papers
Colonel William Holland Thomas Papers
Stephen Whitaker Papers
Samuel Wheeler Worthington Collection
William R. Perkins Library, Manuscript Department, Duke University,
    Durham, N.C.
  William G. Brownlow Letters
  Campbell Family Papers
  Jefferson Davis Papers
  John Buchanan Floyd Papers
  Edmund Kirby Smith Papers
  Andrew Jay McBride Papers
  William E. McCoy Papers
  James Bennet McCreay Diary
  Samuel Powel III Papers
  William B. Reynolds Papers
  James Taylor Papers
  James Whary Terrell Papers
  William Holland Thomas Papers
  Sarah Thompson Papers
  James H. Wiswell Papers
Southern Historical Collection, University of North Carolina Library,
    Chapel Hill
  Edward P. Alexander Papers
  Alexander Donelson Coffee Papers
  Confederate States Papers, Opinions of the Attorney General, 1861–65
  Duke-Morgan Papers
  Joseph S. Espey Letters
  Joseph S. Fowler Papers
  Franklin Gaillard Letters
  Gale and Polk Family Papers
  John Wilson Hines Papers
  Martha Holland Letters
  David McKendree Key Papers
  Edmund Kirby Smith Papers
  Lenoir Family Papers
  Cornelius J. Madden Papers
  Basil Manly (Sr.) Papers
  John Hunt Morgan Papers
  J. G. M. Ramsey Autobiography
  J. G. M. Ramsey Papers
  Jacob Siler Papers
  Paul Turner Vaughn Letters
  Chauncey B. Welton Letters
  Mary Ann Covington Wilson Letters

Tennessee State Library and Archives, Nashville
Chapman Family Papers
Clift Family Papers
Doak Family Papers
Henry M. Doak Memoirs
Fergusson Family Papers
Andrew Jackson Fletcher Correspondence
Jill Garrett Collection
William P. Grohse Papers
Isham Green Harris Papers
Susan McCampbell (Heiskell) Diary
Hill Family Papers
Walter King Hoover Collection
Thomas Smith Hutton Diary
Abraham Jobe Diary
Andrew Johnson Correspondence
Lillard Family Papers
Chris D. Livesay Papers
Curtis McDowell Papers
McIver Collection
Paine Family Papers
Papers of the Governors, William G. Brownlow
Papers of the Governors, Isham G. Harris
Mary Jane Reynolds Letters
Abraham Ryan Correspondence
Scales and Campbell Family Papers
Shahan Family Papers
Sneed Family Papers
William B. Stokes Correspondence
Wells Family Papers
Civil War Collection
Mary E. Couch Scrapbook
John Calvin Gruar Papers
Joel Haley Jr. Letters
Landon Carter Haynes Letters
Milton P. Jarnagin Reminiscences
James E. Rains Letters
William Sloan Diary and Memoirs
Confederate Collection
William Gibbs Allen Memoir
David Shires Myers Bodenhamer Memoir
Small Collections
James P. Brownlow Papers
William G. Brownlow Papers
Stockly Donelson Papers
Havron Collection
Robertson Topp Papers

University of Tennessee Library, Special Collections, Knoxville
Samuel Mays Arnell Papers
Margaret Barton (Crozier) Diary
William G. Brownlow Papers
Samuel P. Carter Memoir
John Eaton Papers
Thomas Doak Edington Diary
Samuel P. Johnson Papers
S. C. Howard Lewis Diary
Horace Maynard Papers
Robert A. Ragan Letters
Ramsey Family Papers
Mary Jane Reynolds Letters
Rhea Family Papers
John Shrady Letters
Oliver P. Temple Papers
William Walker Ward Diary
Edwin Floyd Wiley War Memoirs

PRINTED SOURCES

Barton, William F. *The Cumberland Mountains and the Struggle for Freedom.*
Boston: n.p., 1897.
Berlin, Ira. *The Destruction of Slavery.* Series 1, vol. 1 of *Freedom: A
Documentary History of Emancipation, 1861–1867.* New York: Cambridge
University Press, 1985.
———. *The Wartime Genesis of Free Labor: The Upper South.* Series 1, vol. 2 of
Freedom: A Documentary History of Emancipation, 1861–1867. New York:
Cambridge University Press, 1993.
Brents, John A. *The Patriots and Guerrillas of East Tennessee and Kentucky.* New
York: John A. Brents, 1863.
Brownlow, William G. *Sketches of the Rise, Progress, and Decline of Secession.*
Philadelphia: J. B. Lippincott, 1862.
Burns, Amanda McDowell, and Lela M. Blankenship. *Fiddles on the
Cumberland.* New York: Richard S. Smith Co., 1943.
Carter, William Randolph. *History of the First Regiment of Tennessee Volunteer
Cavalry in the Great War of the Rebellion.* Knoxville: Gant-Ogden, 1902.
Duke, Basil. *Morgan's Cavalry.* Bloomington: Indiana University Press, 1960.
Ellis, Daniel. *Thrilling Adventures of Daniel Ellis.* New York: Harper, 1867.
Federal Writers Project. *Slave Narratives: A Folk History of Slavery in the United
States from Interviews with Former Slaves.* Washington, D.C.: Government
Printing Office, 1941.
Graf, Leroy P., Ralph Haskins, and Paul H. Bergeron, eds. *The Papers of
Andrew Johnson.* 13 vols. Knoxville: University of Tennessee Press, 1967.
Hancock, Richard R. *Hancock's Diary: Or, a History of the Second Tennessee
Confederate Cavalry.* Nashville: Brandon Printing Company, 1867.

Humes, Thomas Williams. *The Loyal Mountaineers of Tennessee*. Knoxville: Ogden Brothers, 1888.

————. *Third and Fourth Reports to the East Tennessee Relief Association at Knoxville*. Knoxville: Brownlow & Hous, 1868.

Hurlbut, J. S. *History of the Rebellion in Bradley County, East Tennessee*. Indianapolis: Downey & Brouse, 1866.

Longstreet, James. *From Manassas to Appomattox*. Bloomington: Indiana University Press, 1960.

Partain, Robert, ed. "The Civil War in East Tennessee as Reported by a Confederate Railroad Bridge Builder." *Tennessee Historical Quarterly* 22 (1963): 238–58.

————. "The Wartime Experiences of Margaret McCalla, Confederate Refugee from East Tennessee." *Tennessee Historical Quarterly* 24 (1965): 39–53.

Poe, Orlando M. *Personal Recollections of the Occupation of East Tennessee*. Detroit: Ostler Printing Company, 1889.

Ragan, Robert A. *Escape from East Tennessee to the Federal Lines*. Washington, D.C.: J. H. Doney, 1910.

Records of East Tennessee, Civil War Records. Nashville: Historical Records Survey, 1939.

Rowell, John W. *Yankee Cavalrymen*. Knoxville: University of Tennessee Press, 1971.

Scott, Samuel W., and Samuel P. Angel. *History of the Thirteenth Regiment, Tennessee Volunteer Cavalry, U.S.A*. Knoxville: n.p., 1903.

Skipper, Elvie Eagleton, and Ruth Gove, eds. "'Stray Thoughts': The Civil War Diary of Ethie M. Fonte Eagleton." *East Tennessee Historical Society Publications* 40 (1968): 128–37; 41 (1969): 116–28.

Sullins, David. *Recollections of an Old Man: Seventy Years in Dixie*. Bristol, Tenn.: King Printing Company, 1910.

Temple, Oliver P. *East Tennessee and the Civil War*. Cincinnati: Robert Clarks Company, 1899.

————. *Notable Men of Tennessee from 1833 to 1875*. New York: Cosmopolitan Press, 1912.

Thatcher, Marshall P. *A Hundred Battles in the West: The Second Michigan Cavalry*. Detroit: Marshall P. Thatcher, 1884.

Trowbridge, Luther S. *A Brief History of the Tenth Michigan Cavalry*. Detroit: Friesman Brothers, 1905.

U.S. Census Bureau, *Statistics of the United States in 1860, Compiled from the Original Returns of the Eighth Census*. Washington, D.C.: Government Printing Office, 1866.

The War of the Rebellion. A Compilation of the Official Records of the Union and Confederate Armies. 128 vols. Washington, D.C.: Government Printing Office, 1880–1900.

Wilson, Suzanne Colton, comp. *Column South: With the Fifteenth Pennsylvania Cavalry*. Ed. by J. Ferrell Colton and Antoinette G. Smith. Flagstaff: J. F. Colton & Company, 1960.

Bibliography

Abernathy, Thomas Perkins. *From Frontier to Plantation in Tennessee*. Chapel Hill: University of North Carolina Press, 1932.

———. "The Origins of the Whig Party in Tennessee." *Mississippi Valley Historical Review* 12 (1925–26): 504–22.

Alexander, Thomas B. "Ku Kluxism in Tennessee, 1865–1869." *Tennessee Historical Quarterly* 8 (1949): 195–219.

———. "Neither Peace nor War: Conditions in Tennessee in 1865." East Tennessee Historical Society *Publications* 21 (1949): 33–51.

———. "Persistent Whiggery in the Confederate South, 1860–1877." *Journal of Southern History* 27 (1961): 305–29.

———. *Political Reconstruction in Tennessee*. Nashville: Vanderbilt University Press, 1950.

———. "Strange Bedfellows: The Interlocking Careers of Andrew Johnson, T. A. R. Nelson, and William G. (Parson) Brownlow." East Tennessee Historical Society *Publications* 24 (1952): 68–91.

———. "Thomas A. R. Nelson as an Example of Whig Conservatism in Tennessee." *Tennessee Historical Quarterly* 15 (1956): 17–29.

———. *Thomas A. R. Nelson of East Tennessee*. Nashville: Tennessee Historical Commission, 1956.

———. "Whiggery and Reconstruction in Tennessee." *Journal of Southern History* 16 (1950): 291–305.

Allen, V. C. *Rhea and Meigs Counties (Tennessee) in the Confederate War*. N.p.: V. C. Allen, 1908.

Ambrose, Stephen F. "Yeoman Discontent in the Confederacy." *Civil War History* 8 (1962): 259–68.

Anderson, Charles C. *Fighting by Southern Federals*. New York: Neale Publishing Company, 1912.

Ash, Stephen V. *Middle Tennessee Society Transformed, 1860–1870: War and Peace in the Upper South*. Baton Rouge: Louisiana State University Press, 1988.

———. *When the Yankees Came: Conflict and Chaos in the Occupied South, 1861–1865*. Chapel Hill: University of North Carolina Press, 1996.

Ayers, Edward L. *Vengeance and Justice: Crime and Punishment in the Nineteenth-Century American South*. New York: Oxford University Press, 1984.

Bailey, Fred Arthur. *Class and Tennessee's Confederate Generation*. Chapel Hill: University of North Carolina Press, 1987.

Barrett, John G. *Civil War in North Carolina*. Chapel Hill: University of North Carolina Press, 1963.

Bergeron, Paul H. *Antebellum Politics in Tennessee*. Lexington: University Press of Kentucky, 1982.

Black, Robert C., III. *The Railroads of the Confederacy*. Chapel Hill: University of North Carolina Press, 1952.

Bowen, Dan R. "Guerrilla War in Western Missouri, 1862–1865: Historical Extensions of the Relative Deprivation Hypothesis." *Comparative Studies in Society and History* 19 (1977): 30–51.

Bowen, David W. *Andrew Johnson and the Negro*. Knoxville: University of
Tennessee Press, 1989.

Brown, Campbell H. "Carter's East Tennessee Raid: The Sailor on Horseback
Who Raided His Own Backyard." *Tennessee Historical Quarterly* 22 (1963):
66–82.

Brown, Richard Maxwell. *Strain of Violence: Historical Studies of American
Violence and Vigilantism*. New York: Oxford University Press, 1975.

Brownlee, Richard S. *Gray Ghosts of the Confederacy: Guerrilla Warfare in the
West, 1861–1865*. Baton Rouge: Louisiana State University Press, 1958.

Bryan, Charles F., Jr. "A Gathering of Tories: The East Tennessee Convention
of 1861." *Tennessee Historical Quarterly* 39 (1980): 27–48.

———. "'Tories' Amidst Rebels: The Confederate Occupation of East
Tennessee, 1861–1863," East Tennessee Historical Society *Publications* 60
(1988): 3–22.

Bullard, Helen, and Joseph Marshall Krechniak. *Cumberland County's First
Hundred Years*. Crossville, Tenn.: Centennial Commission, 1956.

Burns, Inez. *History of Blount County, Tennessee*. Nashville: Benson Printing
Company, 1957.

Burt, Jesse C. "East Tennessee, Lincoln, and Sherman." East Tennessee
Historical Society *Publications* 34 (1962): 3–25; 35 (1963): 54–75.

Burton, Orville Vernon, and Robert C. McMath Jr. *Class, Conflict, and
Consensus: Antebellum Southern Community Studies*. Westport, Conn.:
Greenwood Press, 1982.

Byrum, Stephen C. *McMinn County*. Memphis: Memphis State University
Press, 1984.

Camp, Henry R. *Sequatchie County*. Memphis: Memphis State University
Press, 1984.

Campbell, James B. "East Tennessee during the Federal Occupation,
1863–1865." East Tennessee Historical Society *Publications* 19 (1947):
64–80.

Campbell, John C. *The Southern Highlander and His Homeland*. New York:
Russell Sage Foundation, 1921.

Campbell, Mary Emily Robertson. *The Attitude of Tennesseans toward the Union,
1847–1861*. New York: Vantage Press, 1961.

Carter, Dan T. *When the War Was Over: The Failure of Self-Reconstruction in the
South*. Baton Rouge: Louisiana State University Press, 1985.

Castel, Albert. "The Guerrilla War, 1861–1865." *Civil War Times Illustrated* 13
(1974): 1–50.

Clark, Blanch Henry. *The Tennessee Yeomen, 1840–1860*. Nashville: Vanderbilt
University Press, 1942.

Cole, Arthur C. *The Whig Party in the South*. Washington, D.C.: American
Historical Association, 1913.

Connelly, Thomas Lawrence. *Army of the Heartland: The Army of Tennessee,
1861–1862*. Baton Rouge: Louisiana State University Press, 1967.

———. *Autumn of Glory: The Army of Tennessee, 1862–1865*. Baton Rouge:
Louisiana State University Press, 1971.

Cooling, B. Franklin. *Forts Henry and Donelson: The Key to the Confederate Heartland*. Knoxville: University of Tennessee Press, 1987.

Coulter, E. Merton. *William G. Brownlow: Fighting Parson of the Highlands*. Chapel Hill: University of North Carolina Press, 1937.

Cozzens, Peter. *The Shipwreck of Their Hopes: The Battles for Chattanooga*. Urbana: University of Illinois Press, 1994.

———. *This Terrible Sound: The Battle of Chickamauga*. Urbana: University of Illinois Press, 1992.

Creekmore, Betsy Beeler. *Knoxville*. Knoxville: University of Tennessee Press, 1958.

Crofts, Daniel W. *Reluctant Confederates: Upper South Unionists in the Secession Crisis*. Chapel Hill: University of North Carolina Press, 1989.

Crouch, Barry. "The Merchant and the Senator: An Attempt to Save East Tennessee for the Union." *East Tennessee Historical Society Publications* 46 (1974): 53–75.

Current, Richard Nelson. *Lincoln's Loyalists: Union Soldiers from the Confederacy*. New York: Oxford University Press, 1992.

Davis, William C. *Breckinridge: Statesman, Soldier, Symbol*. Baton Rouge: Louisiana State University Press, 1974.

Degler, Carl. *The Other South: Southern Dissenters in the Nineteenth Century*. Boston: Northeastern University Press, 1982.

Dickson, Bruce, Jr. *Violence and Culture in the Antebellum South*. Austin: University of Texas Press, 1979.

Dillon, Merton L. "Three Southern Anti-Slavery Editors: The Myth of the Southern Anti-Slavery Movement." *East Tennessee Historical Society Publications* 42 (1971): 47–56.

Dugger, Shepherd M. *The War Trails of the Blue Ridge*. Banner Elk: North Carolina Pudding Stone Press, 1932.

Dunn, Durwood. *Cades Cove: The Life and Death of a Southern Appalachian Community, 1818–1937*. Knoxville: University of Tennessee Press, 1988.

Dyer, Frederick H. *A Compendium of the War of the Rebellion*. 4 vols. New York: Thomas Yosiloff, 1959.

Dykeman, Wilma. *The French Broad*. New York and Toronto: Rinehart & Company, 1955.

———. *Tennessee: A Bicentennial History*. New York: W. W. Norton & Company, 1955.

Eaton, Clement. "Mob Violence in the Old South." *Mississippi Valley Historical Review* 29 (1942): 351–70.

England, J. Merton. "The Free Negro in Antebellum Tennessee." *Journal of Southern History* 9 (1943): 37–58.

Escott, Paul D. *Jefferson Davis and the Failure of Confederate Nationalism*. Baton Rouge: Louisiana State University Press, 1978.

———. *Many Excellent People: Power and Privilege in North Carolina, 1850–1900*. Chapel Hill: University of North Carolina Press, 1985.

Feierabend, Ira K., Rosalind L. Feierabend, and Ted Robert Gurr. *Anger, Violence, and Politics*. Englewood Cliffs, N.J.: Prentice-Hall, 1972.

Fellman, Michael. *Inside War: The Guerrilla Conflict in Missouri during the American Civil War*. New York: Oxford University Press, 1989.

Fisher, Noel C. "Definitions of Loyalty: Unionist Histories of the Civil War in East Tennessee." *Journal of East Tennessee History* 67 (1995): 58–88.

———. "'The Leniency Shown Them Has Been Unavailing': The Confederate Occupation of East Tennessee." *Civil War History* 40 (1994): 275–91.

Folmsbee, Stanley J. "The Beginnings of the Railroad Movement in East Tennessee," East Tennessee Historical Society *Publications* 5 (1933): 81–104.

———. *Sectionalism and Internal Improvements in Tennessee*. Knoxville: East Tennessee Historical Society, 1939.

Folmsbee, Stanley J., Robert E. Corlew, and Enoch L. Mitchell. *History of Tennessee*. 4 vols. New York: Lewis Historical Publishing Company, 1960.

———. *Tennessee: A Short History*. Knoxville: University of Tennessee Press, 1969.

Franklin, John Hope. *The Militant South, 1860–1861*. Cambridge: Belknap Press of Harvard University Press, 1956.

Freidel, Frank. "General Orders 100 and Military Government." *Mississippi Valley Historical Review* 32 (1946): 541–56.

Freytag, Ethel, and Glenn Krels Ott. *A History of Morgan County, Tennessee*. Knoxville: Specialty Printing Company, 1971.

Garner, Captain James G. "General Orders 100 Revisited." *Military Law Review* 27 (1965): 1–48.

Gates, John M. "Indians and Insurrectos: The U.S. Army's Experience with Insurgency." *Parameters* 13 (1983): 57–68.

Genovese, Eugene D. "Yeoman Farmers in a Slaveholding Democracy." *Agriculture History* 49 (1975): 331–42.

Govan, Gilbert, and James W. Livingood. *The Chattanooga Country, 1540–1956*. New York: E. P. Dutton & Company, 1952.

———. "Chattanooga under Military Occupation, 1863–1865." *Journal of Southern History* 17 (1951): 23–47.

Graf, Leroy P. "Andrew Johnson and the Coming of the Civil War." *Tennessee Historical Quarterly* 19 (1960): 208–21.

Graham, Hugh Davis, and Ted Robert Gurr, eds. *Violence in America: Historical and Comparative Perspectives*. Beverly Hills and London: Sage Publications, 1979.

Grant, C. E. "Partisan Warfare Model 1861–1865." *Military Review* 38 (1958): 42–56.

Grimsley, Mark. *The Hard Hand of War: Union Military Policy toward Southern Civilians, 1861–1865*. New York: Cambridge University Press, 1995.

Gurr, Ted Robert. *Why Men Rebel*. Princeton: Princeton University Press, 1970.

Hackney, Sheldon. "Southern Violence." *American Historical Review* 74 (1969): 906–25.

Hahn, Steven. *The Roots of Southern Populism: Yeomen Farmers and the Transformation of the Georgia Backcountry*. New York: Oxford University Press, 1983.

Hall, Clifton R. *Andrew Johnson: Military Governor of Tennessee*. Princeton: Princeton University Press, 1916.

Hall, Kermit L. "West Humphreys and the Crisis of the Union," *Tennessee Historical Quarterly* 34 (1975): 67–69.

Haskins, Ralph W. "Internecine Strife in Tennessee: Andrew Johnson vs. Parson Brownlow." *Tennessee Historical Quarterly* 24 (1965): 321–40.

Hattaway, Herman, and Archer Jones. *How the North Won*. Urbana: University of Illinois Press, 1983.

Heilbrunn, Otto. *Partisan Warfare*. New York: Frederick A. Praeger, 1962.

Henry, J. Milton. "The Revolution in Tennessee, February 1861–June 1861." *Tennessee Historical Quarterly* 18 (1959): 99–119.

Hesseltine, W. B. "The Underground Railroad from Confederate Prisons to East Tennessee." East Tennessee Historical Society *Publications* 2 (1930): 55–69.

Hibbs, Douglas A., Jr. *Mass Political Violence*. New York: John Wiley & Sons, 1973.

Holland, Cecil Fletcher. *Morgan and His Raiders*. New York: Macmillan Company, 1942.

Holland, James W. "The Building of the East Tennessee & Virginia Railroad." East Tennessee Historical Society *Publications* 4 (1932): 83–101.

———. "The East Tennessee & Georgia Railroad, 1836–1860." East Tennessee Historical Society *Publications* 3 (1931): 89–107.

Holt, Edgar A. *Claiborne County*. Memphis: Memphis State University Press, 1981.

Holt, Michael F. *The Political Crisis of the 1850s*. New York: Wiley, 1978.

Humphrey, Steve. *That D–d Brownlow*. Boone, N.C.: Appalachia Consortium Press, 1978.

Hyman, Harold. *Era of the Oath: Northern Loyalty Tests during the Civil War and Reconstruction*. Philadelphia: University of Pennsylvania Press, 1954.

Inscoe, John C. *Mountain Masters: Slavery and the Sectional Crisis in Western North Carolina*. Knoxville: University of Tennessee Press, 1989.

Jones, Archer. *Civil War Command and Strategy*. New York: Free Press, 1992.

Jones, Virgil Carrington. *Gray Ghosts and Rebel Raiders*. 2 vols. New York: Ballantine Books, 1973.

Kephart, Horace. *Our Southern Highlanders*. New York: Outing Publishing Company, 1913.

Klingberg, Frank Wyser. "The Case of the Minors: A Unionist Family within the Confederacy." *Journal of Southern History* 13 (1947): 27–45.

Klotter, James C. "Feuds in Appalachia: An Overview." *Filson Club History Quarterly* 56 (1982): 290–317.

Knox County History Committee, East Tennessee Historical Society. *The French Broad-Holston Country: A History of Knox County, Tennessee*. Ed. by Mary U. Rothrock. Knoxville: East Tennessee History Society, 1946.

Lacy, Eric R. "The Persistent State of Franklin." *Tennessee Historical Quarterly* 21 (1964): 321–32.

———. *Vanquished Volunteers: East Tennessee Sectionalism from Statehood to Secession*. Johnson City: East Tennessee State University Press, 1965.

Lane, Roger, and John J. Turner. *Riot, Rout, and Tumult: Readings in American Social and Political Violence*. Westport, Conn.: Greenwood Press, 1978.

Law, Henry L. *A Brief Geography of Tennessee*. Clarksville: Queen City Book Company, 1949.

Lewis, Lloyd. *Sherman: Fighting Prophet*. New York: Harcourt, Brace & Company, 1958.

Lillard, Roy G. *Bradley County*. Memphis: Memphis State University Press, 1980.

Linderman, Gerald F. *Embattled Courage: The Experience of Combat in the American Civil War*. New York: Free Press, 1987.

Livingood, James W. *A History of Hamilton County, Tennessee*. Memphis: Memphis State University Press, 1981.

Lonn, Ella. *Desertion during the Civil War*. New York: Century Company, 1928.

McCague, James. *The Cumberland*. New York: Rinehart and Winston, 1973.

McCormick, Richard P. *The Second American Party System*. Chapel Hill: University of North Carolina Press, 1966.

McCuen, John J. *The Art of Counterinsurgency War*. Harrisburg, Pa.: Stackpole Company, 1966.

McDonough, James L. *Schofield: Union General in the Civil War and Reconstruction*. Tallahassee: Florida State University Press, 1972.

———. *Shiloh: In Hell before Night*. Knoxville: University of Tennessee Press, 1977.

———. *War in Kentucky: From Shiloh to Perryville*. Knoxville: University of Tennessee Press, 1994.

McKee, James W., Jr. "Felix K. Zollicoffer: Confederate Defender of East Tennessee." *East Tennessee Historical Society Publications* 43 (1971): 34–58; 44 (1972): 17–40.

McKenzie, Robert Tracy. *One South or Many: Plantation Belt and Upcountry in Civil War Era Tennessee*. New York: Cambridge University Press, 1994.

McKinney, Francis. *Education in Violence*. Detroit: Wayne State University Press, 1961.

McKinney, Gordon B. *Southern Mountain Republicans, 1865–1900: Politics and the Appalachian Community*. Chapel Hill: University of North Carolina Press, 1978.

McKitrick, Eric L. *Andrew Johnson and Reconstruction*. Chicago: University of Chicago Press, 1960.

Madden, David. "Unionist Resistance to Confederate Occupation: The Bridge-Burners of East Tennessee." *East Tennessee Historical Society Publications* 52 (1980): 42–53; 53 (1981): 22–39.

Marvel, William. *Burnside*. Chapel Hill: University of North Carolina Press, 1991.

Maslowski, Peter. *Treason Must Be Made Odious: Military Occupation and Wartime Reconstruction in Nashville, Tennessee, 1862–1865*. Millwood, N.Y.: KTO Press, 1978.

Mering, John V. "The Slave-State Constitutional Unionists and the Politics of Consensus." *Journal of Southern History* 43 (1977): 395–410.

Miles, Emma Bell. *The Spirit of the Mountains*. Knoxville: University of
Tennessee Press, 1975.

Mooney, Chase C. "The Question of Slavery and the Free Negro in the
Tennessee Constitutional Convention of 1834." *Journal of Southern History*
12 (1946): 487–509.

Moore, Albert Burton. *Conscription and Conflict in the Confederacy*. New York:
Macmillan Company, 1924.

Neely, Mark E., Jr. *The Fate of Liberty: Abraham Lincoln and Civil Liberties*.
New York: Oxford University Press, 1991.

Noe, Kenneth W. *Southwest Virginia's Railroad: Modernization and the Sectional
Crisis*. Champaign: University of Illinois Press, 1994.

O'Dell, Ruth Webb. *Over the Misty Blue Hill: The Story of Cocke County,
Tennessee*. N.p.: Ruth Webb O'Dell, 1950.

Owsley, Frank L., and Harriet C. Owsley. "The Economic Structure of Rural
Tennessee, 1850–1860." *Journal of Southern History* 8 (1942): 161–82.

Paget, Julian. *Counterinsurgency Operations*. New York: Walker & Company,
1967.

Paludan, Philip Shaw. *Victims: A True Story of the Civil War*. Knoxville:
University of Tennessee Press, 1981.

Parks, Edd Winfield. "Zollicoffer: Southern Whig." *Tennessee Historical
Quarterly* 11 (1952): 346–55.

Parks, Joseph H. *General Edmund Kirby Smith, C.S.A.* Baton Rouge: Louisiana
State University Press, 1954.

———. *John Bell of Tennessee*. Baton Rouge: Louisiana State University Press,
1950.

———. "The Tennessee Whigs and the Kansas-Nebraska Bill." *Journal of
Southern History* 10 (1944): 308–30.

Patton, James Welch. *Unionism and Reconstruction in Tennessee, 1860–1869*.
Chapel Hill: University of North Carolina Press, 1934.

Pustay, John S. *Counterinsurgency Warfare*. New York: Free Press, 1965.

Rable, George C. "Anatomy of a Unionist: Andrew Johnson and the Secession
Crisis." *Tennessee Historical Quarterly* 32 (1973): 332–54.

Radley, Kenneth. *Rebel Watchdog: The Confederate States Army Provost Guard*.
Baton Rouge: Louisiana State University Press, 1989.

Ramage, James A. *Rebel Raider*. Lexington: University Press of Kentucky, 1986.

Ramsdell, Charles W. *Behind the Lines in the Southern Confederacy*. New York:
Greenwood Press, 1944.

Raulston, J. Leonard, and James W. Livingood. *Sequatchie: A Story of the
Southern Cumberlands*. Knoxville: University of Tennessee Press, 1974.

Rhea, Gordon C. *The Battle of the Wilderness, May 5–6, 1864*. Baton Rouge:
Louisiana State University Press, 1994.

Ridenour, G. L. *The Land of the Lake: A History of Campbell County, Tennessee*.
LaFollette, Tenn.: LaFollette Publishing Company, 1941.

Sellers, Charles Grier, Jr. "Who Were the Southern Whigs?" *American
Historical Review* 59 (1954): 335–46.

Sensing, Thurman. *Champ Ferguson, Confederate Guerrilla*. Nashville:
Vanderbilt University Press, 1942.

Seymour, Digby Gordon. *Divided Loyalties: Fort Sanders and the Civil War in East Tennessee*. Knoxville: University of Tennessee Press, 1963.

Sheeler, J. Reuben. "The Development of Unionism in East Tennessee, 1860–1866." *Journal of Negro History* 29 (1944): 166–203.

Smith, Wayne W. "An Experiment in Counterinsurgency: The Assessment of Confederate Sympathizers in Missouri." *Journal of Southern History* 35 (1969): 361–80.

Stamper, James C. "Felix K. Zollicoffer: Tennessee Editor and Politician." *Tennessee Historical Quarterly* 28 (1969): 356–76.

Starr, Stephen Z. *The Union Cavalry in the Civil War*. 3. vols. Baton Rouge: Louisiana State University Press, 1985.

Stryker, Lloyd Paul. *Andrew Johnson: A Study in Courage*. New York: Macmillan Company, 1929.

Tatum, Georgia Lee. *Disloyalty in the Confederacy*. Chapel Hill: University of North Carolina Press, 1934.

Taylor, Oliver. *Historic Sullivan*. Bristol, Tenn.: King Printing Company, 1909.

Thornton, J. Mills III. *Politics and Power in a Slave Society: Alabama, 1800–1860*. Baton Rouge: Louisiana State University Press, 1978.

Trefousse, Hans. *Andrew Johnson: A Biography*. New York: Norton, 1989.

Trelease, Allen W. *White Terror: The Ku Klux Klan Conspiracy and Southern Reconstruction*. New York: Harper & Row, 1971.

Van Noppen, Ina. *Stoneman's Last Raid*. Boone, N.C.: North Carolina State College, 1961.

Walton, Brian G. "The Second Party System in Tennessee." East Tennessee Historical Society *Publications* 43 (1971): 18–33.

Watson, Henry L. *Jacksonian Politics and Community Conflict: The Emergence of the Second Party System in Cumberland County, North Carolina*. Baton Rouge: Louisiana State University Press, 1981.

Williams, A. J. *Confederate History of Polk County, Tennessee, 1860–1866*. Nashville: McQuiddy Printing Company, 1923.

Williams, Samuel Cole. *History of the Lost State of Franklin*. New York: Press of the Pioneers, 1933.

Williams, T. Harry. *Lincoln and His Generals*. New York: Grosset & Dunlap, 1952.

Winston, Robert W. *Andrew Johnson: Plebian and Patriot*. New York: Barnes & Noble, 1928.

Woodworth, Stephen E. *Jefferson Davis and His Generals: The Failure of Confederate Command in the West*. Lawrence: University Press of Kansas, 1990.

Wooster, Ralph A. *Politicians, Planters, and Plain Folk: Courthouse and Statehouse in the Upper South, 1850–1860*. Knoxville: University of Tennessee Press, 1975.

———. *The Secession Conventions of the South*. Princeton: Princeton University Press, 1962.

Wyatt-Brown, Bertram. *Southern Honor: Ethics and Behavior in the Old South*. New York: Oxford University Press, 1982.

Beamer, Carl B. "Gray Ghostbusters." Ph.D. diss., The Ohio State University, 1988.

Bellamy, James W. "The Political Career of Landon Carter Haynes." M.A. thesis, University of Tennessee, 1952.

Bentley, H. Blair. "Andrew Johnson, Governor of Tennessee, 1853–1857." Ph.D. diss., University of Tennessee, 1972.

Bryan, Charles Faulkner. "The Civil War in East Tennessee: A Social, Political, and Economic Study." Ph.D. diss., University of Tennessee, 1978.

Campbell, James B. "Some Social and Economic Phases of Reconstruction in East Tennessee, 1864–1869." M.A. thesis, University of Tennessee, 1946.

Carroll, Mary S. "Tennessee Sectionalism, 1796–1861." Ph.D. diss., Duke University, 1931.

Cotten, W. D. "Appalachian North Carolina: A Political Study, 1860–1869." Ph.D. diss., University of North Carolina, 1954.

Daniel, John S., Jr. "Special Warfare in Middle Tennessee and Surrounding Areas, 1861–1862." M.A. thesis, University of Tennessee, 1971.

DeBerry, John H. "Confederate Tennessee." Ph.D. diss., University of Kentucky, 1967.

Garrett, Beatrice Lydia. "The Confederate Government and the Unionists of East Tennessee." M.A. thesis, University of Tennessee, 1932.

Groce, W. Todd "Mountain Rebels: East Tennessee Confederates and the Civil War, 1860–1870." Ph.D. diss., University of Tennessee, 1993.

Hsiung, David C. "Isolation and Integration in Upper East Tennessee, 1780–1860: The Historical Origins of Appalachian Characterizations." Ph.D. diss., University of Michigan, 1991.

Lowrey, Frank Mitchell. "Tennessee Voters during the Second Two-Party System, 1836–1860: A Study in Voter Consistency and in Socio-Economic and Demographic Distinctions." Ph.D. diss., University of Alabama, 1973.

Russell, Mattie. "William Holland Thomas: White Chief of the Cherokees." Ph.D. diss., Duke University, 1956.

Smith, Frank Prigmore. "The Military History of East Tennessee, 1861–1865." M.A. thesis, University of Tennessee, 1936.

Turner, Ruth Osborne. "The Public Career of William Montgomery Churchwell." M.A. thesis, University of Tennessee, 1954.

Webb, Basha R. "The Attitudes of Members of Congress of Tennessee on the Slavery Question, 1820–1855." M.A. thesis, University of Tennessee, 1931.

Whelan, Paul A. "Unconventional Warfare in East Tennessee, 1861–1865." M.A. thesis, University of Tennessee, 1963.

Williams, Cratis D. "The Southern Mountaineer in Fact and Fiction." Ph.D. diss., New York University, 1961.

Jackson, Brig. Gen. Alfred E., 162, 164

Jackson, Andrew, 10

Jameson, R. E., 121

Jamestown, Tenn., 51

Jefferson County, Tenn., 20

Johnson, Andrew: and Democratic Party, 11; conflicts with William G. Brownlow, 14–15; support for East Tennessee statehood, 15; and 1860 election, 23; opposition to secession, 26; campaign against secession, 29–33; escape from East Tennessee, 49; appointment as military governor, 49, 104; support for East Tennessee invasion, 52–54, 110, 122–23; concern with secessionist guerrillas, 82; family expelled, 107; property siezed, 107; recruitment of troops, 130; policies in Middle Tennessee, 131–32; and hostage taking, 148; special pardons of, 161, 163; support for Emancipation Proclamation, 166, 169; opposition to African-American franchise, 168–69; opposition to franchise restrictions of Gov. William G. Brownlow, 168–69; and death of Brig. Gen. John Hunt Morgan, 186–87

Johnson, Robert, 159

Johnson County, Tenn., 33, 42, 65, 76, 83–85, 118

Johnson's Island, Ohio, 136, 151

Johnston, Maj. Gen. Albert Sidney, 60

Johnston, Lt. Gen. Joseph, 154

Jones, Maj. Gen. Sam: operations against Unionists, 74, 78; appointment to East Tennessee, 110; views of Unionists, 111–12; attempts to recruit Unionist leaders, 111–14; attempts to end partisan conflict, 114–15; attempts to suspend conscription, 115–16; concern with theft by Confederate soldiers, 117; departure from East Tennessee,

118; advocacy of restraint, 120, 175; operations against Army of the Ohio, 126–27

Jonesborough, Tenn., 12, 16, 17, 33, 73, 79, 85, 91–92, 113, 156, 160–61, 169

Kansas-Nebraska Act, 20

Keith, Col. James, 78

Kentucky, 1, 35, 41, 51–53, 64–68, 110, 118, 123, 131, 140, 154–55

Kephart, Forest, 72–73

Key, Col. David M., 31, 157, 160, 162, 164

King, John G., 158

King's Mountain, Battle of, 7, 21, 179

Kingsport, Tenn., 33

Kingston, Tenn., 17, 42, 69, 82

Kirby Smith, Maj. Gen. Edmund: operations against Unionists, 68–71, 78, 107–8; antebellum military career of, 102–3; views of secession, 103; reorganization of East Tennessee command, 103–5; views of Unionists, 105; arrests of Unionist leaders, 105–7; offers of amnesty, 108; suspension of draft, 108–9; defense of East Tennessee, 109–10; invasion of Kentucky, 110; departure from East Tennessee, 118; advocacy of restraint, 120, 175; indicted for treason, 162

Kirk, Col. George, 68, 87

Klein, Lt. Col. Robert, 89

Knox County, Tenn., 33, 65, 79, 105, 134, 155, 164

Knoxville, Battle of, 128

Knoxville, Tenn., 1, 12–14, 15, 17, 22, 24–26, 33, 37, 42, 43, 44, 51, 54, 56–57, 79, 85, 88, 104, 105, 113, 121, 126, 138, 141–42, 147, 156–58

Knoxville Convention, 34–35, 87, 106

Knoxville Register, 34, 112–15

Knoxville Whig, 13–14, 34, 124

Montgomery, Tenn., 51, 69, 155
Morgan, Brig. Gen. George W., 73, 87, 89, 109, 120, 122, 148
Morgan, Brig. Gen. John Hunt: excesses against Unionists, 117–18, 130; and hostage taking, 149–52; indicted for treason, 162; death of, 186–87
Morgan County, Tenn., 16, 19, 68–69, 73, 75, 91, 155
Morristown, Tenn., 75, 80, 105–6, 113, 157–58
Mossy Creek, Tenn., 70
Murfreesboro, Tenn., 110

Nashville, Tenn., 15, 48, 54, 59, 122, 139, 147, 150, 158, 167
National Guard of Tennessee, 133–35, 144–45
Nelson, David, 31, 113–14
Nelson, T. A. R.: candidacy for U.S. Senate, 15; opposition to sectional conflict, 22; campaign against secession, 29–33; radical proposals at Greeneville Convention, 38–40; election to U.S. Congress, 1861, 47; capture by Confederate troops, 48; submission to Confederate government, 48–49, 142–43; discussions with Maj. Gen. Sam Jones, 112; reaction to Emancipation Proclamation, 112–14, 166, 169; complaints concerning Union foraging, 146–47; post-war court suits, 158, 160; split with radicals, 166–70; opposition to Lincoln, 167; opposition to Unionist violence, 169–70; conservatism of, 176
Nelson, Brig. Gen. William, 52
Netherland, John, 15, 112, 142
New Market, Tenn., 67, 84, 159
Newport, Tenn., 74–75
Ninth Pennsylvania Cavalry, 81–82
Ninth Tennessee Cavalry, 92, 155
Noe, Kenneth, 6
North Carolina: operations of

Unionist guerrillas in, 3; governance of early East Tennessee, 7–9; vote on secession, 37; Unionist raids in, 56, 66, 87; Unionist partisans in, 76, 78; deserters in, 81; secessionist bases in, 83–85

Ohio River, 136
Overton County, Tenn., 155

Paine, Oliver, 117
Parrotsville, Tenn., 118
Parsons, Col. James, 92, 154
Partisan war: in the South, 3; and conventional war, 3–4; organization of partisan forces, 41–42, 63–64; violence between East Tennessee Unionists and seccessionists, 42, 68–69, 82–85, 157–59; fighting between Unionists and Confederate troops, 42–44, 69–70, 74–78, 86–87; cooperation between Unionist partisans and Union Army, 51–54, 64–65, 71–73, 79, 87, 133–35, 143–45; Unionist sabotage, 52–56, 70–71; significance of, 62–64, 92–95, 159–64; and escape network, 65–68; role of African Americans in, 73–74; role of white women in, 74, 79, 137–38, 186–87; secessionist sabotage, 79–80; fighting between secessionists and Union troops, 79–82, 89–92, 154–55; and East Tennessee churches, 85–86; and crime, 87–89; and damage suits, 159–61; and secessionist exodus, 159–64; economic effects of, 165; political effects of, 165–71
Patterson, David T., 58, 142, 164
Patton, James, 180
Pennsylvania, 6
Perryville, Battle of, 118
Pickens, Levi, 58, 160
Pilots, 65–68
Polk, Maj. Gen. Leonidas, 46
Polk, William H., 47